RODIN

BY JUDITH CLADEL

This full-length biography of the great sculptor, by a woman who knew him since her childhood, will stand as a sound piece of work, well documented and carefully written. For many years, Mlle. Cladel served Rodin as secretary, supervised exhibitions of his work, and lectured on it. She paints an interesting picture of his private and artistic life, with a wealth of material on the complicated relationships between him and the world.

The story is told from the time of Rodin's humble beginnings and through his struggles for recognition, which came when he was old; but the most compelling part of the book is that which deals with the days of his late success.

Many of Rodin's letters help to reveal the man—his tender love for his wife, his absent-mindedness, his susceptibility to being cheated by unpleasant and dishonest hangers-on, his friendships, his passion for work.

RODIN

by Judith Cladel

TRANSLATED FROM THE FRENCH
BY JAMES WHITALL

NEW YORK
HARCOURT, BRACE AND COMPANY

first edition

Typography by Robert Josephy

PRINTED IN THE UNITED STATES OF AMERICA

BY QUINN & BODEN COMPANY, INC., RAHWAY, N. J.

To you, sculptors of the twentieth century who are valiantly struggling against poverty in a world unaware or little concerned with the things of the mind, and who are maintaining the great traditions to which Rodin gave new life, this book is dedicated.

Il n'y a pas de souvenirs superflus quand on a à peindre la vie de certains hommes.

CH. BAUDELAIRE

ACKNOWLEDGMENTS

I HAVE attempted to reconstruct those periods of Rodin's life, in which I was not personally involved, with the help of documents, but my chief aid has come from the sculptor's relatives, friends and assistants. A long acquaintance with him has enabled me to judge of the material obtained, and only that which seemed to ring true has been made use of.

My sincere thanks is offered to Rodin's intimates, as well as to all those whose eager and unfailing assistance has made possible the writing of this book. M. Ferdinand Brunot, head of the *Faculté des Lettres,* and M. Albert Dauzat, professor in the *Ecole pratique des Hautes Etudes* at the Sorbonne, enlightened me as to the etymology of Rodin's name; MM. Emile and Henri Cheffer, the sculptor's first cousins, supplied me with much valuable information about his youth. Mme Marcel Tirel generously loaned me Rodin's letters to Rose Beuret which Auguste Beuret had given her, and many facts about the latter's life were supplied by his cousins, M. and Mme Cazaud-Beuret.

Frequent conversations with Alfred Boucher and Jules Desbois produced much detailed information about the years in Paris after the sculptor's return from Belgium. To Mr. R. P. Bedford, curator of architecture and sculpture at the Victoria and Albert Museum in London, I owe an account of the competition for the *Monument Byron* in which Rodin took part; and to Dr. Edouard Grinda, a description of the decorative work on the Villa Neptune at Nice, of which he is the present owner. MM. Hans Haug, director of the Strasbourg museums, and Robert Heitz, art critic, have searched eagerly for the unsigned works produced by Rodin in that city in 1879-80 without obtaining so far any definite results. MM. Ferdinand and Julien Tempelaere showed me many letters from Rodin to his friends and through M. Tison, archivist of the Municipality of Calais, I had access to the long series written to M. Dewavrin, mayor of that city.

Mr. Jules E. Mastbaum, founder of the Rodin Museum of Philadelphia, put his collection of documents at my disposal; and Mr. Francis Barrett sent me Sir Lionel Earle's account of the sculptor's visit to London to decide upon a place for *Les Bourgeois de Calais*. The art dealer, Eugene Blot, the sculptors Louis Dejean, Halou, Séraphin Soudbinine, who did marble-cutting for Rodin, P. F. Berthoud, Limet, his finisher, Guilloché, his caster for twenty-eight years, have all cordially complied with my requests for information.

Finally, it would not have been possible to write a life of Rodin without the assistance of a catalogue of his works in their chronological order. The only satisfactory catalogue of this kind is the one which is being continually revised and augmented by successive editions for the museum in the rue de Varenne by M. Georges Grappe. This eminent curator has also verified much of my documentation.

J. C.

CONTENTS

ILLUSTRATIONS

Titles in parentheses are those which appear in the official catalogue of the Musée Rodin (1931). Where no title appears, either the French title is identical with the English or the work is not in the Paris collection but in the collection of the Metropolitan Museum of New York. Grateful acknowledgment is made to the Musée Rodin and the Metropolitan Museum for permission to reproduce these photographs of Rodin's works.

RODIN

I. YOUTH

ON the fourteenth of November, 1840, Jean-Baptiste Rodin, a humble employé at the Prefecture of Police, went to the Mairie of the twelfth district of Paris—now become the fifth— to register the birth of his son, François-Auguste-René; the event had occurred at noon two days before at 3 rue de l'Arbalète. The father was thirty-eight; the mother, Marie Cheffer, thirty-four. The infant was therefore not the son of young parents, but of two people who had attained a certain maturity of mind. Two neighbours witnessed the declaration: Denis-Xavier Moine, an architect living at number 19 of the same street, and Jacques Guillier, a baker from the rue Mouffetard.

Jean-Baptiste Rodin had come to Paris from Yvetot in Normandy; he was descended from a family of cotton-merchants whose name was of Nordic origin and remotely signified red, in the sense of strong and powerful. By a picturesque coincidence his son had fiery red hair until middle age. Jean-Baptiste had been for a time with a Christian Brotherhood as a lay brother, before entering the Prefecture in 1827 where he obtained the position of office messenger at a salary of eight hundred francs a year. A daughter, Clotilde, was born of his first marriage and of his second, to Marie Cheffer from Laundorff in Lorraine, near Metz, were born Maria in 1838 and François-Auguste in 1840. Jean-Baptiste and his second wife were a very pious couple and it is rather surprising that they did not have their second child baptized until he was more

3

than two months old. This delay may have been due, however, to Marie Cheffer's ill health after her son's birth.

The christening took place on January 24, 1841, at the Church of Saint-Médard. The godfather was Auguste Levis, a shop clerk in the rue Cossonerie, doubtless one of Jean-Baptiste's friends from the Halles quarter where he was then employed; and the godmother was Françoise Adam, a lady's maid in the rue Madame. The fact that people of lowly origin were chosen seems to show that the parents expected to rely upon their own courage and industry for the child's up-bringing.

Rodin's birthplace, according to information obtained from the Hôtel de Ville, is no longer 3, but 7 rue de l'Arbalète, owing to a renumbering of the street. To those questioning him, Rodin used to declare that it had been torn down and the ground appropriated for the erection of a school. Perhaps he wished thus to forestall the public indiscretions that he feared would be committed. It is probable that he was born at number 7, on the fifth floor of the tall many-windowed building which today adjoins the more recently erected *Institut Agronomique*.

The street has undergone extensive reconstructions, but near the corner of the rue Mouffetard where number 7 is situated it has kept its original character, its shabby irregularity; some of the tumble-down dwellings are low and squat; others are narrow and tall, seeming to look down over the heads of their neighbours upon what is happening at their feet.

Fate decreed wisely that the son of parents from Normandy and Lorraine should be born in this old poverty-stricken quarter, occupied since the fifteenth century by artisans and later by ordinary workers. The Rodins never left it, the nearest they came to so doing in the course of their frequent changes of abode being when they lived in the remote rue de la Tombe Issoire leading to Montrouge, where their yearly rental was two hundred francs. They dwelt for a long time in the rue des Fossés-Saint-Jacques; then they ascended the rue Saint-Jacques, halting three times, till they finally settled in the rue du Faubourg Saint-Jacques, next to the

4

Hôpital Cochin. Upon these slopes of the Mont de Paris—a quarter filled with old churches and convents, but now being rapidly spoiled by modern buildings—the child could unconsciously absorb the proportions of formal and domestic architecture from the middle ages up to the eighteenth century. During those years he became familiar with Saint-Etienne-du-Mont: the Renaissance smiling amid the austerities of Empire and Restoration University buildings; with the Panthéon: once again the church of Sainte-Geneviève; with Saint-Séverin: a shrine of Gothic art; with the sanctuary of Saint-Julien-le-Pauvre; and finally with Notre-Dame, which he was far from admiring or understanding then; but he was susceptible, and the beauty of these buildings was secretly imprinted upon his mind. Rodin himself realized this in later life while ruminating on "memories of my youth when I could only go where there was no entrance fee, but came away with countless ideas."

The greater part of his life was spent in a neighbourhood of little dance-halls and shops with low, wide windows, dating from the time of the guilds, behind whose little square panes at night glowed the faint golden illumination that one sees in paintings by the Dutch masters. The Saint-Marceau quarter was shabby and constricted, especially the rue Mouffetard, which, except for its roofs, resembled an oriental market. Its narrow passages and alleys, bearing names that charmed the imagination: rue du Pot-de-Fer, Marché des Patriarches, rue Tournefort, place de l'Estrapade, swarmed with people carrying on their business, exhibiting their wares on the pavements: groceries, fruit, milk, fried fish, coal, wines, second-hand clothing, and junk of every description. They were active and alert, never still for a moment, and full of witty repartee.

Rodin was a son of the people and spent his youth among the people. They shaped him and impregnated him with their virile qualities. Had he been born of a bourgeois family, he would not have been Rodin; his fearless and resigned acceptance of life's ordeals, his inflexible endurance, his robust realism which required

5

an ideal and a faith, his profound simplicity, his credulity, his naivety reinforced with shrewdness—all these qualities would have been lacking. From his mother, who was an extremely religious woman, he inherited an inclination towards mysticism. Marie Rodin gave her two children a careful religious training; every Sunday the family went to mass at Saint-Médard, the ancient parish church of the Convulsionists, and when they were living in the rue des Fossés-Saint-Jacques they went to Sainte-Geneviève, and finally to Saint-Etienne-du-Mont. Until the age of nine, Auguste attended a school run by the Brotherhood occupying a building in the rue du Val-de-Grace which had been at one time a part of the military hospital. He must have received poor instruction there, or perhaps he was slow witted—frequently the case with those endowed with a great gift whose maturing consumes their vitality—for he learned almost nothing. On the other hand, a taste for drawing had begun to declare itself. He saved the paper bags and newspapers in which the provisions his mother bought had been wrapped, smoothed them out carefully, studied and copied the pictures he found thereon; such were his first models.

Jean-Baptiste Rodin had a brother Alexandre, reputed to be very intelligent, who was the head of a rather successful institution at Beauvais which he ran in competition to the grammar school there. He offered to take in young Auguste and also his cousin, Auguste Cheffer, five years older. This cousin was the eldest son of one of Marie Rodin's sisters, Thérèse Cheffer, an important member of the family circle. There were five sisters, daughters of an old soldier, and they were all women of courage and sensitivity. One married the proprietor of a little café at Metz: Monsieur Butin; another, Madame Cordonnier, helped her husband who was a hairdresser in the same city; Madame Hildiger was housekeeper for Auber, the composer; Marie married Jean-Baptiste Rodin; and Thérèse, the youngest, did house-work for Michel Drolling. When a young woman finds herself in the household of a painter, it often happens that she poses for him. Drolling did not fail to make use of her in this way; in one of his pictures in the Louvre—the interior of a dining-room—one can see the silhouette of Thérèse at work, with a handkerchief about her head. He also made a pencil portrait of his servant's son.

Once familiar with the irreproachable good manners of Auguste Rodin and with the humble walk of life from which he emerged, it is difficult not to admire the force of tradition in French life of that time. Rodin himself recognized it: "I was given an eighteenth-century education," he often said. He barely escaped that century of grace and courtesy which produced his parents. Was not his father born "on the 29th day of the Pluviose in the eleventh year of the French Republic," that is, in 1802?

Thérèse Cheffer brought up her three sons, Auguste, Emile, and Henri, according to moral and religious principles, and with admirable courage, for their father seems to have failed to assist her. But endless effort and labour held no terrors for this French-woman. The two families were closely united. The Cheffer boys soon showed artistic leanings and all the evidence points to the fact that Rodin received whatever gift he was born with from the maternal, the Lorraine side of his family. Auguste Cheffer wanted to learn engraving and came to live with his uncle Jean-Baptiste during his student years. Emile was similarly inclined and took up commercial design, handing the gift on to his two children who both became artists. Henri became a typographer and bought a little printing business in the rue Saint-Placide which he kept until his death.

Auguste Cheffer, who had married Alexandre Rodin's daughter Anna, resembled his illustrious cousin Auguste Rodin both in feature and figure. I had an opportunity to discover this for myself once when Rodin sent me upon a diplomatic mission to his relative. I was to obtain from M. Cheffer, who was then seventy, a little sketch-book dating from Rodin's early youth. The old engraver-heraldist kept the sketch-book in the safe at his shop in the rue Saint-Sulpice. He showed it to me willingly, but would not exchange it for a piece of sculpture, as Rodin proposed he should do. The precious album is now in the Rodin Museum in Philadelphia, but the Paris museum has others like it.

At Beauvais, Uncle Alexandre's teaching was of no more use to his nephew than that of the Brotherhood. No one realized that the boy was shortsighted, and this disability, which made it difficult and sometimes impossible for him to read writing on the blackboard, gave him a distaste for arithmetic and solfeggio, and he was mortally bored for three years. Nevertheless he was studious and attentive.

How can it be otherwise explained that, after several years of school, he remained almost illiterate, completely unable to spell words or put them together? He remedied these shortcomings later himself by means of extensive reading, and learned to express himself with charming originality and an astonishing sense of brevity and exactness. The spelling remained uncertain and the style unorthodox, but what a savour it had! I used to find him seated at his studio table with five or six freshly written letters spread out before him: "Will you read these and correct the spelling for me?" he would ask with that half-smile that made everything all right. And he would add, calmly philosophical, "After all, mistakes in spelling are like the mistakes that other people make in drawing."

The man who, in his maturity, became embarrassed at the thought of speaking in public, was, when young, tempted to go in for oratory. At Beauvais during recreation hours he would enter the empty class-room, seat himself at the teacher's desk, and harangue the vacant benches.

He continued to devote himself to drawing. But he was not happy; the gentle, well-mannered boy was horrified by the brutality of the young males with whom he lived. He missed the civilized refinements of his home and the school seemed to him almost like a convict-prison. The beauty of the architecture at Beauvais, even the choir of the Cathedral which was to dazzle his vision later, escaped him then—failed to console him in his exile. He adopted the prevailing habit of defaming the works of antiquity and regarded them with bored indifference.

8

He returned to Paris in his thirteenth year, delighted to be with his own people again, with his sister Maria to whom he was attached by a deep reciprocal affection, and with his cousins. The atmosphere of home, though poverty-stricken, was harmonious, and his mother made their dwelling attractive by keeping it neat and clean. Maria was all gentleness, kindness, and devotion. Jean-Baptiste Rodin, though not very clever, had great originality; he was good-tempered and gay, and got on well with his wife. Maria, just fifteen, had her mother's tender heart, adored her parents, and was the joy of the household.

On Sundays they saw the Cheffers who lived successively in the rue des Bernardins, the rue Guisarde, and the rue des Canettes, close to Saint-Sulpice. The two families went together to the Jardin des Plantes; sometimes to Clamart. Jean-Baptiste often acted with Maria and amused everyone with his witty burlesques. Auguste was quieter, more thoughtful, and would sit with his mother whom Jean-Baptiste rebuked affectionately for being a little peevish now and then. These recreations were what Rodin, at the height of his career, called *les petits bonheurs*.

There were also the important family occasions, such as New Year's Day which never passed without the usual exchange of good wishes. Madame Rodin received her nephews affectionately and gave them each one franc fifty, while they brought her a half dozen oranges. Then there were the first communions; Henri Cheffer kept for a long time a rosary and a prayer-book which his cousin Maria had given him on that great day. She was obliged to earn her living and was selling religious articles, chiefly medals. Unlike her brother she had been a good student and was later to become a teacher in a religious community. A cousin of Rodin's, named Coltat, the son of one of Jean-Baptiste's sisters and reputed to be intelligent, was also a dealer in medals and sold them from a little stall in the rue d'Enfer, near the Foundlings' Home.

There was a family secret in the possession of these good people: Clotilde, Jean-Baptiste's daughter by his first marriage, lived in a way that roused the reprobation of her relatives, and they never

9

discussed, even among themselves, this Fantine, who was making severe atonement for her sins.

Auguste Rodin was now fourteen; he would have to learn a trade; the family's resources were very limited and it was thus necessary for him to provide for his own needs. He announced that he wished to learn to draw and at first his father resolutely opposed his determination; later he said that if his son was really a born draughtsman he could make practical use of his gift and consented to his entering the school of Decorative Arts. When Rodin attended the *Ecole Impériale spécial du Dessin et de Mathématiques,* commonly called the *Petite Ecole* to distinguish it from the *Grande* (the *Beaux-Arts*), it occupied a beautiful seventeenth-century house in the rue de l'Ecole de Médecine—in 1928 it was transferred to the rue d'Ulm. Founded in 1765 under the name of *Ecole Royale gratuite du Dessin* by Jean-Jacques Bachelier, favourite painter of Madame de Pompadour who made him art director of the Sèvres Manufactory, the *Petite Ecole* kept its eighteenth-century traditions. In 1854 when Rodin entered it, instruction in the fine arts had had for about twelve years the impetus of an exceptional man, Horace Lecoq de Boisbaudran, who was to become its director in 1866. Uncompromising in his adherence to the unalterable principles of art, he possessed an extraordinary flair for discovering the gifted among his pupils and for helping them to develop without curbing their individuality. "I have retained most of what he taught me," wrote Rodin towards the end of his life in a letter-preface to the new edition of Lecoq de Boisbaudran's book, *L'Education de la Mémoire Pittoresque.* "At that time, Legros and I and the rest of the youngsters did not realize, as I do now, our good fortune in coming under the influence of such a teacher."

Lecoq's instruction, extraordinarily fruitful because his method was spirited and original, stirred up bitter animosity among his colleagues who were steeped in academic dogma; and their sly, spiteful opposition finally, after a struggle of several years, ousted this unrivalled educator. All the artists of Rodin's generation went through the *Petite Ecole*. He was the fellow-student of Jules Dalou, of Alphonse Legros, who was to be a great etcher, of the painter Cazin, of the sculptor and medallist Chaplain, and, among many others, one might name Guillaume, Frédéric Régamey, Fantin-Latour, and Lhermitte. A few years after Rodin, his cousin Emile Cheffer joined the drawing course and his abilities took him immediately into the advanced classes.

On the ground floor under the rotunda the youngsters worked all morning. They were not very numerous at those hours. They copied eighteenth-century engravings, red chalk drawings by Boucher, Bachelier, and Carle Van Loo; they drew from Bouchardon and from living models as well. The tall figure of Lecoq, to whose face age had brought a likeness to Veronese, moved among them, bending over their work and suggesting alterations with the point of his pen-knife. In the evenings the hemicycle was encumbered with crowds of noisy, restless amateurs, mostly artisans: ornament-workers, marble-cutters, iron-workers, weavers, who had come there after their day's work was over to develop their taste and improve their technique. No one was comfortable and it was impossible to see the model from all angles because of the crowding draughtsmen with their boards on their knees; but the regular students made up for their lost time during the morning hours.

At the *Petite Ecole,* between the years 1854 and 1857, Rodin did the thirteen academy figures now in the museum in the rue de Varennes. These he kept throughout his eventful career with its innumerable changes of abode. From these vigorous drawings, the shrewd Lecoq realized what an unusual pupil had been entrusted to his care.

Up to that time the young man knew nothing of the different artistic mediums; he was not aware that sculptors, before cutting stone or marble, moulded a figure in clay and then took a cast of it in plaster. One day he went up to the modelling room where some students were working from the antique. He was astounded by the sight of the soft clay being kneaded and modelled. How delightful must be this means of reproducing figures, and what joy to see them come to life in one's hands! He determined to try it immediately and his first attempts enchanted him. This would be his life work. Before reaching his fifteenth year, his course was chosen.

At first he modelled fragments: hands, feet, torsos, heads; then he attacked whole figures. He had no disappointments or difficulties; he found at once that he understood the structure of the human body. In studio parlance: "his people hung together." He was a born sculptor.

Thenceforth all his time was devoted to study. Every day at dawn he went to the studio of an old painter named Lauset, a family friend, to work at some canvas or other; from eight until noon he was busy at the *Petite Ecole* where two instructors, Fort and Lahémelin, had become interested in him. He was fortunate enough to have his work criticized by Carpeaux, the great Carpeaux who on his return from Rome had asked for the modest position of assistant professor and had been given it without those in authority trying to find anything better for him. The students scarcely appreciated the luxurious gift this painter possessed, but they admired his extraordinary dexterity and the justness of the corrections he made under their eyes.

At the stroke of noon Rodin hurried across the Seine to another task, lunching on rolls and a cake of chocolate as he went. He drew from the antique at the Louvre, or went to the Galerie des Estampes in the Bibliothèque Impériale and asked for albums of engravings after Michael Angelo and Raphael, and a huge work entitled *L'Histoire du Costume romain* from which he studied the representation of drapery. More than once he was distressed at having the precious collections refused him. His poverty-stricken appearance and his timid, uneasy demeanour did not inspire confidence on the part of the librarians. When he was able to obtain them his attention was so rapt that he seemed to be waking out of a dream when the words "Closing time, Gentlemen" echoed through the rooms. From the rue de Richelieu he went halfway across Paris, always on foot of course, to attend a course in drawing at the Gobelins Manufactory from five to eight. There he worked from the nude under the instruction of Lucas.

At home in the evenings he put the finishing touches to his sketches of the afternoon, and, following a practice advocated by Lecoq de Boisbaudran, he drew from memory things he had seen during the day, continuing without interruption far into the night. His health suffered, for he brought his drawing to the dining-table despite the fact that the dinners were scant and quickly eaten. Severe dyspepsia soon resulted, an affliction from which he suffered for years.

He began his career not as a dilettante, but as a workman—a plebeian. Poverty saved him from the sort of artificial education that often weakens the strongest characters. It had prepared him for the struggle and he could have said with Kléber: "My poverty has served me well; I'll stick to it."

Jean-Baptiste Rodin wondered where this frenzy of work would lead his son. When he asked the thin, solemn-faced boy about it, he received the invariable answer: "I intend to be a sculptor." A sculptor, an artist! What madness! It was tempting misfortune. He was displeased and scolded the boy. Madame Rodin, from whom Auguste had obtained the use of a locked cupboard in which to keep his first attempts at sculpture, grumbled: "When are you going to take away all those lumps of plaster? You'll be filling all the corners soon; they'll be under the beds next."

He confided in his sister, told her how it distressed him to have his career thwarted. He did not then realize that opposition strengthens the determination and causes one's desire to take deeper root. At that moment he was miserable. Maria was his only confidante, and she was a kind and understanding friend.

Enchanted vistas began to open for him. At the *Petite Ecole,* his intercourse with the educated students made him aware of his own ignorance. He was greatly upset by the discovery and, impatient

13

to put matters right, he began to read furiously, intoxicated himself with poetry; Hugo, Musset, and Lamartine excited him tremendously, filled him with the desire to know their predecessors, Homer, Virgil, and Dante. Homer immediately burned into his youthful imagination like red-hot iron. He studied literature and history at the *Collège de France;* he read Edgar Quinet and Michelet, and with young and unsuspecting enthusiasm admired the genial historian, though thirty years later he reproached Michelet bitterly for having defamed the Middle Ages, in which French art was at its peak. He passed celebrated men in the Luxembourg Gardens, and, not daring even to greet them, he glanced timidly at them and went his way.

At seventeen his preliminary studies were completed; he wished to leave the *Ecole de Dessin* and enter the *Beaux-Arts*. His mother, doubtless carefully worked upon by Maria, did not oppose the idea and left the decision to her husband. Jean-Baptiste was anxious at least to get an expert opinion of his son's ability. A friend who had been told of the family's problem offered to help; she arranged for the young man to meet Hippolyte Maindron, who had produced *la Velléda,* a much-talked-of statue in the Luxembourg Gardens, and many other widely discussed works, among which were the two monumental groups on either side of the portico of the *Panthéon*. In 1906 Rodin's *le Penseur* was placed at the foot of the portico steps, where it united these two groups; it remained there until 1922.

Maindron made laudable efforts, not always successful, to avoid the tedious technique so admired under Louis-Philippe and Napoléon III. He was struck by the exceptional qualities which the beginner's work revealed and declared his belief in a future for him. Young Rodin was forever grateful for this favourable opinion which obtained for him Jean-Baptiste's consent.

The young sculptor was therefore free to present himself at the *Grande Ecole* which in the opinion of everyone was the only school that could prepare him properly for an artist's career. He entered the lists and was refused. He competed a second time with the same result. What was the reason for his failure? Neither he nor his fellow-students could understand it. While he worked in the modelling rooms they would make a circle round him to admire his visual precision and his already surprisingly skilful hands, assuring him that he would be accepted at the next trial. He failed a third time. At last a student who was shrewder than the others solved the enigma. Dating from Louis David's directorship of the *Beaux-Arts,* the school turned away from eighteenth-century art which, for all its superficial appearance, is full of vitality and measured force. Now Rodin, thanks to the gentle domination of Boucher, Van Loo, Clodion, and Houdon whose work he had so often copied, was a student of the century admired by the *Petite Ecole* but scorned by the *Grande* which was supposed to have been rehabilitated by David. David was an admirable painter of portraits, but disastrous as an educator. "The evil genius of French painting," was Rodin's mature criticism of him. The supple technique of the candidate was the opposite of the stiff composing and surface modelling favoured by the disciples of David. Rodin was not working according to the precepts of the *Grande Ecole* and, fortunately, he never did. Dalou, who had undergone the depleting effects of official instruction, once declared, "Rodin was lucky never to have entered the *Ecole des Beaux-Arts.*"

He was accordingly refused, as Fantin-Latour was refused, numbered forty-first and rejected for good, as many independent and eminent artists have been and will be rejected. It was the first phase of the struggle between Rodin and the Academicians, a struggle which continued to the end of his life, punctuated by some dramatic episodes.

He was not discouraged by his failure and this opposition probably cleared things up for him. His life flowed smoothly and unswervingly, free from the anxieties and conflicting aspirations of most beginners. What unaffected self-confidence for so shy a boy! What resolution had this son of obscure birth, who drew genius

15

in the divine lottery! We have vivid testimony to these qualities in the form of a self-portrait in pencil, very like a beautiful eighteenth-century drawing: a beardless, almost childish face, square brow, wide temples, straight nose with still undeveloped nostrils, mouth tightly closed upon the secret of an unbreakable determination, and, particularly, the converging arch of the eyebrows denoting a will that would never weaken.

He nevertheless regretted his gentle voice, his clear eyes, and his light hair, because he imagined dark-haired men were more successful with women. He was attracted to women, but they frightened him more than they attracted him, and in his young days an overwhelming sense of his poverty kept him from finding out anything about them.

The family had difficulty in living on Jean-Baptiste's increased salary of eighteen hundred francs, so that Rodin had to get a job without further delay. He obtained one with a master-mason named Blanche at five francs a day. Ornamental masonry was wrongly considered to be an inferior art, but the precocious Rodin held that no art was inferior and resolved to give the best that was in him. He became by turns ornament-worker, sculptor's caster, and model-maker for jewellers and cabinet-makers. He was employed successively by the decorators, Bièze, Blanche, and Cruchet. The latter lived in the rue Pétrel in Montmartre and asked him to his apartment. Rodin showed his appreciation of this kindness by making a little bust of Madame Cruchet. He only earned five francs a day, but he gained a manual dexterity which could cope with any plastic difficulty.

One of the workshops in which he was employed opened into a neglected garden, choked with trees and shrubs. Rodin and his fellow-workers, instead of producing ornaments all alike and therefore stale and lifeless, found models in this garden. One of the older and more expert of these, Constant Simon, a native of Touraine, who had done work on the Saint-Michel fountain and

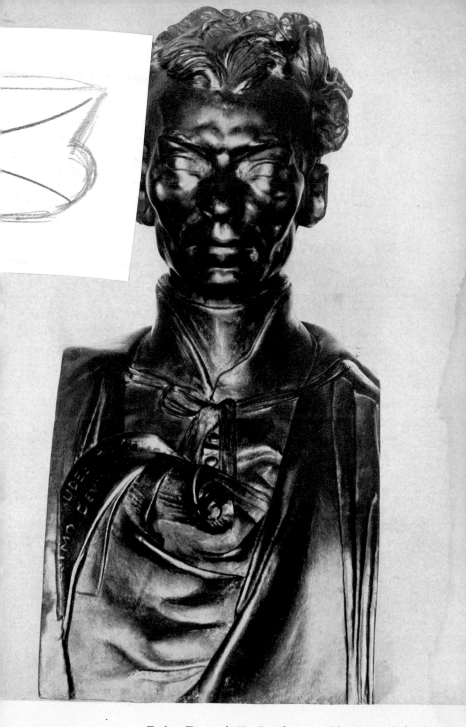

Father Eymard (*Le Bienheureux Père Pierre-Julien Eymard*). COURTESY OF THE MUSEE RODIN

Mignon. COURTESY OF THE MUSEE RODIN

on the restoration of the Medicis fountain in the Luxembourg Gardens, was aware both of his young comrade's cleverness and of his inexperience; he said to him, "You're doing it wrong; don't have your leaves lying flat, they look dull, like bas-relief. Turn up the edges; that'll look like sculpture." This principle of all good sculptors, so simply phrased, became Rodin's from that moment and amazing progress resulted. He always spoke with deep gratitude and emotion of the little man from Blois whose advice spared him years of searching and groping.

He came under the propitious influence of Klagman, the founder of *l'Union Centrale des Arts* and without doubt unjustly forgotten today. Rodin praised the elegance of his statues which were greatly appreciated at the time, also his work on the Louvois fountain.

When Rodin had assured himself of a livelihood he undertook some things for himself. One piece of work done in his twentieth year, the earliest one knows of, shows not only his tendencies but a talent that was already remarkable; it was a bust of his father, the likeness of a fine character done in the antique style—smooth-shaven, as he was then, a civil servant careful of his appearance.

The Rodins were living now in the rue des Fossés Saint-Jacques on the third floor of an old house just behind the Mairie of the fifth arrondissement. From their windows they could see the extensive gardens and walls of a convent for penitents. As is the case with most families, this one had its period of misfortune. Jean-Baptiste, who had been employed successively at the Sorbonne police headquarters, at the Boudreau House of Correction, and at Saint-Denis, was finally made a municipal police inspector, but in August of 1861 he reached the age for retirement and the family resources were thus cut down to his yearly pension of nine hundred francs. Then the blow fell. Maria became infatuated by a friend of her brother's, Barnouvin, who had painted a charming portrait of him at the age of eighteen or nineteen. He also painted one in 1861 of the girl herself, an extraordinary likeness with the grey-blue eyes of her young brother—sober, solemn as a Chassériau or an Italian primitive. This monk-like austerity—a distinctive characteristic of the family—was strikingly noticeable upon Rodin's face with the arrival of maturity. Maria's expression is not that of a happy person. . . . Barnouvin loved another and married. In her despair—no doubt urged by her mother who was completely immersed in religious matters—the forsaken girl decided to take the veil. After a two-year novitiate under the name of Sister Saint-Euthyme her health failed and before she had made her vows she returned to her home where she died of peritonitis towards the end of 1862.

Maria had been everything to her brother, the companion of his infancy and his youth, his guide and his comfort. Auguste's grief was so profound that one feared for his reason. A friend of his mother's, a priest, besought him to have courage and accept the will of God. It was useless. No amount of exhortation could soothe his pain; his art, his work now meant nothing to him. Then, under the influence of the priest, he took the path which desperate people follow if they have faith; he, in his turn, resolved to take orders and went to the *Pères du Très-Saint-Sacrement* for his novitiate under the name of Brother Augustin. The order was housed in a building now demolished in the rue Saint-Jacques. On Christmas night his family saw him in his surplice kneeling upon the flagstones of the chapel, serving mass. (In mature years, though without any formal belief, Rodin remained essentially, he said, deeply religious, and he bestowed upon Nature the love that his early education had urged him to consecrate to God. In this bestowal, however, confusing the works of God with God Himself, he often evoked the Almighty in his artistic conceptions. "The first thing God thought of when He created the world was its modelling," he unhesitatingly declared.)

But his first vocation was not easily laid aside. His passion took possession of him again and he asked permission of his superior to draw and model. Father Eymard, founder of the order of the *Très-Saint-Sacrement,* was a man of great intelligence who has since been beatified by the Church. He arranged for a shed in the garden to be put at the novice's disposal, and when he became aware of the young sculptor's seriousness, of his eagerness to work, he consented to sit for a bust. What is more, the sureness of the beginner's eye and his manifest power made matters clear to Father Eymard, and, several months after Rodin had entered the monastery, he was told that his true destiny lay not in the Church but in the world where, with determination, he would probably become a great artist. The bust that Rodin made of his wise counsellor reproduced in striking manner the strange intelligent features which remind one of certain portraits by Daumier.

Rodin returned to his parents and took up his laborious existence: workman by day and artist by night. He managed somehow to continue his studies, sketching at street corners, at the Horse Market in the Boulevard Saint-Marcel where he was often jostled by the dealers and by their horses, and at the Museum where he worked at the anatomy of animals with Barye.

Emile Cheffer had made friends with the sons of the great animal sculptor. They lived with their father in the rue de Pontoise and he joined their games in the adjacent cloître des Bernardins. The serious and retiring young sculptor did not take part in these games, but he became intimate with the eldest Barye boy and went with him to the Museum. The course in drawing was conducted in the library and there were so many amateurs and women that the boys were uneasy and installed themselves in the cellar which was damp and dreary; Barye lent them some fragments of animal skeletons. They would have preferred to draw from animals in the menagerie, but their instructor ordered them to begin with this rudimentary work since anatomy, the key to plastic art, could in no other way be learned. He came to see them in their retreat, offered brief criticisms, and departed in dreamy silence. He was an unpretentious man, very like a college tutor in his worn frock coat, but he made a powerful impression upon his pupils without their understanding why. Rodin was slow to appreciate this grave, sombre man. All through the year 1864 he attended the course at the Museum; perhaps he would one day be doing groups that included animals; perhaps he would realize the dream that had begun to haunt him: the execution of an equestrian statue. He took a course in anatomy at the *Ecole de Médecine* and worked at the *Dupuytren,* an anatomical museum near the *Ecole des Arts Décoratifs.* Osteology, myology, and neurology stimulated his power of penetration which gave strength to his compositions and prevented him from representing the surface of the human body except as the outer manifestation of its interior structure.

But during all these months he had to earn his living. For one of his employers he worked on the pediment of the *Panorama des Champs-Elysées,* executed a chimney-piece in the lobby of the *Gaîté* theatre, and some caryatides for the *Gobelins* theatre. The Rodin family had moved to the last-named quarter and were now living at 91 rue de la Tombe Issoire. While working at the *Gobelins* theatre, a friend of Rodin's who kept a dress-shop in the rue de Tiers introduced him to a seamstress named Marie-Rose Beuret.

At the age of twenty, Marie-Rose Beuret was more than a pretty woman; she had strong features, big brown eyes that glowed at the slightest trace of emotion, luxuriant dark hair quaintly arranged, and, though she was simplicity itself, her costume which was usually completed by a wide-brimmed hat, gave her an extremely individual appearance. Her father was Etienne Beuret, a vine-grower from Champagne; her mother, Scholastique Clausse. Rose was born in June, 1844, at Vecqueville in the commune of Joinville, Haute-Marne, near the Lorraine border. She used to say, not without pride: "I come from Jeanne d'Arc's country." Certainly the bust she sat for three or four years later which Rodin called *Mignon* and which reproduces her vivid, somehow inspired, features and her roughly braided hair, should have been given the name of the heroine from Lorraine.

Simple, courageous, deeply in love with one another, these two set up housekeeping without binding themselves by legal ties or thinking about the question of money. They were young and healthy; they would work hard. A year and several months later,

on the 18th of January, 1866, a son was born to them at a lying-in
hospital. Auguste-Eugène was given his mother's surname and
only his father's Christian name. What was Rodin's reason for not
acknowledging the infant and not regularizing his own matri-
monial status until nearly the end of his life? Was he waiting for
better times, and, after they came, was it merely carelessness on
his part? Did he become later so enamoured of power, so determined upon complete obedience that he preferred a docile mistress
to a legal wife? No one has ever been able to settle this point.
Those who knew him well at that time and throughout the remainder of his life declare that he was so absorbed in his difficult
career that he never gave the matter a thought.

He was obliged to enlighten his family and spoke first to his
aunt Thérèse Cheffer. Since Maria's death she had been the one
to receive his confidence. The generous heart of this simple woman
enabled her somehow to understand the strange boy who, to everyone else, seemed almost unbalanced, or at least very eccentric.
Nevertheless, his gentleness and his attachment to his family remained. On Sundays in the rue de la Tombe Issoire, his mother
put on the soup pot, Thérèse brought a cake, and they all dined
together, the cousins discussing among themselves their intentions
to find professions that would bring them in money immediately.
It was at one of these gatherings that they saw Rose for the first
time. Rodin had never mentioned her, and when he did speak to
his Aunt Thérèse it was to tell her that he had a son.

Rose continued to earn her meagre wages, doing day's work in
the dress-shop or bringing garments home to sew. There is a
family tradition that Rodin used to help her by putting on the
buttons himself. The young woman also posed for her companion
and this had to be accomplished at dawn and at night, for both
had their regular work to do. Rodin endeavoured not to tire her
with sittings that were too long and she, full of confidence in him,
though unaware of the gift that was maturing before her eyes, and
regarding him simply as a conscientious workman, did not com-

plain; she did not ask what the material benefits of all this hard work would be and she never spared herself.

Sundays, especially in summer, were holidays for both, but the mornings were devoted to leisurely sittings during which the artist could abandon himself to the joy of creation with a free mind. In the afternoons he rewarded his companion by taking her to the suburbs of Paris which were all green groves and gardens, still unspoiled by modern building. In this way was developed a taste for long walks which throughout their lives supplied their favourite recreation.

Rodin now accomplished his greatest desire: he was at last able to rent a studio. Until that time he had been obliged to work in cramped quarters without the space necessary for standing off and comparing his work with his model. Now he had a studio, and what a studio! It was a stable in the rue Le Brun in the Saint-Marcel quarter, and it cost him 120 francs a year. The badly fitting door and the antiquated roof made it terribly draughty, and in one corner there was a well which breathed forth a cold dampness all the year round. Rodin was fully aware of the disadvantages, but they did not matter; the place had enough light and space. The intoxicating fermentation of genius was taking place within him and he accumulated masses of work. Rose sat to him for a large figure, a *Bacchante* which took him two years to complete, and he felt that he was acquiring day by day a mastery of his art. Unfortunately he could not afford to have his things cast; they dried, cracked, and fell apart. Most of his early work was lost in this way. Such was the fate of *la Bacchante*, so tenderly executed. When Rodin was obliged to change studios, some clumsy movers lifted the figure roughly, despite his warnings; the armature gave and the cracked clay fell in pieces. He never got over it.

But he enjoyed recalling the incidents of these poverty-stricken years, found them amusing in retrospect. . . . A friend of the family had succeeded with difficulty in arranging for him to do a bust of a young lady for a modest sum. A cruel difficulty arose: how was the studio to be heated for the sittings? He was too poor to buy the necessary fuel and hit upon the idea of going to a junk dealer in the quarter and buying a bundle of old shoes for a few sous. These could be burned in his stove. But alas, the burning leather gave forth such a foul odour that the young lady fainted. The stimulant required to revive her cost more than a bag of coal.

The year 1864 contained two other important events besides his meeting with Rose Beuret: he entered the studios of Carrier-Belleuse, with whom he remained until 1870, and he sent his first work to the Salon.

Carrier-Belleuse, then in full public favour, became the most highly esteemed decorative sculptor of the end of the Empire and the first years of the Republic. He was also an excellent modeller. Besides hundreds of figures for large-scale decorations or for commercial reproduction, statues and busts of distinction left his studios in the rue de la Tour d'Auvergne. Certain of these are still famous: such as *Le Messie* in the church of Saint-Vincent-de-Paul, *L'Hébé endormie* now in the Louvre, and the busts of Renan, Marie-Laurent, Croizette, George Sand, Théophile Gautier, Napoléon III, Eugène Delacroix, Hortense Schneider; these testify to his clever and flexible talent.

The Goncourts speak of him cruelly as "the pedlar of the nineteenth century and the copier of Clodion" and several eulogists of Rodin have been unjust to this charming artist. When Rodin became a master sculptor he said of the man who was really his first employer: "Carrier-Belleuse had something of the beauty of the eighteenth century in his blood. There was also something of Clodion in him; his studies were admirable, though they lost a little in execution, but he was an artist of great worth."

Rodin was introduced to Carrier by the sculptor Halou, a former comrade at the *Petite Ecole*. In return, forty years later, he took Halou's son as his assistant; he admired his talent and entrusted him with the execution of several important works.

23

At Carrier's studios he made friends with one of the Danielli brothers, a sculptor whose fine head was the inspiration for a boldly treated bust—perhaps the *Buste de M——*, shown at the Salon in 1878, which appeared five years later in bronze. Figures, groups, and smaller objects, fashioned with Carrier's elegance of manner but with a distinctly personal quality were Rodin's share of the output. He also produced many *motifs* to be used in the decoration of Paris buildings, particularly those to be seen on the roof of the small house built for the Marquise de Païva on the Champs-Elysées.

His position with Carrier being now firmly established, Rodin moved across the river and settled in the rue Hermel, in Montmartre, in order to be nearer to the studios. In 1864 he made his first try for the Salon.

In the Saint-Marcel quarter lived an old man, well-known to all the artists there; he posed for them, and between sittings he swept out studios and did errands. They called him Bibi. His air of misery and resignation, his flattened nose and his strange resemblance to a Thessalian shepherd tempted Rodin to do a bust of him with a narrow band encircling his head. One freezing day in the rue Le Brun, the clay cracked and there was nothing left of the bust but the old man's face. He cast this in plaster, called it *l'Homme au Nez Cassé,* and offered it to the jury at the Salon. It was refused.

Several years later, Jules Desbois, a sculptor ten years younger than Rodin, was working by the hour for Legrain who had been entrusted with work for the Exposition of 1878; Desbois noticed the expertness and speed with which one of his comrades executed two large masks for a fountain at the Trocadero Gardens; he, himself, did a third and complimented his colleague; Rodin introduced himself and took Desbois to his studio which was then in the rue des Fourneaux. While looking at Rodin's work, Desbois saw the mask of Bibi on the floor in a corner of the room and picked it up. "I found the extraordinary fragment," the famous sculptor told me just before his death, "and asked Rodin if he would allow me to have it for a few days in order to take an impression. 'By all means,' he said with characteristic and charming generosity. And what humility, what timidity, despite his gifts! He was amazing! The next day I took the mask to the *Beaux-Arts*. 'Look,' I said to my fellow students, 'at this superb antique I've just found at a second-hand shop.' They were full of admiration and the news spread through the school. Everybody came to see it. Then I said: 'Well, the man who did that mask—his name is Rodin—was rejected here three times and the fragment you all take for an antique was refused by the Salon.' " And Desbois concluded his remarks with delightful modesty: "I have remained Rodin's friend; he was from that time my master. Everything that I know I learned with him."

The work has come to be known as *l'Homme au Nez Cassé*, and now has its place in most of the museums of the world.

Rodin's attempt to get into the Salon in 1864 represents the second battle in his unconscious warfare against the Academicians. Apparently, just as with the first, he lost it.

II. BELGIUM

L'Age d'Airain

WHEN the war broke out, Rodin was still working with Carrier-Belleuse. He had left the rue Hermel—the Clignancourt quarter was too far from his employer's studios—and was living in the rue des Saules at the top of the Butte. Montmartre was then a charming village dotted with parks and gardens full of birds and wild rabbits.

The war put an end to all public works and this meant poverty for artists. The young sculptor's household and that of his parents were severely affected by the calamity. At first Rodin was drafted into the 158th Regiment of the National Guard and became a corporal. The neighbours christened him *le grave caporal,* for he smiled less than ever; they also called him *le caporal en sabots,* because he suffered so severely from cold feet during the terrible winter of 1870-1871 that he had to wear this very un-military type of shoe. Owing to his poor eyesight he was soon invalided out of active service. The man whose gaze seemed as sharp as a diamond was very near-sighted, and this deficiency explains perhaps his passion for penetrating to the inmost molecular structure of the human body. All the Rodins had poor eyesight; Jean-Baptiste went blind; also a Coltat cousin. And in several photographs of the sculptor, taken towards the middle of his life, one is struck by the unhealthy state of his eyes and his enflamed eyelids.

Shortly after the declaration of war, Carrier-Belleuse was called to Belgium by the architect Suys to undertake some important decorations for the Bourse at Brussels. He took Belgian artists into his studios: the sculptor Julien Dillens, and a clever modeller named Van Rasbourg who had worked for him in Paris. But when he learned that Rodin was free from military service and absolutely without the means of keeping alive, he sent for him. This meant a period of security for the obscure sculptor, but it also meant separation from his family. In February, 1871, almost immediately after the armistice, Rodin obtained a passport and departed, leaving Rose and little Auguste with nothing to live on, and his parents, who were enfeebled by the privations of the siege, with only Jean-Baptiste's nine-hundred-franc pension.

Before leaving he had wanted to visit Henri Cheffer who was in the *Garde Mobile* of the Seine and was stationed at the *Plateau d'Avron,* a strategic point in the defence of Paris. Emile, the elder of these two cousins, a quarter-master, had been taken prisoner at Sedan. Rodin and his Aunt Thérèse made the journey together, partly in a delivery van and partly on foot. The young sculptor was in civilian clothes except for his corporal's cap. The soldiers of the *Garde Mobile* were suffering from food shortage and had nothing to eat but an insufficient quantity of bad bread, so Mme Cheffer and the two young men set out to look for a tavern where they could have lunch. Rodin had a fondness for such places, to which, as a workman, he had become accustomed because they were within his means. Finally one was discovered, but the only food was bread. However, the cellar produced a bottle of wine and, with some black radishes which Mme Cheffer had had the foresight to bring with her, something like lunch was possible, and the hungry, frozen boys were restored. Rodin was somehow in very good spirits now, and he "began to joke and tell stories," a mood that, for him, was more than rare.

How long would he be in Belgium? Perhaps several months. . . . He stayed there for six years.

At the age of thirty, serious, reserved, proud in his poverty, he exerted a considerable influence among his young comrades in the Carrier studios. They were daily witnesses to his extraordinary skill which rendered the more impressive his inspired gifts; and they made continual demands upon his knowledge and experience. He became intimate with Julien Dillens, his junior by ten years, who, though very talented himself, was filled with admiration for the French sculptor. Rodin worked ceaselessly, as was his habit, under the direction of Carrier by day and for himself in the evenings. In addition to the work for the Bourse, he modelled little busts and groups which Carrier retouched, signed, and turned over to his bronze caster for reproduction.[1]

Rodin was much alone now, badly dressed, absorbed in his thoughts, living in one modest room and eating his meals in small cafés. In Belgium, the land of cleanliness, these were prepossessing with their spotless windows, their polished pewter, their white table-tops which had been scrubbed with sand; and until October, 1871, Rodin dwelt in one of them: the *Estaminet du Pont Neuf* at number 36 in the street of that name, in the centre of town and fairly close to the Bourse. The opening up of wide avenues was just beginning to give the quarter a modern appearance, but this old Brussels street has kept the unpretentious aspect which it had in Rodin's youth.

He was overwhelmed by alarm for his family. What was happening to his loved ones through these months of calamity? How could they keep alive? The money he made was just enough for his own subsistence, and he had been unable so far to send them anything. The terrors of the war were followed by those of the Commune, and he was even more detached from the family circle. Letters from Paris were lost or greatly delayed; he was panic-stricken and wrote an agonized letter to Rose Beuret:

> 36, rue du Pont Neuf
> 3 June, 1871

My darling angel,
   I write you with death in my heart. My poor Rose, where are you? Write me at once. I have written to my parents. What has become of them?

[1] V. Sandor Pierron: *Etudes d'Art*, "*Rude et Rodin à Bruxelles*," 1903.

28

Write me immediately and tell me how you are. I hoped that things were going to be better for me, but now I'm indifferent to everything here.

Write quickly—I will be able to send you a little money soon. If only I could hold you in my arms.

Always yours,

A. Rodin

News came finally. The terrible second siege of Paris by the Versailles Army was over. The whole family was safe. During the war, Rose had gotten work from a Military Supply depot; she had made shirts for the soldiers at a wage of a little over a franc a day, and by working from dawn till night she had been able to keep herself and the child. She also found time to stand in line at the butcher's and baker's with Auguste on her shoulders, in order to get her 250 grams of meat and her bit of bad bread. But at the moment when Rodin learned of the safety of his brave wife he was himself in a most perilous position: he had quarrelled with Carrier-Belleuse. In order to augment his wages by a few sous, he had sold a little figure, modelled and signed by himself, to the bronze caster who issued his employer's works. The latter took offence and discharged his assistant, leaving him with neither work nor money, destitute, and suffering from hunger. Early in July he gave Rose some idea of his plight, but told her that things would soon be better:

My angel,

I am so happy that you are safe and sound. But please tell me more; I am so greedy for news. You don't answer all my questions. Give me details so that I can know what you have been doing through all these dreary weeks. I can comfort you in advance by telling you that I'll be sending you some money in a few days. I think my affairs will soon be in better shape. Keep on hoping, my angel. And if I stay in Brussels I will send for you. I am unhappy without you. You say nothing of M. Garnier, or of M. Bernard to whom I am going to send some money. Go to see

29

him soon and also to the studio. Is anything broken there?

I sent a long letter in reply to yours of a month ago. Did you get it? I want to know about our rooms, the studio, everything. What letters have you received?

I've had a lot of trouble, Rose darling. No work for almost three months, and you can imagine what a hard time it's been. There has been a quarrel with M. Carrier, but things will be better. You'll have to wait a little longer, Rose. I haven't a sou now. A chemist here and also one of my colleagues have helped me. Without them I can't imagine what would have happened. I asked you, in that long letter I wrote, to pawn my trousers; that would be money easily earned. What about M. Tyrode? Tell him that I'll send him some money as soon as I can. I don't see how we can keep such an expensive place. But in a month I'll be able to tell whether I'm to stay in Belgium or come back to Paris. Go to M. Garnier [2] and ask him to write me; tell him he ought to have his busts baked, and that I sent this message to him through you. Ask Bernard to write me. Also M. Schavary, the wine-merchant.

Tell me everything you can think of.

I love you with all my heart.

Your,

Auguste Rodin

Thus Rose, with all her other occupations, was appointed guardian of the studio in Paris. It seemed to her perfectly simple: had not her husband assured her that her efforts would soon be rewarded? The conjugal union of two courageous people is a wonderful thing: each inspiring hope in the other and hoping for the other's welfare.

Rodin's great expectations were to be realized, without, however, the large material benefits that he anticipated. At the end of the Commune, Carrier-Belleuse, also impatient to rejoin his family, returned to Paris. He had recommended the Belgian, Van Rasbourg, to Jean Rousseau, the director of the Fine Arts adminis-

---

[2] There were several sculptors of Rodin's generation named Garnier. It has not been possible to determine to whom this refers.

tration, as quite capable of completing the work for the Bourse. Though a skilful modeller, Van Rasbourg did not feel himself equal to the task of composing vast decorative ensembles and he availed himself of Rodin's assistance.

The two sculptors made elaborate plans for the future, installed themselves in a studio in the Faubourg d'Ixelles, at 111 rue Sans-Souci, and took in Julien Dillens as temporary assistant. A year's trial must have convinced them that they could work together, for, on the 12th of February, 1873, an agreement was signed by Antoine-Joseph Van Rasbourg and Auguste Rodin of 172 rue du Trône, probably a furnished room or a tavern. The agreement was to be in force for twenty years—actually, the partnership was dissolved on the 31st of August, 1877. The document provided for the signing of the works for which the two collaborators expected to be commissioned in France as well as in Belgium. Each was to sign those destined for his own country, and this clause accounts for the fact that the work done by Rodin at that time bears only Van Rasbourg's name.

The beginning of work did not make it possible for Rodin to send for his wife; he explained the reason for this. Now that the evil days were past, he could speak lightly of them:

My dear Rose,

I have received your letter. It's a long one, thank heaven! But you don't tell me what has happened to the studio. And I want more details about our private affairs, of course. I'm sending you 20 francs; spend them carefully. Also 30 francs for Mamma. My poor darling, if I could only kiss you! I can't have you here with me yet. I can spend almost nothing, because we are not paid immediately for our work. Not long ago I had a meal of ten centimes' worth of mussels and the same of fried potatoes. It's been like another siege. Now I can imagine buying a whole ham, but, though my luck has changed, the money is still to come.

My poor Rose, I think such a lot about you! I blame myself continually for not being with you, but I have no money at all.

My darling, all things have an end, even misfortune. Put your mind at rest and have faith in me.

Bernard must go to the studio. And poor Domasque, I'll soon be sending him some money.

M. Garnier lives at the corner of the rue Antoinette and the Chaussée des Martyrs, near the Mairie—over the grocer.

He was encouraged about his affairs and in August or September of 1871 wrote again—this time a gay and charming letter. What did the makeshift spelling and the non-existent punctuation matter to Rose whose education was greatly inferior to his and who could herself barely write down what she wanted to say? Her heart enabled her to value these communications at their true worth, for she kept them all her life; and we have her to thank for these precious glimpses into the deeply affectionate nature of the man who, later in his life, was so cruelly slandered.

36 rue du Pont Neuf, Brussels

My dear Rose,

I have been thinking about you today—as a matter of fact for several days past you have been continually in my mind. If I had been alone I would have written you a long letter. I was in the country, happy, enjoying the pure air and the sunlight, but my thoughts were far away, with you. It seemed to me that I could hear you saying nice things to me and that you were happy too. And all those thoughts of you made that song you used to sing come back into my mind:

> *Soldats qui m'écoutez*
> *Ne le dites pas à ma mère,*
> *Mais dites-lui plutôt*
> *Que je suis à Breslau,*
> *Pris par les Polonais*
> *Qu'elle ne verra jamais.*

You see, I had an attack of tenderness. I'm so changeable that I too am visited now and then by affectionate little impulses,

Man with a Broken Nose (*L'Homme au Nez Cassé*).
COURTESY OF THE MUSEE RODIN

Caryatid (*L'Un des deux Cariatides de Saint Gilles*).

though I don't want them always with me. When they pay their rare visits I welcome them with delight, but they must not come too often. I don't like tyranny of any sort, even the tyranny of tender emotions. . . . I must stop this chatter. Write me a long letter; I promise you it will please me greatly. Don't spray the clay figure too much or the legs will get soft. I'm glad you are looking after my casts and clay figures. I'll send a little more money in a fortnight. Give my regards to Mme and M. Pouilleboeuf.

I'm sending 65 francs now: 30 for the big Italian, Fortuné Zangrandi, who called to see you. He'll come for it. 30 for my parents, and 5 for your clothes. I'm sending mother's to you so that she won't have to go out with a postal order. I hope Papa is being well looked after. Write me details and ask Bernard to write me at the *Estaminet du Pont Neuf, rue du Pont Neuf.*

Your
A. Rodin

I would like Bernard to finish my marbles. I'll send him some money.

The Bernard now in question was a marble-cutter, a friend to whom he had entrusted the execution of some of his figures. How could he buy the marble and pay the artisan for his work at a time when poverty obliged him to pawn his trousers? And how was Rose able to keep the clay figures in good condition for so long? The spraying was a delicate business and required an experienced hand, but Rodin had doubtless taught her how to do this when they were together. What patience, what diligence, and what love all this required during his long absence! Even in his later days when he had three casters working for him he preferred to let his wife look after his clay figures if he had to leave Paris, so sure was he of her skill. And sometimes she enjoyed showing one of the casters the best way to take an impression.

Rodin had no hesitation in entrusting her with even greater responsibilities: she had to supervise the moving to a less expensive studio. In his letters he overwhelmed her with instructions which he made more explicit by means of little sketches to help her recognize the figures he mentioned. In spite of all this care, many precious fragments were lost, many rough casts were broken in the successive movings, and many portfolios filled with drawings went astray. What became of "the little clay virgin" so strangely dear to Rodin who could resign himself to the loss of the casts of other figures? . . . *L'Alsacienne* about which he seemed anxious was a bust of Rose executed during the siege of Paris; upon the features were engraved the patriotic regrets felt by everyone then, at the thought of the lost provinces:

My dear Rose,

I am sending you 100 francs for M. Tyrode; the rest is for the moving. Leave the *Gladiateur* on account of its weight; also the little torso, *l'Amour*—it is cracked and awkward to manage. It's this one [sketch]. Leave the cast of Père Eymard, but please be careful of the cast of Bibi and of that little clay virgin [sketch]. My poor Rose, you have not written me and I have not been able to send you any money. You could not have had enough, but you know what my expenses are. I couldn't do otherwise. Don't worry; I shall come by the middle of October. We are arranging for a sale at Antwerp; if it succeeds I'll send you a present to buy clothes with. Domasque has still a month to go and that's an expense.

Write me, my dear, and go to see Papa so that you can tell me how he is. Have you some work to do? Write me a long letter at once. I wanted to send you a five-franc piece to spend on a little dinner for Mme and M. Pouilleboeuf, but that will have to be some other time. I want you to do this when I send it.

Good-bye—I am not very well these days.

Affectionately, your

A. Rodin

1st. October 1871

In your next be sure to tell me your address. Mine is changed. Here it is: 346, Chaussée de Wavre. Notice that it is spelled with a W. Be careful of the casts; wrap them each one in newspapers, handkerchiefs, or anything of that sort—especially the cast of *l'Alsacienne*.

In this struggle for material and intellectual subsistence, which of them was the more touching: the artist determined to develop his talent in strict accordance with his conscience, or the woman who offered the support of her unflagging devotion?

An anonymous portrait of Rodin, painted several years later, betrays, with realistic but delicate touch, the traces of this ordeal: the features are pale and the eyes restless, and the flesh has the unhealthy look of a man who has suffered too long from overwork and malnutrition. The author of this poignant document has also noted the nervousness and inner agitation of the artist who does not as yet feel completely sure of himself. The portrait Alphonse Legros painted in 1882 reveals the same disordered health and mental anxiety, and the painful implications of both painters give rise to the thought that the greatest sculptor of his time was not far from collapse before the flowering of his genius.

At the end of 1871 a grievous blow fell: Rodin who was so devoted to his parents lost his mother. Like many other housewives of that period, Marie Rodin and her sister Thérèse fell ill as a consequence of the privations of the war: lack of food and endless waiting in the bitter cold outside shop-entrances. Thérèse recovered, but the sculptor's mother who had had, some years before, a serious attack of smallpox failed to do so and died in her little apartment in the rue de la Tombe Issoire. Though no trace of her grave, or of her daughter Maria's, exists today, it is very probable that she was buried in the neighbouring cemetery at Montrouge. Later, in his days of relative prosperity, Rodin was able to see that his father had a suitable grave, and it must have been a terrible thing for him to be unable to do likewise for the mother he had loved so deeply. But at least there remains a portrait of her, a curious painting done by her son. The features, encircled by short brown hair, have a wild, tormented look, suggesting that of a hunted gipsy. And a strange fact is that the same expression of savage exaltation was often seen on Rose Beuret's face, matured by age and its attendant sorrows. Rodin has reproduced it upon the tragic features of his *Bellone*. After Marie Rodin died, who was to care for her husband whose health and eyesight were failing? Was not Thérèse Cheffer at hand with her inexhaustible kindness? She had remarried, and lived with her husband, M. Dubois, in the rue Dauphine where she had established herself as a laundress. She considered it perfectly natural that the widower should come to live with them, and more than that, when Rodin sent for Rose to join him in Belgium, Thérèse took charge of little Auguste who was six years old. She cared for him for seven years and met all expenses with Jean-Baptiste's nine-hundred-franc pension, adding to it what she could afford.

Her kindness was truly angelic, and when two of her sons returned to Paris, one a freed prisoner and the other having escaped to Havre during the Commune after service at the Federation Headquarters in the Place Vendôme, they found a whole family of poverty-stricken neighbours whom they did not know living with their mother. She was generous even with things that were not hers and gave to all those who desired them the innumerable sketches that Rodin had left behind him or given to his cousins, so that when the latter re-established themselves in their mother's apartment there were none to be found.

It is easy to understand Rodin's deep affection for the woman whose devotion to him was as great as that of his own mother, and one also sympathizes with his anxious protests when she became so old that her sons felt obliged, because of her scattered family, to place her in a home for the aged, kept by nuns in the rue Violet.

The Rodin-Van Rasbourg partnership seemed to function smoothly. For the exterior of the Bourse at Brussels, Rodin modelled, and cut in stone and marble, a group of cupids for the main façade, and two colossal groups—Asia and Africa—for a lateral façade; for the interior, four monumental caryatides depicting Commerce, Industry, and the Arts, and a vast bas-relief of two gnomes supporting a globe—a composition both imposing and charming, set into the pediment above the entrance to the public hall. In 1874 he executed two fine decorative groups of cupids offering trophies for the exterior of the *Palais des Académies,* which, according to the agreement, were signed by Van Rasbourg. And Rodin did not disown this youthful work when he himself showed it to me twenty-five years later; nor was he ashamed of the twelve caryatides embellishing several houses in the boulevard Anspach. For three of these figures, which were over six feet high and took long weeks of labour to complete, the sculptor received 750 francs.

He was also the chief executant of the monument erected by the city of Antwerp to the Burgomaster Loos, for which the painter-sculptor Jules Pécher had been commissioned; it was signed by this artist as being entirely his own work.

This unsigned and unremunerative work kept Rodin alive, but it did not advance his reputation; he seemed in no hurry to acquire fame and fortune. Five or six years later when he returned to Paris, he was still unconcerned by these considerations. One of his Belgian friends, Gustave Biot, the engraver, scolds him affectionately:

"One of my friends, M. Peussens of 29 rue de Berlin, saw your bronze *Nez Cassé* and seemed to be anxious to have it. He asked me its price and I told him that you would like to have it placed somewhere and would let it go very reasonably, for two or three hundred francs, perhaps less. You should fix a price and let him know, or me. I advise you to put a decent figure on it; you can't always work for nothing. After all you have to pay for the pedestal, etc., . . . And maybe Kips will buy something too."

What he wanted—or so it seemed to those who knew him at that time—was the slow but sure mastery of his art. Despite his miserable health, he seemed to know instinctively that his life would be a long one (this was a family trait), that he would have plenty of time for the full development of his genius, and that its splendid progress should not be impeded by haste or impatience. "Until the age of fifty I had all the worries of poverty," he said in his old age. "I have always lived like a workman, but the pleasure of working enabled me to endure everything." His pockets were crammed with books to be read avidly at meal times and even while walking in the streets; the need to cultivate his mind became a passion with him. All his faculties matured simultaneously.

His dreary solitude came to an end at last. Rose joined him in 1872 and he moved to a larger room at 15 rue du Bourgmestre, not far from the studio in the rue Sans-Souci in the Ixelles quarter where he remained till the Belgian sojourn was over and which now has an avenue bearing his name.

Both of them were happy; a little money was coming in, and, with economy, they were able to put by several hundred francs. Life in Belgium was not difficult and the cleanliness of the streets and the houses made it particularly agreeable; the bread, beer, and coffee were excellent, and so cheap! A few very simple people were all they knew: a shoemaker, an upholsterer and his wife whose conversation, though full of the good sense that is common to those who are in daily contact with tangible things, was scarcely able to draw Rodin out of his continual preoccupation. He lived the life of the people and understood it; he had no reason to complain of it. Nor did he ever speak offensively of the Belgians, after the manner of Baudelaire and Verlaine: two aristocrats whom they did not appreciate. On the contrary, he always felt a peculiarly warm friendship for them; he had always found a sympathetic understanding in Belgium.

An accident affecting his health occurred at this time; he expended too much strength one day in moving some blocks of stone and began to suffer internally. He was obliged to consult a doctor who told him a small operation was necessary and performed it himself. When the sculptor had recovered he called to thank the doctor and to enquire anxiously what he owed him. The doctor, taking his obviously small means into account, told him his fee would be twelve francs.

"Twelve francs?" cried the astonished Rodin. "Here they are, but I will do a bust of you if you like."

Thus it was that he executed the bust of Doctor Thiriar, an able surgeon who afterwards became an eminent professor and doctor to King Leopold II. He had a fine head with curly hair and a short beard resembling that of a Roman of the Augustan age. In 1874 the bust figured in the *Salon de Gand* and later a bronze copy was placed in the University of Brussels.

In the rue du Bourgmestre, when not required to be at his studio, Rodin modelled little busts in the Carrier manner—*Dosia* and *Suzon,* for instance—whose voluptuous grace saved them from dulness; these he sold to commercial casters for from fifty to eighty francs apiece. In the same room, Rose did her sewing and mending, also her cooking and washing. She had recovered her gaiety and Rodin heard her singing again:

> *Soldats qui m'écoutez*
> *Ne le dites pas à ma mère,*
> *Mais dites lui plutôt*
> *Que je suis à Bordeaux. . . .*

Sunday mornings were spent in careful study at the *Musée des Moulages* in the *Palais des Académies* before its final removal to the *Parc du Cinquantenaire.* There he compared the works of Antiquity with those of the Middle Ages. Sometimes he took his wife to the collegiate church of Sainte-Gudule. The beauty of Gothic architecture had already conquered him and was to fill his mind for the rest of his life. In the afternoons he and Rose went to the Soignes forest, at one time hallowed by its seven monasteries. The colonnade of beeches, like pillars in a cathedral nave, was stimulating to the imagination of a man given to mysticism. There was no luxuriant vegetation there, none of that graceful, rustling undergrowth so characteristic of the Ile de France. It was an ogival, a Gothic forest for solitary meditation. Rodin's grave spirit, almost as much inclined to religion then as in his younger years, acquired a kind of superconsciousness while walking in it; and he was deeply moved by the vale of Groenendaël, frequented in the fourteenth century by Ruysbroëk l'Admirable, the great contemplative theologian, with its peaceful lakes and flowering meadows like mediaeval tapestries. He never forgot to take his colour-box which Rose delighted in carrying for him, and he painted bits of the Brabantine landscape; but he would often let the day pass without taking out his brushes and abandon himself to the contemplation of his surroundings, to the joy of silence and the pervading forest odours. When in this mood he refused to emerge from his reveries which were perhaps more fruitful than work itself, for his sensitive eye would be absorbed by the proportions of the lofty trees, and by the interaction of light and shadow which produced an atmosphere of consecrated solemnity. The forest made such a powerful impression upon him that when he returned to France it was several years before he could appreciate the less austere qualities, the smiling brightness of the country round Paris.

It was at Brussels—he realized this later—that his spirit reached maturity, that he walked out to meet his genius among those lofty forest trees.

An important work was produced during those years which were perhaps the most moving ones in Rodin's development: *L'Age d'Airain*. Fundamentally, this fine human column is the representation of his own recent personal drama. In the grip of immediate emotion he called it *le Vaincu*, but as soon as the process of creation was over and it had left his hands, it became endowed with a life of its own, took on symbolic proportions and dictated to the sculptor its true title: *L'Homme qui s'éveille à la Nature*.

In the evenings he and Rose would return to the city, after lingering in the villages on the edge of the forest to watch the villagers playing bowls in the café gardens and drinking the excellent light beer of the country. If Rodin had had the time he would have liked to join in their games—exercise as well as recreation—and in his old age he often considered making a bowling-green in the garden at Meudon.

These years, so rich in the joys of work and filled with the intoxicating vigour of youth, put a spell upon him which lasted all his life. Perhaps, too, his grave and tender disposition, Norman mixed with Lorraine, was so in harmony with the Flemish that he believed he had found a second home in the country which was itself compounded of two races.

In Brussels there were vivid reminders everywhere of Rude, a master of French sculpture whose talent, like his own, took definite form in Belgium, but nearly fifty years before. Rude had remained there for twelve years and had produced, for the palaces of Tervueren and Laeken, his most important decorative work—with the exception of the famous *Marseillaise;* though widely scattered throughout the country, almost all of it has been destroyed by fire. Rude became one of Rodin's great admirations.

His reputation now spread among artists and writers; he was intimate with the sculptors Constantin Meunier (as hard-working and as poor as he himself), Dillens, Paul de Vignes and his cousin de Winne, the animal sculptor Bouré; with the engraver Gustave Biot, Jean Rousseau the Fine Arts director, and Camille Lemonnier, admirable art critic as well as prolific novelist; with Léon Gaucher, editor of *L'Art;* and with Charles Tardieu, future editor of *L'Indépendance Belge.* All these men stood by Rodin, several years later, when the affair of *L'Age d'Airain* came to a head. Busts of several of them remain as proofs of his gratitude.

He was well aware that *L'Homme au Nez Cassé,* despite the 1864 jury, was a superior work and he restored the bust, cut it in marble, and sent it in 1872 to the Brussels Salon. In spite of the enthusiastic campaign, headed by Dillens and the painter Bourson, there were no purchasers for it. The same fate awaited it at the Paris Salon of 1875, where, this time, it was admitted without

41

opposition, along with a terra-cotta bust of the sculptor Garnier.

Rodin had made peace with his old employer. Also, he realized now that he had been in the presence of genius while studying at the Museum and he had himself listed in the catalogue as a pupil of Barye and of Carrier-Belleuse.

For several years a two-fold desire had been growing within him: to produce a work which would make an impression on the public, and to see Italy. So far he had had bad luck with his large figures; *La Bacchante* had been destroyed, and a life-size figure for which Rose had sat, treated in the Gothic manner, that is, with long folded draperies, had not been cast in time to avoid cracking. He lamented its loss—a considerable one for posterity, for it was his only draped statue of a woman. But discouragement was unknown to him, and he began a new figure. It was to be an important one, finely wrought to the last detail, and not to be considered finished until the utmost limit of its possibilities had been reached.

He visited the cities and the museums of Belgium, where, he once wrote to Bourdelle, he acquired nothing "but a love of nature during my long walks, and a delight in the austerity of the forests." He studied her artists, particularly Rubens, several of whose paintings he copied while visiting Antwerp. But now that he intended to express himself in an important statue, careful study of the Italian masters seemed indispensable to him. The call of Italy and particularly of Michael Angelo became irresistible. Doubtless the great master had a two-fold fascination for him: that of his personality as well as his genius. There was also in his smouldering imagination an affinity of sentiment, of still hidden gifts, drawing him with the power of predestination towards the amazing Florentine.

He approached him as in former years he had approached God. He convinced Rose of the necessity of this journey, entrusted her

42

once more with the care of his studio, and departed toward the end of the winter of 1874-75.

He went first to Rheims, then crossed the Alps at Mont-Cenis, stopping at Turin, Genoa, and Pisa; he crossed the Apennines on foot and visited Florence and Rome. Rigorously economical with the little hoard he had brought with him, he walked a great deal to save railway fare, but also to acquire an intimate acquaintance with the country. He ate macaroni at street corners, and he saw Italy and the works of art which have made her famous. From Rome he wrote his impressions to Rose, as intimate and witty as those of a workman on a holiday and calculated to make her smile before he began to speak of his discoveries:

"I must tell you that there is a sausage I got at Pontarlier which is beginning to give me trouble. I thought one couldn't eat in Italy and I got this as a final reinforcement. I'm eating well now and drinking quite a lot to your good health. I've just poured myself a glass from a bottle something like a 'Marie-Jeanne.' I had it put in my room so I could keep up my strength for the hard life I'm leading. For I must tell you that I don't always eat regularly. I only bother about my stomach when there is nothing for me to look at. Just like my watch: I forget that it's stopped, or hours fast, and don't understand why the museums are so late in opening.

"I must have brought Belgium with me for there was snow on the way and it's raining here. People tell me that as soon as I go they will have their usual fine weather. I suppose that's how it will be.

"I meet trippers everywhere, almost all of them French, but some English. I've been travelling as though I were in France so far, eating and sleeping as cheaply as I want. All travellers have to be rather bold and I get on very well. The men, my Rosette, are very handsome: brown skin and black moustaches.

"Shall I tell you something about the fine arts now? . . . By the way, take good care of my figure; don't wet it too much. I want

43

it to stay pretty firm. Attend to this yourself and don't let that little idiot Paul touch it.

"First, my journey: Dinant is picturesque, and the cathedral at Rheims of a beauty that I have not yet met in Italy. Your part of the country was very nice. At Pontarlier, where my sausage came from, there were two feet of snow and the Alps from Lausanne were very fine; the view of them was admirable as far as Geneva— a splendid city."

Without knowing it, he restated the celebrated opinions of *le président de Brosses:*

"The railway enters Savoie, a wretched part of the country, whose famed chalets have a suburban look. Nothing but mountains, horrible all the way to Saint-Jean de Maurienne. Within these terrifying walls human beings soon become idiots."

He passed through "the mole hole that pierces Mont-Cenis" and was at last beyond the Alps. His letter continues:

"I stopped here to listen to a fine trio of voices; in Italy the arts have now taken refuge in Music.

"Now I'll take up my story again. The slope toward Italy was incredibly beautiful; the landscape is much more human and just as majestic as Savoie. It rained at Turin; there is contemporary sculpture in all the public squares—very ugly, including the Marochetti, equestrian figure sheathing his sword. Genoa: I had artichokes and peas there (very pretty women, Rosette). Pugets very like Michael Angelo in detail, but they are somehow less Puget than the ones I know . . . I'm going by train to Pisa; there are over a hundred tunnels, little ones. It's like the Alps—you go under mountain spurs along the seashore."

With his passion for precision he completed his account with a little map showing the railway line and announced that he would speak of the works of art at Pisa in another letter. He journeyed to Florence in wonderful weather; it was "an earthly paradise with

44

the green, violet and blue mountains." And now comes the passage which makes this letter infinitely precious to Rodin's biographers, to those who have explained and will explain the development of his art; it is the account of his so ardently desired face-to-face with Michael Angelo; two geniuses: one in the bright radiance of immortality, the other in the darkness of germination; and the humble Rose Beuret was the first one to receive the confidence:

"There has been fog and a little rain in Florence for the last six days. None of the photographs or the casts I have seen give the slightest idea of the San Lorenzo Sacristy. One has to see these tombs in profile and at a three-quarters angle. I have spent five whole days in Florence and only saw the Sacristy this morning. Well, that makes five days without any very great excitement. Now I have three deep and lasting impressions: Rheims, the ramparts of the Alps, and the Sacristy. It is impossible at first to make a clear analysis of what one sees. You will not be surprised when I tell you that the moment I arrived in Florence I began to study Michael Angelo, and I believe the great magician is going to reveal some of his secrets to me. But none of his pupils or his masters could do what he did, and I don't understand that; I have analyzed the work of his actual pupils. The secret was his and his alone. I've made sketches in the evenings in my room, not of his works, but figures that I have imagined and elaborated in order to understand his technique. Well, I think I have succeeded and I believe they have that quality, that nameless something which he alone could give."

He thought he had discovered at once "that nameless something," that secret—purely technical of course—but he was wrong. He believed it to be the animation, or the distinctive individuality of the figure. But it was the modelling, the tremendous power of the modelling, and it took him three or four years of studying and comparing Michael Angelo's figures with living models to find this out. As he said, the great master set him free, gave him his final instruction, handed down to him the masculine method of sculpture.

Some important art critics of Rodin's time refused to admit that he was influenced by Michael Angelo. How could they have been so mistaken? Why did they not question him at this culminating moment in his development, when, at the age of thirty-five, he was still desperately hunting for the truth? He has often told of the long search which obsessed him. In a previous book,[3] I have assembled his detailed accounts of it, and in the following letter to Bourdelle, about 1906, he confirms the result:

"Michael Angelo liberated me from Academic methods. In teaching me (by observation) rules that were diametrically opposed to the ones I have been taught (School of Ingres), he set me free. . . . He held out his powerful hand to me and helped me over the bridge from one school to the other. This mighty Geryon carried me across."

The letter to Rose ends with the full itinerary of his journey and some intimate details:

"Then I came to Rome; Naples next (I'll go back to Florence one day); then Venice, and back to Paris in about a fortnight; I'll stay there two days. Finish Auguste's little overcoat in time for that; it's probably done already. Be careful of my statue and say hello to Joseph [doubtless Van Rasbourg] and his wife, and the neighbours too.

                                        "Auguste Rodin

"It's a pity Joseph didn't come with me; the living is so cheap: 5 francs a day including everything but the museums. [Rodin's trip cost him between five and six hundred francs.] Don't spend more than I gave you unless there is an emergency.

"Don't wet the statue too much. I've been here in Rome two days; write me at the Hôtel de Leone, Via Victoria, as soon as you receive this letter."

[3] Judith Cladel: Auguste Rodin: *L'Oeuvre et l'Homme*.

How unfortunate that we have no further letter giving us his impressions of the city he admired above all others and to which he returned many times, though only after a period of thirty years; and telling us of his reactions to Raphael and the Sistine Chapel. "How eagerly," he wrote at that period, "how eagerly I attacked the museums—and was disarmed!" There are several drawings which were made during his direct contact with the Florentine master's work, one of which seems to have been done from the Vatican Faun and is exceptionally fine. But deep within him, for he was unusually susceptible, he had absorbed much more than he knew. As a result of this transfusion of imponderables, this long communion with the supreme genius of the Renaissance, there was in the very fibres of his being a love of impetuous life, of movement and *relievo*, an obsession with the springing figures which make the ceiling of the Sistine Chapel one of the miracles of art. He never spoke of this and, as far as I am aware, no critic has ever called attention to it. Nevertheless it seems to me that one needs only to look at *La Porte de l'Enfer* to be convinced of it.

He returned to Belgium with his imagination seething and his heart beating fast with the desire to excel. More than ever tormented by his passion to produce something, he began work on the figure he had abandoned for his Italian journey. From that moment a creative frenzy possessed him and statues were executed in rapid succession. He was now halfway through his life which he had consecrated completely to one aim; in his mature years and even in his old age, he was almost as powerful and fertile as the master whom he had chosen.

He needed a model; professionals who had been spoiled by the studios and could only pose conventionally were of no use to him. He made friends with the officers at one of the barracks in the military quarter near his room in the rue du Bourgmestre, and spoke to them of his desire to find a model among the handsome young men under their command. A soldier from the engineering

47

corps, a telegraphist named Auguste Neyt, was authorized to pose for him.

He worked at the statue for more than eighteen months, until December, 1876, because, as he told his young colleagues at the Van Rasbourg studio, "one mustn't be in a hurry . . . an artist's reputation can be made with one statue." He worked at this one from every angle, climbed a ladder in order to determine the exact position of the top of the head, the shoulders, the hips, the feet, and he gave the young soldier a staff for support during the endless posing.

In January of 1877, he sent the finished statue to the show at the *Cercle Artistique* in Brussels, calling it *Le Vaincu*. It was a glorification of luckless heroism which still touched his French heart.

The following paragraphs in the *Etoile Belge* of January 29th caused him surprise and indignation; they contained a mixture of praise and criticism with a perfectly clear insinuation and a decidedly thoughtless turn of phrase:

"M. Rodin, one of our talented sculptors who has heretofore been represented in the Salon by his busts only, shows at the *Cercle Artistique* a statue destined to figure at the *Exposition de Paris*.

"It will not pass unnoticed there, for it not only attracts one's attention on account of its strangeness but holds that attenion on account of a precious and rare quality: life.

"We cannot here discuss how much casting direct from the human body there is in it; we merely wish to mention the figure whose appearance of physical and mental collapse is so expressively portrayed—we have no other information than that supplied by the work itself—that the sculptor seems to us to have endeavoured to represent a man about to commit suicide."

Casting from life, a practice unworthy of a true sculptor and disastrous for art, was nevertheless a common one in the most reputable studios. Rodin's conscience would never have allowed him to indulge in such a makeshift and he could not endure the newspaper's insinuations. On the 2nd of February he sent a pro-

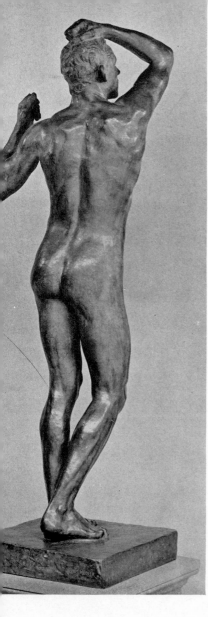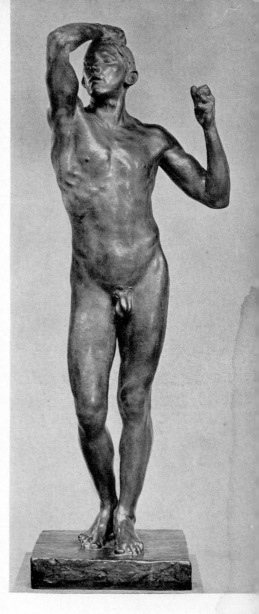

Bronze Age (*L'Age d'Airain*). COURTESY OF THE METROPOLITAN MUSEUM OF ART

Defence (*La Défense*). COURTESY OF THE MUSEE RODIN

test to the *Etoile Belge,* and an anonymous editor deigned to publish a few lines from it with comments that were anything but frank:

"M. Rodin protests against the suggestion that his figure, shown at the *Cercle Artistique,* may have been cast from life. He says, 'If some connoisseur would like to oblige me by satisfying himself on this point, I will arrange for him to see my model, and he will then be able to ascertain how far removed an artistic interpretation must be from a slavish copy.' Our minds are made up, but we must call M. Rodin's attention to the fact that we did not for an instant mean to give the impression that his statue was a slavish copy, and we think it strange to say the least that he should use our perfectly friendly statement as a basis for his reply to doubts which originated at the *Cercle.*"

Thus the accusation spread through professional and official circles. Ignorance could hardly have accounted for its origin; the figure whose anatomy was so exact and whose flesh was so living had a dignity and a nobility which were due entirely to the interpretation. Envy must therefore have been the motive of his slanderers. A little group of writers and artists warmly defended him, but he required indisputable reparation. He sent the statue to the Paris Salon where he expected competent and sincere judgment. Perhaps also, the State would acquire it. What a reply that would be to his defamers!

He went to Paris to wait for the statue, and his friend Tournier, the sculptor, let him have space for it in his studio at 3 rue de Bretonvilliers on the Ile Saint-Louis. On three successive days he went to the station, only to find that it had not come. At last the delicate cast arrived; it was undamaged—not a crack anywhere. He removed the long staff which was actually a useless accessory and chose a new title for his work: *L'Age d'Airain.* Then came one of those periods of depression to which all true artists are subject and the intensity of which cannot be gauged by the uninitiated:

"I've been to the Exposition several times [he said in a letter to Rose]; I'm going to do a little work while waiting for the decision of the jury which will be the 5th or 6th of April. I've been depressed again lately. My figure doesn't seem to me as good as I thought. But Falguière thinks well of it."

Falguière—nine years older than Rodin—was for the first time a member of the jury for sculpture, with Paul Dubois, Eugène Guillaume, and Chapu. The eighty-one voters assembled and *L'Age d'Airain* was admitted; but it was put in a place where the light was poor. . . . From Brussels, like bad seed on an evil wind, the slanderous accusations flew to Paris. The proud vigorous figure with its youthful charm and its mysterious life-giving power seemed to those judges also to be the result of castings from life, a series of impressions cleverly put together. The accusations grew more definite, and it became a question of actually excluding the statue from the Salon.

What unavowed, even unavowable feelings prompted those pontiffs? Was it the fear that the obscure sculptor who had produced this shamefully living statue might revolutionize public taste and thereby spoil a profession which then functioned according to a peaceful routine? Or was it simply, as Rainer Maria Rilke once said, that "genius is always a terror in its day"?

Rodin was cruelly wounded and wrote a depressed but not a bitter letter to Rose:

"I am thoroughly unhappy. Falguière says my statue is beautiful, but it is believed to have been cast from life. Falguière tells me it is a compliment, but a back-handed one."

He knew that almost all the sculptors in Paris as well as in Brussels cast from life, and that many respected painters worked from photographs, but he saw no reason why he should be blamed for a fault that he had not committed and one that revolted his integrity. In a letter to the Under-Secretary of State at the Ministry of Fine Arts, he demanded an inquiry. This high functionary appointed a committee. At last the truth was to be revealed, or so Rodin thought.

Among these new judges were Charles Yriarte, an eminent art critic, and Paul de Saint-Victor, a fine prose writer, both at the Ministry: gifted men but not competent judges, for they were not practising artists. Nor would they have dared openly to contradict the Salon jury. They therefore contented themselves with the prudent statement: "the committee is not convinced that there has been any falsification." Thus the atmosphere was not cleared of doubt.

Rodin protested immediately to the Under-Secretary. Eugène Guillaume advised him to have casts and photographs made of his model for comparison with the statue. More expense and complications. Rose was entrusted with this task:

"It is very annoying [he wrote her on April 13, 1877, in language whose restraint must be admired], when I was so near success. Everyone thinks my statue beautiful and it is persistently considered to be cast from nature. I took the impressions you had made to the Exposition; will they even take the trouble to compare them? I'm exhausted and without money, and I've got to look for another studio. Tournier's is too small."

His Belgian friends, having seen him hard at work on the statue, gave him their warmest support:

"The kind messages that I've had from all parts of Belgium make me happy. Please thank Joseph, Vanderreghen, Auguste Neyt, the pupils and P——. The letters from M. Biot have cheered me; also those from M. Bouré, M. Carlier and Portié."

The young soldier, Auguste Neyt, who had become a friend of his sculptor, offered to hurry to Paris and, repeating the gesture of Phyrne, to let the jury compare his naked body with the statue. But things are never as simple as that; leave of absence, granted as a special favour to the handsome trooper by his superior who had artistic leanings, would have had to be according to the usual

51

routine, and a general knowledge of it might have put the officer in an embarrassing position.

The committee in charge of buying works of art for the museums met and the suspected statue was put aside. The affair dragged cruelly on for the man who was awaiting vindication. But even these serious annoyances could not break down his resistance or prevent him from working and planning for his next statue:

My dear Rose, how are things with you there? Have you been able to get some money? I'm afraid that work here is going to be difficult on account of politics. I don't know what to do with so many expenses and no money; when you come, you'll have to lend me a helping hand. I'll know more on Friday. But the committee did not buy my statue. Beautiful as it is, it was rejected. They say that I made casts from a corpse and put it on its feet—gross stupidity!—and you can see what I am going through; my money will all be spent in another attempt and I may not succeed. The future looks dark and I see poverty ahead for us. If only the jury will be willing to look at the casts and photographs! I'm completely worn out in body and mind, for I've been working hard. If only you were here and I could sleep in your arms! Well, we'll be together soon: about June 5th.

In another letter he reveals to Rose the source of his courage in one sentence: "I have put my confidence in the power of truth."

This power was eventually to bring the affair of *L'Age d'Airain*, which had taken on the proportions of a scandal, to a happy end. One glance at the casts and the photographs would have been sufficient. The difference between their violent realism and the noble transformation accomplished by the sculptor's talent would have been obvious to the most ignorant, but Rodin, in telling of the affair twenty years later, said that the cases sent from Brussels were never opened.

His living had to be earned through all these distressing days, and he began to work for the decorative sculptors. *L'Exposition*

Universelle of 1878 was near at hand and there would be some important orders given out. The sculptor Laouste employed him at his studio in the rue Blomet.

Rodin was working on a group of children holding a shield when chance (perhaps he still called it Providence) brought to Laouste's one day a young sculptor named Alfred Boucher, also looking for work. In the studio he noticed a red-bearded man busy preparing some large clay balls, both round and oval, which he then moulded into heads and plump arms and legs. His sureness and speed astounded Boucher and he asked the sculptor's name. It was Rodin. Rodin, the supposed counterfeiter, of whom the whole art world was talking! Could this be Rodin creating these delicate cherub figures without models? So he was able after all to work without taking casts! How could there be anything in the accusations which had been brought against him?

Alfred Boucher was ten years younger than Rodin; he had been to the *Beaux-Arts,* won the *Prix de Rome,* and another prize at the Salon. He belonged to the Academic group, but he was an honourable man. Going immediately to Paul Dubois, his master and a member of the jury, he told him what he had just seen. Dubois took his friend Henri-Antoine Chapu to Rodin's studio. In the presence of these two sculptors, Rodin executed an improvisation which at once convinced them that he was capable of having modelled *L'Age d'Airain* without fraud. They obtained the support of several other well-known sculptors, including Carrier-Belleuse who had long been aware of Rodin's ability, and a letter was addressed to the Under-Secretary establishing the artists's sincerity and declaring that his statue was very beautiful and the work of a man clearly destined to become a great sculptor. Chapu, Chaplain, Carrier-Belleuse, Delaplanche, Paul Dubois, Falguière, and Thomas signed this splendid exoneration.

To Alfred Boucher, who also achieved fame in his turn, was due the recognition then accorded Rodin, and the latter handsomely acknowledged his gratitude to his young colleague; when he had acquired supporters in the Ministry of Fine Arts, he eagerly used his influence there in Boucher's behalf. "I adore his sculpture and his water-colours," said Boucher, "and he was so generous that I could have had cartloads of his drawings."

L'Age d'Airain did not receive enough recognition to redeem the first injustice. Three years later it appeared in bronze at the Salon, with *Saint Jean-Baptiste prêchant* in plaster, which latter obtained a third medal. *L'Age d'Airain* was purchased by the State for two thousand, two hundred francs—the cost of its casting —and was placed in a rather unfrequented part of the Luxembourg Gardens, near the Boulevard Saint-Michel. It was taken later to the *Hôtel Biron*. Six years after the affair of 1877, the Ministry of Fine Arts begged the curator of the *Musée du Luxembourg*, with the utmost deference, to consider "whether M. Rodin's statue deserves to be placed in the museum, supposing of course that the necessary space is free."

Oddly enough I was once obliged to defend *L'Age d'Airain* against its creator's own criticism. When preparations were being made for the Exposition at Brussels I asked him to include the statue with the others he was sending: "It wouldn't help any," he replied. "I've done better ones since: the *Rochefort* and the *Victor Hugo,* for instance."

These works represented another phase of his art, but to my mind they do not overshadow the genuine beauty of his earlier productions. I tried to get him to change his mind, to be less severe; one day I met him by chance in the Luxembourg and we strolled out into the Gardens where he pointed to the statues of the queens of France, and said: "That's Louis-Philippe sculpture —not very good, even the figures by Clésinger and Préault, but they're well suited to this atmosphere. I saw them so often when I was young that I enjoy them now." I dragged him towards *L'Age d'Airain* which had been named *L'Homme qui s'éveille à la Nature* or *l'Eveil de l'Humanité*. He looked at his statue as though it were the work of another sculptor: "I had begun to forget it . . . it's all right, but my modelling is better today."

He would not consent to its being shown in other countries

until Bourdelle also went with him to look at it and gave him technical reasons for his admiration. His conscience was never satisfied: in February of 1900, he wrote to Roger Marx who was actively devoted to him and who, when in the Ministry of Fine Arts, had proposed that a copy of the statue be bought by a provincial museum:

"I want you very much to see *L'Age d'Airain*. The original will be at my studio in the rue de l'Université. Is it to be done in bronze? If so I must attend to it, and I will be very glad because we can get a fine casting, better than the one in the Luxembourg Gardens."

Rodin emerged from the conflict of 1877 with more definite advantages than a third medal: his name was known to the majority of the artists—those who had already established reputations—and he had come to the notice of the art critics; he had made friends and he had triumphed in his third battle with the Academic forces. But this did not prevent a fresh disturbance each time he produced an important work: there were the affairs of *les Bourgeois de Calais, Claude Lorrain, Balzac, le Monument Sarmiento,* the Exposition of 1900, *l'Homme qui marche,* and, to crown them all, that of the *Musée Rodin* which was not settled until a few days before his death.

During his stay in Paris his disputes with the pundits of the Salon were not the only matters that absorbed him. He was overwhelmed by anxieties and legitimate ambitions. In 1875 the city of London arranged a competition: a monument was to be erected to the memory of Lord Byron. An imposing committee of aristocratic, political, and artistic notables was presided over by Disraeli who became Lord Beaconsfield the following year. Serving on this committee were Tennyson, Longfellow, Swinburne, Robert Peel, Matthew Arnold, and several reputable sculptors. Rodin decided to enter the competition; he had made a model at Brussels, representing the poet standing upon a pedestal which was encircled by two allegorical figures. When he went to Paris he entrusted Paul, one of his assistants, with the task of casting the rough model under Rose's supervision. Rose was responsible for its shipping to England, and his letters to her were crammed with instructions and covered with frenzied sketches to clarify the text:

"The monument must be in London before the 1st of June. . . . Have Paul make the base at once—a big wooden square painted white. This must be done immediately. . . . Have Paul place the main figure and pedestal on this in the position I arranged when I was there—about a three-quarters angle; and he must cut down the corners of the pedestal to go with the base. He must also mark exactly where the other figures go, for they will have to be packed separately. . . . Fix the position of the pedestal like this [a comprehensive sketch] and be sure to put the figures exactly where I had them and mark the places distinctly with red crayon. . . ."

One has the impression that he was consumed by anxiety to see his instructions carried out, and he repeated them endlessly:

"Don't forget to send off the case. Find out from the Verstraetens at Meurs and Son's just how long you have, for it has to arrive in time. It will help greatly if I can get something out of the competition. Send me long letters and write clearly. My father and Auguste are well. Get our affairs in order there and tell me how much money you have given to Auguste Neyt. I suppose the wooden base is finished? Write me details about all that and try to collect some money. It's absolutely necessary for the monument to be in London before the 30th of May; that's what you must ask the shippers about. . . . Pay what it costs—it'll be ten or fifteen francs—for it has to arrive with all shipping charges paid and you haven't much time to spare. . . ."

In order to live, and to pay these charges (which today seem absurdly low), their meagre and hard-won savings had to be sacrificed. With the nervous haste of a pilot at the crucial moment, he ordered:

"The Antwerp bond will have to be sold; use the proceeds carefully. Go to M. Van Berkelaer and try to collect some more. . . . [And in another letter, he wrote:] Sell the second bond. [Again:] The caster asks 150 francs for doing my *Ugolin* and I won't pay him that. Troubles everywhere! I'm all right when I can sleep eight hours, but that doesn't happen often. Try to get some money from M. Berkelaer. Sell the casks if you have to. Studios cost 600 or 700 francs and I'll have to pay that if I want one."

The casks were doubtless those used for modelling stands. To have been obliged to sell them meant that the situation was precarious; and all the trouble and effort went for nothing. The model for the Byron monument was not accepted. Perhaps the country which welcomed Rodin later and overwhelmed him with honours now regrets that it did not recognize the sculptor's gifts in his early obscurity and choose him instead of Richard Belt, whose model was accepted, executed, and placed in Hyde Park in 1880, apparently without the eminent committee ever receiving public approval of its choice. Not only was Rodin's model unnoticed among the thirty-seven submitted to the jury, but so far no trace of it has been discovered in the Paris or the Meudon studio.

None of these worries and vexations could ever take from him the joy of working. He had sent to him from Belgium certain "bits of sculpture: *l'Enfant sur le lion* which is in pieces, *la Femme drapée* which Paul cast in plaster," and particularly his *Ugolin*, "that big figure" which he wished to finish and of which "one leg has not been cast." He was anxious also to know whether the *Josué* had been cast, whether the cracks in the clay had been filled, whether his draped figure was still being sprinkled, whether the broken terra-cottas just back from being fired—and his other clay figures—were being properly cared for. He asked for his card to the *Bibliothèque Nationale* and said that he had got one to the Louvre with permission to work "in the *Musée Egyptien* which is

57

under a different direction." It was a harassed period during which all that his seething imagination contained, his innumerable ambitions and inspired lyricism, seemed determined to spring into being simultaneously. Henceforth his method was planned to meet these urgencies; he worked at ten or fifteen statues at once, resting from one by working on another, refreshing his mind momentarily by forgetting one for the other, so that the execution of each statue, conceived in intense mental excitement and elaborated slowly by means of a terrific exertion of his will, lasted several years.

III. PARIS

La Porte de l'Enfer
Les Bourgeois de Calais

R ODIN was aware that the struggle would continue after they returned to Paris, and he hoped to find plenty of work to do for the decorative sculptors who had orders for the *Exposition Universelle*. When he got back to Brussels he decided to wind up the affairs of the Van Rasbourg-Rodin partnership, and the agreement was broken by common consent at the end of August, 1877. With the betterment of his own affairs he made the Belgian sculptor his associate again and his son one of his regular casters. The latter's daughter, Rosette, was the godchild of Rodin and Rose Beuret, and lavished affectionate care upon them at Meudon in their old age.

Before submerging himself again in work, Rodin was determined to satisfy a desire as urgent as the one which had taken him to Italy two years before. He visited the Gothic and Renaissance cathedrals of Northern France. His passion for them was fed throughout his life by constant journeys into the provinces and endless meditation upon their architecture and sculpture. Edmond de Goncourt spoke, in his *Journal,* of the sculptor Rodin absenting himself from home for several days at a time, without anyone knowing his whereabouts; on his return, when asked where he had been, he would say: "I've just seen some cathedrals." He was already beginning to collect the material for his book, *Les Cathédrales de France,* but it was not until 1914 that he consented to allow the publication of this book of reflections selected from his many notes and sketches. It is impossible to decide which of these are the more delightful: the original judgments or the fascinating architectural drawings accompanying them. His study of mediaeval art lasted throughout the second half of his life.

In the autumn of 1877, Rodin returned to Paris with Rose Beuret, who was overjoyed to see her son Auguste. The boy had been in the care of Thérèse Cheffer during his mother's absence in Belgium. Misfortune had again visited the sculptor's family. After the war, Jean-Baptiste Rodin went blind, and the man who had once had such gaiety and spontaneity and an original turn of mind peculiar to the Rodins was now saddened by adversity, became ill-tempered and mentally unbalanced. One had to fly into a rage in order to get him out of bed in the morning and he had made a thousand difficulties when Mme Cheffer's sons had been obliged to move him from the rue de la Tombe Issoire to their mother's apartment in the rue Dauphine. There was a tendency to senile insanity on that side of the family; a female relative had been paralyzed for forty years; a sister and brother went completely insane and had to be confined in an asylum. Jean-Baptiste's mind began to wander as soon as he lost his sight. Psychiatrists could perhaps determine what mysterious dosage must have been administered to subdue the great artist in him and to transmute the attributes of genius into physiological distress.

The only person who had the power to distract and amuse the old man was his grandson Auguste. The child was amenable and affectionate; he attended a school run by the Little Sisters of the Poor, but he was no student and did not learn very much. If someone scolded him severely, his grandfather would interfere angrily in his favour. When he was allowed the freedom of the streets he loved to do errands for his Aunt Thérèse, to buy the soap and lye needed for her laundry business. But boys of his age are careless and a serious accident occurred. In an attempt to retrieve a little girl's balloon for her, he fell from a third floor window and struck his head on the iron frame of a baker's awning below. Jean-Baptiste was terribly upset and the shock to the boy's organism, already threatened by heredity, caused a permanent impairment of his mentality. Misfortunes abounded in the little group, and M. Dubois, Thérèse Cheffer's husband, came to a tragic end.

Rodin took a tiny apartment in the narrowest part of the old rue Saint-Jacques at the corner of the rue Royer-Collard near the Panthéon. Poor people move often, and by 1883 the sculptor had lived at two other addresses: 268 in the same street opposite the intersection of the rue Feuillatines—the house is now demolished— and 39 rue du Faubourg Saint-Jacques, near the *Hôpital Cochin*. His father and his son were now with them, and Rose, who possessed as he did, a deep sense of filial obligation, cared for the old man until his death on the 26th of October, 1883. The funeral services were held at the church of *Saint-Jacques du Haut-Pas* and Jean-Baptiste Rodin was buried in the Montrouge cemetery. His son, expecting to be laid beside him one day, acquired a ten-year concession as soon as he could afford it (this was eventually taken in perpetuity).

In addition to his 1860 bust of Jean-Baptiste resembling a Roman legislator, Rodin, probably on his return from Belgium, painted a remarkable portrait of his father, this time in oils; the strangely sloping forehead prolonged the line of the prominent nose; the eyes were keen, and the beard white, like tufted wool. Rodin faithfully transferred to that canvas the emotion evoked by the fine head of the man whom both he and his son so closely resembled.

Rodin was now obliged to find a studio. During his sojourn in Brussels he had given the address of a fellow-sculptor for the Salon catalogue: Fourquet, 36 rue des Fourneaux (now the rue Falguière) in the midst of the Vaugirard quarter. It was a street of low houses and workshops with, here and there, a group of studio buildings. In one of these next to Fourquet he found a vacant studio and rented it. The rest of the building was occupied by Jean Escoula, a fine marble-cutter who became Rodin's assistant later, after having been employed by Carpeaux; by the sculptors Millet de Marcilly and Domingues; the mosaic-worker Gouilhet; and the Baroness de Lonlay who had started to do pottery. He kept this studio for several years, during which he had still to endure all the disadvantages of poverty, but when he became familiar with those of fame and relative affluence he thought with regretful pleasure of his years in the rue des Fourneaux, as well as those spent in Belgium, when he was free to devote himself entirely to his art. His wife and his son, who was now a grown youth, helped him with much of the manual work which his profession included. Rose still sprinkled his clay figures and skilfully took impressions of the numerous little pieces conceived in the Carrier-Belleuse manner and for which his friend Legrain executed the floral decoration. She went out, whatever the weather, laden with these reproductions and tried to sell them to a bric-a-brac dealer in the Passage des Panoramas. Auguste swept out the studio, kept up the fire, and prepared the clay balls. Rodin gave him drawing lessons, but, though he showed certain gifts, he had not inherited the energy or the desire to learn possessed by his father. The latter, being unaware of the physiological causes for this, was the more irritated by his son's lack of industry.

Rodin recommended his two-fold activities: work for others which was paid for immediately, and work for himself composed of sculpture and drawing. He did decoration for monuments, life-sized figures, and also models for jewellers and cabinet-makers; he worked by the hour for anyone who would employ him, and everything he did was admirably done, for he was a designer of the first rank. He drew every day like a man keeping a diary. Every impression, whether from art or nature, whether literary or even musical, was graphically recorded. Images evoked in his mind by poetry were immediately given shape with pen or pencil. He drew while meditating on Musset, Shakespeare, or Baudelaïre; he transmitted to paper the turbulent visions that rose up in his mind when he read the Bible and Dante. In the family circle and with

62

friends he spoke little, because he was endlessly *seeing,* conceiving
. . . then he drew.

A former cabinet-maker in the Faubourg Saint-Antoine named
Ginsbach still has two pieces of furniture, dating from that time,
which Rodin was commissioned by him to decorate: one is a heavy
walnut chest—of deplorable Renaissance style, fastidiously brought
up to date by copyists of the period—for which the creator of
L'Age d'Airain modelled a mascaron and two caryatides; the other
is a mahogany bedstead of better composition, embellished with
two lovely infants in high relief—a pleasing allusion to the law of
procreation.[1]

In this same year 1878, the City decided to erect a monument
commemorating the Defence of Paris at the Rond-Point de Cour-
bevoie. Rodin entered the competition and sent a model three feet
high. It was one of his most notable works: *La Défense* or *L'Appel
aux Armes.* The terrible countenance of the winged figure with
mouth wide open, crying out its despair was an interpretation of
Rose Beuret's features. The model was not even among the thirty
which represented the jury's initial choice. The high competence
of this jury resulted in the selection of a dreary bit of pastry by
M. Barrias, winner of the *Prix de Rome* which got him elected
four years later to the *Académie des Beaux-Arts.* Rodin failed
similarly in the competition organized by the city of Nolay for
the statue of Lazare Carnot, for which he made a persuasive model;
he fared no better in the competition for the Diderot statue to be
placed in the Boulevard Saint-Germain, nor in those for the statues
of Jean-Jacques Rousseau and General Margueritte. In 1880, however, he was finally commissioned to do one of Alembert for the
Hôtel de Ville.

The expenses occasioned by these attempts did not discourage
him; he was aware of the power that was in him and also of the
patience that reinforced it. To his cousin Henri, who asked him,
with perhaps a slightly too pitying look on his face, whether he
was satisfied and whether his work was sufficiently remunerative,

[1] V. Mathias Morhardt: *Rodin Ebéniste. L'Art et les Artistes.*

63

he replied in a way that precluded any discussion: "It's not money that I'm working for; it's something else. When I get that, I'll have money too."

He attended the wedding of this relative in October, 1879; he was absent-minded and preoccupied, having already, without knowing it, the other-worldly bearing of a man of genius. "Your cousin has lost his reason," said one of Rodin's aunts to the elder of the two brothers. He scarcely spoke to anyone and sat reading a newspaper in one of the motors which had brought the wedding company to the Mairie; then, **before** the collation, he took his departure. This was not at all because he was ashamed of the humble circle from which he had sprung. Had he not also attended the wedding of one of Thérèse Cheffer's laundresses? Was he not himself a workman employed by the hour? His long years of plebeian existence had given him a deep sympathy with the working classes, and he deplored the wretched lives which the majority of them were obliged to lead. He admired their courage and endurance, and, at the height of his career, he said: "I have a higher regard for the workman who knows his trade well, than for the minister who knows no trade."

In 1875 Carrier-Belleuse was made art director of the *Manufacture Nationale de porcelaine de Sèvres*. He and Rodin had made up their differences and, having discovered that the younger man was still struggling with poverty and realizing what a splendid addition he would be to the studios, Carrier-Belleuse summoned him in June, 1879, "to be a special temporary member of the staff of the manufactory at a monthly salary of 170 francs and an hourly supplement of three francs." Rodin was employed at Sèvres until 1882.

Carrier was both a kind man and an intelligent artist, and the bust that Rodin did of him in 1881 splendidly conveys the twofold nature of his generous employer.

At Sèvres, Rodin began by working as a sculptor, modelling several figures for the large epergne, *Les Chasses,* designed by Carrier. At the instigation of one of his fellow-employés in the studios,

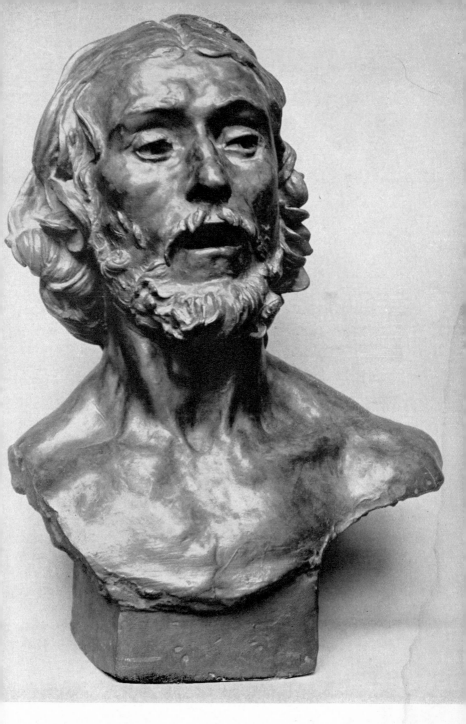

John the Baptist. COURTESY OF THE METROPOLITAN MUSEUM OF ART

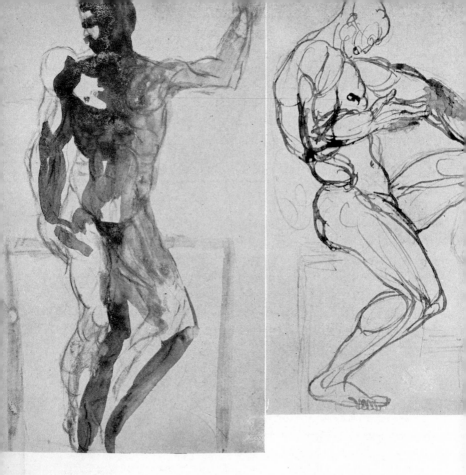

Studies for the Gates of Hell (*Etudes pour la Porte de l'Enfer*).

Taxile Doat, he went in for the decoration of pottery, designed motifs for it, and undertook difficult investigations into the handling of this delicate and friable material. The vases: *les Eléments, l'Hiver, l'Instruction, les Illusions, le Jour,* and *la Nuit* were embellished with dancing nymphs and bacchantes, with the graceful bodies of women and children; and the same amazingly subtle fingers modelled simultaneously the heroic musculature of *Saint Jean-Baptiste.* Roger Marx, an accomplished and accurate historian of this phase of Rodin's life, says with good reason that "no artist has thus communicated sensual ecstasy to inanimate figures since Clodion." [2]

He was an early riser all his life, so he walked out from Paris and submerged himself immediately in work, forgetting the rest of the world completely. "When the lunch hour came," recounts Taxile Doat, "I used to go to his studio to tell him and get him to come out with me. Slowly, he would raise his big bewildered eyes from the work in hand as though he objected to being disturbed and awakened from the dream that filled his mind and might vanish at the intrusion of a stranger. . . . Everything he saw produced many sketches and notes. I remember a plaster vase which Rodin decorated in one hour with an extraordinarily interesting and complete composition the day after he and I had heard Berlioz's *Danse des Sylphes* at a Colonne concert." [3]

At the end of the day his wife frequently joined him and they walked back to Paris along the banks of the Seine, enjoying the green slopes and the islands with their flowering meadows and groves of trees—adored and extolled by all artists in those days and visited by all foreigners, but today shamefully devastated, if not completely demolished by industrialism with the complicity of idiotic city councils.

Carrier-Belleuse had enough discernment to want to keep Rodin permanently on the staff at Sèvres. But despite the fact that the Sèvres museum today is proud of being able to show several pieces

[2] V. Roger Marx: *Auguste Rodin céramiste.*
[3] *Ibid.*

of pottery decorated by Rodin at that time and that his colleagues understood and appreciated him, there were certain people in the employ of the manufactory who had nothing but contempt for the work of the still unrecognized sculptor; it was even put on the floor and several pieces were kicked and broken. His other important work was too engrossing and he refused his employer's offer, begging him to get Jules Desbois in his place. The latter executed, along with other work, some pieces of pottery for which Rodin had designed the decorative scheme. The two artists were bound by mutual affection and admiration, and when Rodin's reputation grew to such proportions that he could not himself fill all the orders he received, he sought the assistance of Desbois, to whose nervous vigour and delicate facility he entrusted the interpretation in stone or marble of several of his statues, or the modelling of certain portions of his larger works. This collaboration lasted without interruption until the time came for the inevitable quarrel —Rodin's disposition became difficult in later life and caused the estrangement one after the other of all his friends.

During this period of pottery decoration which required the light fingers of Ariel, Rodin was simultaneously engaged upon the elaboration of one of his most powerful statues: *Saint Jean-Baptiste prêchant*.

In April, 1877, during the disputes over *L'Age d'Airain,* he kept writing to Rose in Brussels about the *Josué* which was still not cast and—forebodings of a too familiar misfortune—was beginning to crack: "See that the *Josué* does not crack any more . . ." "Be careful not to let it fall. Have Paul and Louis make me a rough-cast of it showing the position of the limbs, to be ready when I come." "Has the rough-cast been made?" None of his works bears this title, but in the Salon of 1880 there appeared a six-foot figure, of which a plaster bust, coated with zinc by Danielli, had been shown the year before; it was the *Saint Jean-Baptiste prêchant.* As all his past work had been and as all his

66

future work would be, this statue was the result of numerous studies and sketches. Possibly one of these bore the name: *Josué,* which admirably suits the movement of the statue in its definitive form, for it embodies the vehemence and the violent determination of the man who commanded the sun to stop in its course. Rodin later deplored the destruction of this *Josué*—possibly it had occurred during the move from the Brussels studio—which must have been a work of equal importance with *L'Age d'Airain.* Perhaps the broken figure was the preliminary study for *Saint Jean-Baptiste;* perhaps it was the admirable and well-known torso, half life-size, with long legs, but neither head nor arms, called *L'Homme qui Marche;* this realistic name was given it spontaneously by Rodin's casters. It shows the influence of antiquity and the great art of the Renaissance, and when, about 1905, the sculptor put his practice of "enlargement" into effect, his studies were all done to the new smaller scale; they were as exact and vigorous as the bronzes of Herculaneum. Such was his method after *L'Age d'Airain:* a study, rigorously executed, one third or half the height of the final statue; then, finally, the "enlargement," followed by several reworkings.

Rodin relied upon nature for everything, obtruding nothing of his own, and nature rewarded him with inexhaustible and unexpected expressions and actions. Thus, neither the *Saint Jean* nor any of his other works represented the execution of a preconceived idea.

One day two models knocked at the studio door: one of them had already posed for him; he was "the big Italian," Fortuné Zangrandi, of whom Rodin had written to Rose from Belgium, and there was a friend with him, a robust peasant named Pignatelli, just arrived from the Abbruzzi, his native country. He took off his clothes, mounted the model-stand, and stood there erect with head thrown back, talking and gesticulating with such fiery passion that Rodin told him to hold his pose. His bristling hair and flashing eyes made him look like a kind of savage. While he worked, Rodin listened and studied the man; he was shy, with almost animal instincts, but now and then he became excited and spoke as though he were haranguing a mob, like an ageless mystic, a prophet from the Bible, the Precursor come to life. Rodin modelled him in this passionate attitude, his legs apart and firmly planted, one arm lifted, and his mouth open.

From this magnificent model he also created *Ugolin au milieu de ses enfants morts.*

The *Saint Jean* which was shown in 1880 with the bronze of *L'Age d'Airain* received a third medal, the only award ever made to him by the ancient *Société des Artistes français* under the direction of the Institute; he showed his work there until 1888. Foreign juries, especially in Belgium, were juster and more discerning, and they awarded the highest gold medal in their Salons to the creator of the *Saint Jean.*

The man who produced these masterly statues was still obliged to do artisan's work and went into the provinces to undertake jobs for other people. In addition to the pecuniary advantages of these journeys—and how small they were!—he availed himself of the chances to visit museums and monuments.

The decorative sculptor Cordier, a pupil of Rude, had had great success in the Second Empire with his gilt and polychromatic figures of Negroes, Chinamen, and Turks, which, though cleverly treated, conformed to the bad taste of the period. He had received the commission to decorate an elegant private dwelling at Nice for a rich connoisseur; it was the Villa Neptune on the Promenade des Anglais and was to be presented to Schoen, the famous singer. Cordier employed Rodin. The façade towards the sea was richly embellished with a tribune resting on corbels and surmounted by a mask of Neptune. Upheld by this was a wide framed bay with uprights formed by two caryatides resembling graceful young tritons. The sculptor gave to this decoration a voluptuous flavour, for, when seen from within, the two charming figures are discovered to have women's bodies, whose life-like delicacy reminds one of Giorgione and Correggio. Perhaps Rodin's collaboration here would never have been known, if, thirty years later at Nice, when staying with M. Gabriel Hanotaux in his villa at Cabé-Roquebrune, the great sculptor had not shown his host these two figures which were his, though signed only by Cordier. The museum in the rue de Varenne contains the first study for them; it is named *Torse d'Adèle,* after the model who posed for it.

Rodin worked at Nice during the summer of 1878. He wrote joyfully to Rose:

". . . nothing between me and the sea but oleanders, palms, and cactuses; it delights me every time I look at it. The passing ships seem just as lazy as the blue water that floats them. I've had a bathe, holding onto a rope and turning my back to the waves which would have carried me out if I had not clung tightly. If I had the courage to do this every morning I would get strong, but it's too cold when one doesn't swim."

During the journey from Paris to Nice he saw "some charming cities: Vienne, Orange, and Arles, where all the beautiful women of the Midi seem to be gathered—don't let that make you cross," he teased; Rose became jealous easily. He stopped at Marseilles and was curiously unaffected by its natural beauty and its Grecian atmosphere; his attention was concentrated upon the monuments and works of art, and he said that the ancient city was without interest for an artist. He did, however, see a Puget there: *La Peste de Milan* in the *Consigne.* But in a letter:

"The museum where I saw Puget's *Satyre* (which is in almost the same pose as my big figure) is arranged with incredible stupidity. Truphème and the other sculptors are well placed, but poor Puget is in a corner and too high; you can't get behind the figure. Stupidity is decidedly the refrain of our great song of Progress. Au revoir, my little housewife. Take care of yourself and Papa. Tell Auguste to be a good boy and give him some paper. Try to get him to work enough to fill fifteen sketchbooks for me. Let him draw men on horseback. . . . My best love, and I wish you were here with me to enjoy the sights, though it's no better than Belgium."

The big figure which Rodin speaks of as being in the same pose as Puget's *Satyre* was the *Adam*. He had done it soon after his return from Rome and during his rigorous search for "the secret of Michael Angelo." Being unsatisfied, he had abandoned it, but he worked at it again later, and it is possible that Puget's *Satyre* influenced him. It was cast in bronze and renamed: *La Création de l'Homme*. Soon after his sojourn at Nice, he went to Strasbourg and stayed with one of his friends who was, he said, "very nice to me, but I have not yet made my expenses." He went eagerly to work, his lodging cost him thirteen francs a month, and for one franc fifty he was "excellently fed." . . . "Strasbourg is a paradise of delight," despite the fact that he was not very well, and he teased Rose, who was lonely in Paris, by threatening to stay there for at least a year. Up to the present time it has not been possible to discover what work the Hercules of modern sculpture did at Strasbourg, and when he returned there almost thirty years later he himself was unable to find the building in whose decoration he had had a part.

He began to be spoken of in the sacred precincts where reputations are made; how and thanks to whom is not known. One of his friends, anxious to do him a service, introduced him to Mme Edmond Adam in whose drawing-room he would be likely to meet literary, artistic, and political notables, particularly Gambetta who was the presiding lion. Gambetta had heard Rodin's unfamiliar name mentioned enthusiastically and he wanted to see the man himself. The meeting took place at a large evening party given by Mme Adam. Gambetta was favourably impressed and spoke of the sculptor to his Minister of Fine Arts, Antonin Proust, who helped him effectively later and who began by getting the State to buy the bronze of *Saint Jean-Baptiste* from the Salon of 1881.

At Mme Adam's parties Rodin met several politicians and eminent administrators of Gambetta's entourage, including Waldeck-Rousseau and Eugène Spuller, several times Minister of Fine Arts with Castagnary as Under-Secretary. Castagnary was an important art critic whose bust the sculptor executed later, in order to show his gratitude for the continual support he received from this high functionary.

At Sèvres, he made friends with a young painter, named Maurice Haquette, in the art department of the Manufactory, a brother-in-law of the then Under-Secretary at the Ministry of Fine Arts, Edmond Turquet. This former brilliant lawyer and magistrate upon whom politics had fortuitously bestowed the post, liked to surround himself with painters, sculptors, and writers, and to help them. Haquette was struck by Rodin's talent, charmed by a personality which was, so to speak, still unpublished, and touched by the idea of such an artist, at the age of forty, being still obliged, as Rodin put it, to work at "the masonry of art" and to receive no credit for his labours. Haquette spoke of him so warmly to Edmond Turquet that the Under-Secretary, realizing how fully his young relative's admiration was justified, wanted to give Rodin a handsome recompense for the ordeal he had undergone in connection with *L'Age d'Airain*. He resolved to give him an important commission and, through his brother-in-law, requested him to make official application for it. Maurice Haquette knew the workings of the high administrative mind, its occasional habit of restraining the impulses of its own chiefs, and its preference for dodging responsibility by acting only on the advice of qualified groups. He urged Rodin to get the backing of several of his sculptor friends who were in favour. In January of 1880, being slightly embarrassed by his own stylistic short-comings, Rodin wrote to the painter, telling him that he relied on his friendship and asking him to draw up something in his favour which Paul Dubois would willingly sign; he hoped to be able to add to this name "those of MM. Chapu, Falguière, Moreau; also those of M. Carrier-Belleuse and

M. Chaplain, and thus to have valuable supporters with the minister;" he thanked Haquette in advance for his efforts in behalf of those "who have the good fortune to be among your friends."

Edmond Turquet received Rodin cordially. It was proposed to build the *Musée des Arts Décoratifs* on the site of the old *Cour des Comptes,* destroyed by fire in 1871, but which still lifted its crumbling masonry on the left bank of the *Seine* where the Gare d'Orsay is now to be seen; Chassériau's frescoes were still within the four walls of the vast ruin, mong the bushes and the rank vegetation growing up through the tumbled stones. The new building was to have a monumental entrance of a highly decorative character. Rodin was entrusted with this task which was worthy of a Pisano or a Ghiberti.

The project dazzled the man who had been to Rome and Florence, and the vision of a great work rose up before his eyes.

"I'll do a great many small figures," he said to the minister, "and then no one can accuse me of casting from life."

Such was the origin of the sculptor's most lavish conception, and he remained sincerely attached to the man who made it possible for him to accomplish it and who became his unfailing friend. Twenty years later, at the time of the *Balzac* affair, Edmond Turquet was one of the first to protest vigorously against the ill treatment received by the illustrious sculptor.

To Haquette he owed another firm and lasting friendship: that of Emile Bergerat. As Rodin left the office of the Secretary of State, Bergerat, who was himself waiting for an interview, saw for the first time the man whose name he did not even know. Haquette introduced them, and, some eighteen months later, the celebrated journalist wrote in *Le Voltaire* the first, or one of the first, articles on Rodin's *La Porte de l'Enfer,* which was followed by so many others full of glowing admiration.

The studio in the rue des Fourneaux was too small for the execution of a work which was to be over twenty feet high. Fortunately the ministers of the Republic, like their predecessors, had the privilege, dating from Louis XIV, of allotting to a few artists the studios in the rue de l'Université at the Dépôt des Marbres where the government kept the blocks of marble it had purchased and would distribute among the sculptors it wished to subsidize. Thanks to Edmond Turquet, Rodin found himself privileged to occupy studio J, and later, studio H as well. These he kept until his death. Jean-Paul Laurens worked there too, and Eugène Guillaume who became, after years of incomprehension, one of Rodin's great admirers; and several statue-makers whose names had better not be given.

Maurice Haquette was responsible for this first smile of Fortune, and Rodin wrote to him at once:

"Thanks, my dear friend! You had a part in all this and have helped the sculptor to extricate himself from his difficulties. I shall never forget what I owe to you."

He began work by going through hundreds of accumulated sketches and he made innumerable further ones every day in his note-books. Even at dinner in the evenings, sitting between his wife and his son, he covered scraps of paper with eager scratches; he filled penny exercise-books with them. Long afterwards, in 1897, when his friend Fenaille brought out an expensive and admirable volume containing a selection from these projects, the ruling on the humble sheet of paper upon which they were drawn could be seen beneath the pencil or India ink. Strange drawings they were, following no known formula; visions sprung from a brain of totally unsuspected turbulence. To look at these biting lines that seem to strip human bodies down to their very skeletons, these violent wash-drawings, lit by planetary gleams and flashing starry trails, is to think of Victor Hugo's prophetic vision and of his drawings which also seem to have taken form during divinatory trances.

The work of great epic poets, especially the Divine Comedy, inspired Rodin. Dante's poem had haunted him since his first

73

serious reading, and it was not to rival Carpeaux—he was too profoundly modest—that he modelled a *Ugolin* in 1876, but because of the portentous Florentine's power over him. There were mysterious similarities between Dante and Rodin: a combination of imagination and realism, a conciseness of thought which preserved only the essential part of human passion. The eternal quality of Dante's poetry seduced and conquered the sculptor.

He too was an "essential man" who owed his selective portrayal of typical characteristics to mature intelligence and to the power of genius. Never allowing himself to become simply an illustrator, he stripped Dante's synthesis of all its transitory elements and limited himself to the presentation of the psychical world which the poet created. The monument he was to erect would represent the inner conflict, the revolt of man against the supreme power which had obsessed his young religious mind years before; it was to be *La Porte de l'Enfer*. His art allowed him but two ways of translating it: by the movement, and by the expression of living bodies whose spirit, the sculptor from within, fashioned in its own likeness.

After a preliminary sketch, suggesting the entrance to a church of the fifteenth century, came a second one which outlined the final conception, and he was soon deep in the execution of the tremendous task. The frame was of a powerful simplicity, twenty-one feet high and eight feet wide, surmounted by a splayed pediment for the group of *Ombres* beneath which was the seated figure of the *Poète,* leaning, with elbow on knee, towards the lake of fire and the countless writhing figures of the damned. Not countless, for there were only one hundred and eighty-six, but so full of movement, so diversified in attitude, and so well massed that they seemed to be nearly a thousand strong. Rodin's conception had exceeded the limits of his commission. *La Porte* was not merely the entrance to a public building; it was a monument in itself. On either side of the frame were statues of *Adam* and *Eve,* over life-size; their execution was not included in the sketch he had submitted to the Ministry of Fine Arts and he could not himself assume the extra expense. Again he called upon his friend Haquette:

My dear Maurice, I hear that there is a chance of M. Turquet's resigning in a few days. . . . Will you be kind enough to speak to him—tonight or tomorrow if possible—about those two figures on either side of my *Porte* which were neither ordered nor officially commissioned. You can understand that this is a serious matter for me and that you are the only person able to accomplish anything. My friendliest greetings to you.

Rodin acknowledged Haquette's kind intervention in his customary manner: he did a portrait bust of him—a typical painter of the late nineteenth century.

To anyone but Rodin, the 30,000 franc commission, of which 27,000 were paid to him in four instalments between 1881 and 1888, would have seemed a magnificent windfall. But his slow method of work, his long and expensive experimentation had to be taken into account. As soon as he had any money, he began to work expensively. He was rigorously economical as to his own material existence, in his rare and sober relaxations; but he never hesitated to spend in matters which concerned his profession. He arranged endless sittings, had endless castings made, and he wanted it clearly understood from the outset that this was his method of work. A rich collector ordered a bronze copy of his *Bellone,* and three times the sculptor recommenced the patina, asking, quite naturally, a higher price for the bronze than the one agreed upon. "But isn't your word of any value?" asked the disgruntled amateur. "It's not my word that's valuable; it's my bust," replied Rodin curtly.

La Porte occupied him for twenty years and during the first of these he worked at it with a kind of concentrated fury. He got up at six in the morning, was at his studio by seven, and with a short interruption for lunch he pursued, sometimes even by candle-light, "standing or perched on a ladder, the labour which left him exhausted when evening came and sent him to bed after an hour's reading." [4]

In 1903, the Ministry of Fine Arts, believing, not without reason, that it had been unusually patient since 1880, especially so, considering their further contribution of 35,000 francs for the casting of the work, asked for its delivery. In 1900 at the Place de l'Alma *La Porte* was shown, but with its panels denuded of the clustered figures which hung from them as from the branches of a huge vine. According to Rodin, the work had a breadth and unity which was spoiled by the ornamentation that had previously covered it. Several visitors criticized it, particularly Bourdelle whose hobby was Architecture; he deplored the excessive cavities and projections, and Rodin the perfectionist began to be anxious. He tried to be detached about the work. "It's too full of holes," he said to those who stood before the empty panels and exclaimed: "But as it is now, it's not finished." Then he said calmly: "And are cathedrals finished?"

In January of 1904, the Ministry of Fine Arts decided to revoke the measures taken in Rodin's behalf. He returned the sums he had received and kept *La Porte,* or at least the enjoyment and use of it, since he was to bequeath it during his life to the State along with the rest of the contents of his studios.

About 1912, when the project for the museum at the Hôtel Biron took shape, I asked him about the panels that were destined to be its most important work of art, and he replied: "I'm no longer interested in them." I was sorry that he should speak in this way of such an extraordinary production, a symbol of one of the most intense phases of his career, and, as I had done some years before when talking with him of *L'Age d'Airain,* I insisted upon the fact that man's mind has its seasons as well as the earth. I felt the awakening of his affection for *La Porte* and was convinced that if he should get back the tranquillity he seemed then to have lost he would decide to complete it.

La Porte occupies, from several points of view, a place of capital

[4] Edmond de Goncourt: *Journal.*

importance in his work as a whole. The something like two hundred figures it included constituted a fund from which he was continually drawing; his most celebrated statues and groups were taken from it and adapted, transformed, "enlarged." They were at the disposal of the great plastic dramatist: a troupe of experienced actors. *Le Penseur, Les Ombres, La Cariatide, La Femme Accroupie, Les Métamorphoses, Les Faunesses, La Belle Heaulmière*, the group of *Le Baiser*, the figures of *Adam* and *Eve*, and many others—all are fragments of *La Porte*. If there were any need to establish Rodin's sincerity, these two last-named works would furnish striking proof of it. He executed the *Eve* from an exceptionally beautiful Italian model with firm and elastic muscles; "a panther," he called her; there were many sittings and he noticed that the young woman's figure was becoming more abundant every day. Accordingly, he altered his modelling until the time came for her to confess that her approaching confinement would oblige her to interrupt the sittings. She then departed for Italy with her Russian lover and never returned. Rodin could not make up his mind to complete the statue without his model, so he left certain parts of it in a slightly unfinished state. Nature, as always, came to his aid, for the gentle sagging of the body enlarged by approaching maternity gave a distinctive quality to this majestic *Eve*, the mother of Humanity. But his vexation at being deceived was so violent that, later on, fearing the same thing would happen again, and being profoundly naïve, he explicitly forbade his young secretaries to have anything whatsoever to do with his models— even to converse with them.

The figure of *Adam* was posed for by a circus athlete named Cailloux. He may have been able to balance 220 pounds on his chin, but as a model he was, according to Auguste Beuret who had known him, "as limp as a rag." Rodin reproduced the abandon of this big nerveless body, transforming it into dejection at having just emerged from primordial slime and a craving to return to it.

The *Adam* showed such conformity to the manner of Michael

Angelo that the casters named it offhand, *L'Esclave*. It appeared in plaster in the Salon of 1881.

The secondary import of *La Porte* in the career of its great creator was the overwhelming enthusiasm it drew from all the artists and writers; it excited the professional admiration of some; it moved others to the depths of their imaginative susceptibility and enabled them to reach heights of lyricism which they had hitherto only dreamed of. Actually, no work of this sweep and breadth had been produced for several hundred years. Everyone talked of it. People who did not know the sculptor sought his acquaintance. On Saturdays his studio was packed with astonished visitors. Men of letters voiced their admiration in the press. "This prodigious achievement," as Léon Cladel called it, affected the public more than a twenty years' production of separate statues and busts. From that time and without prearrangement, an indefatigable band formed itself for the support and defence of Rodin, and the unrelenting violence of their attacks upon his detractors was never forgiven.

The journey to Italy had convinced him that he was taking the right course. Michael Angelo, whose counsel he had so passionately sought, had shown him that "his secret" lay in the vigour of the modelling and that the right sort of modelling was to be found in the human body itself. Rodin, in his slow acquisition of knowledge, now understood that he had gone to Florence and to Rome to seek for something that was at his disposal in Paris and everywhere else: the living and vigorous modelling of the human body. His talent had fully revealed itself at the time of the Italian journey —*L'Age d'Airain* and *Le Saint Jean* were sufficient proofs that he would become a great sculptor—but after *La Porte* his genius was completely manifest. He was a giant of his art with a productive power akin to that of a Rubens, a Balzac, a Hugo. And now his work, until then marked by a gravity—except for the small figures of the Carrier-Belleuse period—and an inherited austerity, began to overflow into the realm of love and the flesh, depicting passionate impulsiveness and the carnal hungers of the soul. *La Porte* became a great poem of extraordinary sensuality whose characters desired, possessed, and destroyed one another; it was a mirror held up to lustful humanity, and Rodin was now crowned by writers as the poet of the flesh, the sculptor of voluptuousness.

This phase, marked by excess of production, coincides quite naturally with the culminating period of his sex life; it was the flowering of his entire procreative power, forces that were accumulated by Nature in men of her choice. An absorbing love affair occupied his mind—the complement of his artistic activities—but he did not speak of it till many years later when the inevitable upheavals occurred. An atmosphere of mutual passion and admiration, the phenomenon of love, enveloped him, and the next fifteen years saw an unbelievable profusion of works: twenty-five or thirty busts including several masterpieces, hundreds of figures, numberless studies, and large statues and groups such as *Le Baiser, Les Bourgeois de Calais,* the *Bastien-Lepage,* the *Claude Lorrain,* and the *Monuments de Victor Hugo* with their noble allegories, *La Muse Tragique, La Voix Intérieure, Iris, messagère des dieux, Les Sirènes,* and finally, the *Balzac.*

The production and the care of this multitude of statues obliged Rodin to acquire more space than that afforded by his studios at the Dépôt des Marbres. The advances he had received and the sale of his works to private individuals made this possible. He rented several studios on the outskirts of the city, remote at that time because of the scarcity of transportation; one of these was at 117 Boulevard de Vaugirard: a huge lofty room extending back "from this outer boulevard to a slum garden . . . the interior was cold and grey like that of a church and crowded with modelling

stands, maquettes, and sketches, dominated by a *Patrie Vaincue*." [5]
In that studio were to be produced *Les Bourgeois de Calais* and the
Claude Lorrain, and there in 1886 Bracquemond brought Edmond
de Goncourt to see him. Goncourt was surprised at the haphazard
installation, "walls spattered with plaster, a dreary little casters'
furnace, casts of heads, arms, and legs everywhere—and in the
midst of it all two scrawny cats whose meagre shapes stood
out like fantastic griffons." [6] And the writer admired "the life-size
clay figures of the six hostages of Calais, powerfully and realistically modelled with an accentuation in their bodies of those graceful cavities that Barye put in the flanks of his animals." Goncourt
does not mention a work which was in that studio at the time—
the sculptor undoubtedly failed to show it to him. It was a large
figure of Christ which Jules Desbois remembered distinctly and
praised. As model for this figure Rodin had the noble-featured
Italian who had posed for the head of *Saint-Jean après la Décol-
lation* and whose body had the same nervous beauty as his face.
Instead of fixing his Christ upon a cross made, according to the
current fashion, of two planks, he had riveted it upon one made
of two thick beams. The cross-beam was placed in front of the
upright, bringing the head forward on a different plane from the
rest of the body. This arrangement gave the figure a vigorous
quality which was profoundly dramatic. What has become of
Rodin's Christ? Undoubtedly he made use of it ten years later in
the group called *Le Christ et la Madeleine,* but how one would
like to know the original work! There is a story to the effect that
Rodin executed a Christ during his novitiate with the Holy Fathers
of the *Très-Saint-Sacrement* and that this figure first attracted the
attention of the Father Superior. It cannot have been the one referred to by Jules Desbois and surely conceived much later. Rodin
greatly admired Préault's *Christ* in the Church of Saint-Gervais, but
he never spoke to me of his own.

He occupied another studio at the Clos Payen, 68 Boulevard

[5] Gustave Geffroy: *La Vie Artistique, 2e Série.*
[6] Edmond de Goncourt: *Journal, t.VII.*

The Gates of Hell (*La Porte de l'Enfer*). COURTESY OF THE MUSEE RODIN

The Thinker (*La Penseur*). COURTESY OF THE METROPOLITAN MUSEUM OF AR

d'Italie, near the Bièvre. It had once been the Directoire summer abode or *folie* of Corvisart, the Emperor's physician, and was even then half in ruins, its garden choked with rank undergrowth. The atmosphere of romance and mystery that survived, despite the demolition of the original building, suited Rodin exactly, and at first no one was admitted except an artist whose studio was in the same street. He was so distressed at the destruction of this bit of architecture that he bought in some of the materials.

He even took studios that appealed to him, without ever occupying them. Once, during a family visit to Fontainebleau, we went to Nemours, *Ursule Miroüet's* part of the country, and the woman in charge of its old fifteenth-century tower with dim and empty interior said to us, "Its occupant at present is an artist from Paris, M. Rodin." We asked the sculptor about this when next we saw him, and, like Cooper's Leatherstocking, he laughed silently at his little extravagance.

In 1882 he took tentative steps towards a relationship with England which was to be kept up for a long period and which his part in the competition for the Byron monument had not established. He was urged to come to London by Jules Dalou and Alphonse Legros, both of whom had been his fellow-students at the *Petite Ecole*. Gustave Natorp, a young American sculptor who was for a time his pupil, also begged him to come. Natorp and Legros both offered him hospitality.

The sober art of the famous Burgundian engraver and painter —he was also a good sculptor—had always appealed to Rodin who valued his friend's faultless technical conscience, his original judgments, and his amusingly caustic manner of speech. Legros had found it impossible to make a living in France; he had experienced frightful privations, but his courage and natural gaiety were unimpaired. He had gone to London in 1863 on the advice of Whistler who did everything in his power to enable Legros to earn his living in the English capital. He was warmly welcomed by English artists and was sufficiently appreciated to be given a professorship at South Kensington where he lectured on art and taught engraving. Ten years later he was able to help his exiled friend Dalou, who, on his recommendation, was made professor of modelling at South Kensington, and ten years after that, his friend Rodin for whose work he found buyers; he also introduced him to famous people, particularly to the poet and prose writer W. E. Henley, editor of the important *Magazine of Art,* and to the latter's celebrated friend and collaborator, Robert Louis Stevenson. Henley had written repeatedly about Rodin's work, which he had followed in the Paris Salons, and was beginning to make a reputation for the French sculptor not only in Great Britain but in all Anglo-Saxon art circles; he took Stevenson to Paris to visit the studios in the rue de l'Université. Rodin was appreciative and generous as usual, and in 1882 he modelled a splendid head of Legros, who in return painted his portrait; in 1884 he did a bust of Henley and presented a copy of *Le Printemps* to Stevenson. When the venturesome novelist finally abandoned his country and went to live in Polynesia among the primitive people of the Samoan Islands, he perhaps felt intuitively that he would die there and wished to have all his possessions with him during his last years, for he took his furniture, and with it, *Le Printemps.*

Rodin not only admired Legros's work, but was curious as to the technique of engraving, so exciting to those who devote themselves to it. The great etcher gave him a brief explanation, persuaded him to try his hand at it, and went off to his duties at the Slade School, leaving the sculptor in his studio with some tools and a copper plate before him. "I understood it immediately," Rodin told me one day, still with an air of surprise at his good luck, as though he had forgotten that his amazing knowledge of drawing gave him an understanding of all the graphic arts. On the back of a copper plate already used by Legros he rapidly executed a charming little design: *Les Amours conduisant le Monde,* and on his return to Paris, delighted with a technique new to him but mastered at once, he made, between 1881 and 1886, a dozen drypoints among which the finest and most sought after are the portraits of Henry Becque and Victor Hugo. Also, at the time of his passion for the engraver's art, he produced, with a pen as vigorous and as subtle as the graver, a series of drawings which for beauty of conception and perfection of execution could take their places among the finest achievements of the great Classic Schools.

Henley's articles made Rodin known in English artistic circles and obtained for him an invitation to exhibit his work at the Royal Academy in 1884. The emotional response to *L'Age d'Airain* in England was greater than it had been in France. Since then the British public's regard for Rodin and his appreciative friendship for England have been glowingly expressed.

During the years 1881, 1882, and 1883 important busts were produced, evoking the proud nobility of Donatello: the thoughtful *Legros;* the agitated *Dalou* with ravaged features and a restless heart within his bared breast; *Jean-Paul Laurens,* the artist who was his neighbour at the Dépôt des Marbres and who became his life-long friend; the *Carrier-Belleuse;* the *Haquette;* the *Victor Hugo,* which was to be followed by a still finer statue of the poet; and many studies for *La Porte*. Rodin's fame spread to foreign countries; he established relations with the son of President Vicuña, who represented Chili at the French capital at that time, and with his young wife who was a relative of General Lynch, the liberator of his country. The Chilian Republic had decided to erect monuments to these patriots; Rodin was commissioned and produced two maquettes. Acceptance would enable him to satisfy one of his great desires—all the desires of this iron-willed man were great and powerfully urgent. Quite properly, he represented the soldier on horseback in the classic attitude of authority, one arm forward in a gesture full of force and vitality, accentuating the significance of the subject. Thus he was finally to produce the equestrian statue of his young dreams while sketching at the Horse Market in the Boulevard Saint-Marcel. The Vicuña statue included, in addition to the figure of the statesman, that of the grateful country offering a palm branch to her chosen hero. The maquettes were sent to Chili, but owing to its perpetual state of political revolution they went astray and, if one is to believe the reports, were never paid for. Fortunately, Rodin had taken a cast of the maquette for the Lynch statue. The sculptor's desire could not be accomplished at that time, and the opportunity never offered itself again.

Another project immediately took its place in Rodin's heart; he had received permission to do a bust of young Mme Morla Vicuña; she was beautiful and a woman of taste and cultivation. This marble bust, done in 1884, did not appear in the Salon until 1888. It was an enchantment. The sensuous mystery of her delicate features was perceived clearly by the sculptor who also gave expression to his discovery of the secrets of her femininity. The voluptuousness of palpitating flesh was imparted to the marble; flowers laid upon the breast were a pretext for the trembling of the nostrils; the complete success of the bust dazzled the sensibilities of the perceiving. Rodin was forty-eight; but the jury, undoubtedly cherishing a grudge against him on account of the injury it had done him ten years before, awarded him nothing for it.

In 1885 Auguste Beuret entered the army. His father advised him to earn his stripes and to enlist for an indefinite period; a military career, he said, was the only one for which the young man was fitted. He had hoped to develop his son's gift for drawing and had begun to teach him engraving; it will be remembered that he told Rose to make the boy fill "fifteen exercise-books with men on horseback." The household was run according to the strictest economy and the sculptor, like many other people of his class with small means, wore paper collars and cuffs which cost but a few sous and kept down the laundry bills. Nothing could be wasted, so, after they had been worn, Rodin made the boy use them to sketch on. Garlands of flowers were drawn upon the collars

The Three Shades (*Les Trois Ombres*). COURTESY OF THE MUSEE RODIN

The Weeping Lion (*Le Lion qui Pleure*). COURTESY OF THE MUSEE RODIN

with bits of charcoal, and upon the cuffs the human body divided into its seven parts. Later, Auguste was given Doctor Leon Deschamps' *Memento Anatomique Instantané,* a series of superposable coloured plates; he also attended courses in anatomy.

Unfortunately, the poor boy was beyond all discipline. He was idle and capricious, disliked all rules and was incapable of making any sustained effort. His parents had sent him first to his mother's native village, Vecqueville, in the Haute-Marne, to live with a young maternal uncle. He was happy and unrestrained in the country with these peasant folk to whom his studies seemed of slight importance. He ingratiated himself with his mother's relatives and the memory of those happy years of freedom was evoked with much feeling during his last days. He proved to be just as incorrigible in the country as in the city, and he indulged in the most diabolical practical jokes which are still remembered in that remote corner of Champagne. He returned to Paris without improvement: "When I send him out with two francs to buy me a packet of tobacco," Rodin confided to a friend, "he comes back with no money and no tobacco." Unaware of the physiological causes of his son's deficiencies, he kept hoping that he could be corrected. He rented him a room in the rue de l'Exposition in the Gros Caillou quarter and the boy would let weeks pass without coming to see his parents, despite his fondness and respect for them.

One day Jules Desbois was working in his studio in the rue des Fourneaux; someone knocked and he went to the door to find a man standing there in clothes that were horribly shabby and torn. He asked to see "Monsieur Rodin" who was there with Desbois; whereupon the sculptor, after a short conference in undertone, disappeared with him into the street. Presently he brought him back to the studio, having fed him at a neighbouring café and bought him a decent-looking suit at a second-hand shop to replace his rags. "Sit down and get to work," Rodin commanded. But in a half-hour he took his departure, saying he had an errand to do. "That was my son," said the great man with melancholy resig-

85

nation. "He'll come back again when he has sold the suit and spent the proceeds."

In the midst of his varied activities, Rodin learned that Calais had decided to erect a monument to honour its heroic citizens who, in the fourteenth century, had offered their lives to the King of England in order to save their besieged city from destruction.

The project had been long considered; in 1845 David d'Angers had been requested by a local *Comité* to come to Calais to choose a site suitable for a statue of Eustache de Saint-Pierre, the most celebrated of the six heroes. But it had not been possible to raise sufficient funds. During the Empire, two of this sculptor's pupils also failed, and the efforts of Clésinger, who hoped to bring the project to a successful conclusion, were interrupted by the war of 1871 and he never got farther than the submitting of maquettes. In August of 1884, the Calais Municipal Council took up the idea again and formed a committee with the Mayor, M. Omer Dewavrin, as chairman. This body of men was instructed to perpetuate the memory, at a time when the last remaining fortifications of the old city were about to sink beneath the flood of modernization, of one of the noblest chapters in its history. M. Alphonse Isaac, a native of Calais, told his friend Rodin of this, urged him to try for the commission, and promised him his earnest support. At a meeting of the Council on the 26th of September the project was broadly outlined; it was decided that the expenses of the monument should be met by a national subscription and that the city of Calais should make an initial contribution of five thousand francs.

Rodin resolved to familiarize himself with the subject historically. He read the old chronicles, particularly that of Froissart who lived at the time; he was full of admiration for the historian's simplicity of style and the fresh vitality of his narrative—qualities which were fundamental in his own artistic nature. He was immediately possessed by a passionate desire to represent this noble action. Had not these Calais citizens and the narrator of their deed been con-

temporaneous with the great builders of cathedrals? Had they not
lived in a century which, for him, was marked by the greatest
achievements of French Art? Would not the execution of this
monument enable him to walk in the footsteps of those ancient
cutters of stone whom he held in such veneration? The springs
of his unconquerable will were tightly wound up. In a man whose
calmness and gentleness charmed all who came in contact with
him this tense determination was rather frightening. Several portraits of him reveal something of this; behind the low stubborn
forehead under its thick shock of badger's hair, and in the steel-like
glance of his eye, resided a strength which he could not control, just
as capable of destruction as of creation; it was the strength of a man
determined to conquer and it was just as unrelenting as that of a
man determined to kill.

On the advice of M. Isaac, the Mayor of Calais, M. Omer
Dewavrin, came to Paris and visited the sculptor's studio. He was
filled with admiration, he "almost gave me the order for the monument, but," wrote Rodin, "he has asked other sculptors to submit
maquettes," particularly Chatrousse; Marqueste, winner of the
Prix de Rome and later a member of the Institute, also entered
the lists. Rodin, always lavish in effort and just as impetuous in
the inventive stage as he was slow and careful in the execution,
made a rough model during the autumn of 1884. He announced
the fact to the Mayor and a correspondence began between them
which was to last eleven years and to comprise no less than fifty-six
letters from the sculptor. The first ones were written on paper
with a wide black border; he was in mourning for the death of his
father the preceding year.

3rd. January, 1884 [7]

Dear Sir,

Since receiving your honoured visit I have been applying myself
to the monument and I have been lucky enough to hit upon an
idea which I like and which will be original when executed. I have
seen nowhere any arrangement so suited to its subject or one that

[7] Correspondence preserved in the archives of the city of Calais.

will be so absolutely appropriate. It will be all the better because all the other cities usually have the same monument, except for a few minor details. . . . [His facility of execution was more alert than his style and his modelling more explicit.] I have just made a rough model in clay and it has been cast. . . . The idea seems to me totally original both architecturally and sculpturally. In any case the subject is heroic and demands a heroic conception, and the group of six figures offering themselves has communicative expression and emotion. The pedestal is triumphal in order to support, not a chariot, but human patriotism, abnegation, and virtue. I have rarely carried out a rough model with as much enthusiasm and seriousness. Eustache de Saint-Pierre alone, by the dignity of his animation, controls and inspires his companions. . . . I am also sending you today a drawing, another idea; but I prefer the plaster model. . . . What I have sent is merely a suggestion of the thoughts I will express; but the arrangement of the figures appealed to me at once for I know what sameness there is in all monuments to great men.

Therefore, dear sir, if my idea is acceptable to you and your committee the expense will be profitable; it is seldom that one hits upon such a splendid idea and opportunity to arouse patriotism and abnegation. . . .

He spoke to his friends of his great expectations, particularly to Alphonse Legros who, being sincerely devoted to him, enlisted the support of the painter Cazin, their fellow-student at the *Petite Ecole;* and he brought him and Rodin together. During visits to London, Cazin had resumed his friendship with Legros and the two met frequently on the Channel coast. Jean-Charles Cazin's family came originally from the Pas-de-Calais where he now lived most of the time, and Legros always spent his vacations at Boulogne where his old mother, having deserted her native Burgundy, had installed herself permanently in order to be near her son. At the end of December the two artists paid a visit to the Mayor of Calais and asked to see Rodin's model. The great etcher realized what an opportunity it would provide for the sculptor, and on his return to England, taking Cazin's influence upon his fellow Calaisians for granted, he wrote to him: "Did your stay in Calais help Rodin? He could produce a masterpiece from that model if he were given the chance."

Cazin was just as enthusiastic about the model as Legros and he told Rodin so immediately. The latter wrote to him on December 29, 1884:

My dear friend,

How delightful your letter is! I feel there is real friendship in it and I am deeply touched and honoured that an artist, a master, should devote so much of his precious time to me. . . . My model which you say you liked—and that is a good omen for the work— can be executed for 35,000 francs. That is not expensive; the founder will charge me at least 12 or 15 thousand francs; 5 thousand will go for a block of that hard local stone for the base which must be given a triumphal suggestion if I can manage it. There would be 15,000 left for me, to include casting costs: not much, since I would have to supervise the architect.

M. Liouville must speak to the Pas-de-Calais Deputy, M. Ribot, and tell him that you and Legros think my model well-conceived.

He was still a long way from securing the commission. At the end of January, 1885, M. Dewavrin concluded that it would be advisable for Rodin himself to appear before the committee in defence of his project and explain it in detail. The sculptor succeeded in communicating his faith and in convincing them, for, on the 28th of January, a mutual agreement was signed and he received the definite promise of an initial payment of 15,000 francs, in regular instalments, for the modelling of his group; the work would be completed, he said, during the early months of 1886. He was delighted and expressed to the Mayor both his appreciation and a desire to execute a bust of him; this he did during the year 1886.

While prices were being agreed upon with the casters, and particularly with the founder who was to be entrusted with the ticklish matter of casting the huge group in bronze, Rodin enlarged his maquette, taking such pains over each figure that, as he wrote to Calais, "In this second plaster model, enlarged and carefully elaborated, you will find all my work towards the final composition in definite form." Before starting the actual execution of the figures, which were to be not less than 6½ feet high, it was imperative that the model be definitely accepted by the Calais committee, the Prefect of the province, and the Ministry of Fine Arts. Rodin asked that two or three thousand francs be allowed him for this first piece of work and, justly cautious, he added:

"But at the same time I hope that you can undertake not to have the model executed by another artist if it should receive your votes, for I always work gradually and the final expression and nuances are not given until near the end."

At the end of July, 1885, he sent this second model; the figures were now thirty-two inches high.

The City had at first expected to erect a statute of Eustache de Saint-Pierre alone, evoking the memory of his companions by means of bas-reliefs placed around the pedestal, but Rodin proposed, for the meagre sum voted, to produce six full-length figures. The great imaginative realist was so invaded by the Froissart narrative that he could only see the project in terms of the whole group, "showing the six citizens about to set forth from Calais, clad only in smocks, the gallows ropes about their necks, and the keys of the city in their hands; surrounded by their starving fellow-citizens, shouting, weeping, and gesticulating with clenched fists." The members of the committee, accustomed to the false and conventional sculpture of the nineteenth century, were confused by so many figures and by the sober opulence of the conception. They knew of no other monument with which to compare it, despite its resemblance to the great religious groups of the Renaissance, French and Italian *pietas,* and the ancient crucifixions—particularly that of Ligier Richer which the Calaisian aldermen had perhaps never had the opportunity to admire. Rodin felt that he would be severely criticized and wrote to the secretary of the committee:

My dear Monsieur Desfontaine:

Will you kindly send me the committee's comment. I hope I am not to be bothered too much with alterations. You know the danger of disturbing the harmony of a piece of sculpture; it is like a tragedy or an opera—you take something away and the whole work is thrown out of proportion; then months of work are required to recapture the balance. It is not that I am afraid of work, but I have developed my project so carefully—it has taken me five months—that if I have to repeat this labour much time will be lost and I am not likely to hit upon a better idea.

The committee's comment was received and it contained even more objections than he had expected. Disappointment was acknowledged:

"We did not visualize our glorious fellow-citizens proceeding to the King of England's camp in this way. Their dejected attitudes offend our religion. . . . The silhouette of the group leaves much to be desired in the way of elegance. The sculptor should be able to undulate the surface of the base which supports his figures and even break the monotony and the harshness of the main outlines by varying their height. . . . We notice that Eustache de Saint-Pierre is clothed in a thickly folded material which does not suggest the thin garments recorded by history. We feel bound to insist that M. Rodin shall undertake to alter the positions of his figures and the silhouette of the group as a whole."

A local newspaper took up these complaints. What the committee had hoped to obtain was one of those pyramidal monuments vulgarized in the nineteenth century which were more akin to circus acrobatics than to genuine sculpture. Rodin was staggered by this volley of criticism and advice, and replied with a long

91

passionate letter which was a noble and restrained assertion of his convictions and actually a declaration of his artistic faith:

Dear Mr. Chairman,

I have just re-read a statement by the "Calais Patriot" which more or less repeats the criticisms already made, but which emasculates my work. If the heads were to form a pyramid (the Louis David method) instead of a cube—straight lines—I would be following the dictates of Scholastic principles to which I am absolutely opposed. They have been prevalent in our century and are in complete contradiction to the great epochs in the art of the past, and they give works conceived under their influence a cold lifeless conventionality.

2nd. Eustache de Saint-Pierre seems to the critic to be already in the presence of the King. What, then, would the others be doing? No; he is leaving the city to go down to the King's camp and that is what gives to the whole group its appearance of walking, of movement. Eustache is the first to go and he must be in this attitude for the sake of my lines.

3rd. The monument should be in a public garden or be given an architectural setting. It really ought to be in the centre of an open square.

The man flinging himself down in despair is the only figure that can be altered. If you insist on this alone, my group is saved. Your colleagues do not realize that this is not a discussion about doing the work over again.

I am the enemy in Paris of this pompous and Scholastic kind of art. You want me to be a follower of people whose conventional style I despise.

This declaration excited him so much that he added a long postscript, even more vehement in phrasing. He had been full of anxiety during the period of research and composition, but now that he had finally made up his mind about his work, he was immovable. One feels that if he had been forced to make drastic changes he would have withdrawn it, as he was to do later with

Eve. COURTESY OF THE MUSEE RODIN

Ugolino (*Ugolin*). COURTESY OF THE MUSEE RODIN

the *Balzac*, despite the serious question for him of expenses already incurred:

"I have done a considerable amount of work on the figures as yet unclothed; Saint-Pierre is already done to scale. In spite of my conflict here with worn-out Scholastic technique in sculpture, I can proceed as I please with my *Porte*, and I would be glad if I could do the same with Saint-Pierre.

"The cube gives the expression I want; the cone is the hobby-horse of students competing for the *Prix de Rome*.

"MM. Lafenestre and Guillaume [curator of the Louvre and member of the Ministry of Fine Arts respectively] are going to Antwerp. I don't know if Lafenestre will be in Calais—he told me he was going to stop there—but, though a friend of mine, he is too Scholastic and of the Administration for me to care greatly about his seeing my model."

It required the convinced eloquence of M. Dewavrin and the vigorous intervention of Jean-Paul Laurens to reassure the Calais aldermen and to have Rodin authorized to proceed with the execution to scale of his group. At a final meeting of the committee, the precise dimensions and composition of the finished monument were decided upon: "the figures not to be less than 6½ feet high, and the execution to be finished and perfected with the same care as that given to works accepted by the annual Salons.

Rodin kept the Mayor informed of the progress of his work:

"I have finished the nudes, that is, the figures are done so as not to have to lose time reworking them when clothed. You see, this means that the essential work is finished, though later it will not actually be seen."

This was his invariable method with draped figures: before clothing them he modelled the nudes with the utmost care. He asked Cazin to pose for the head of his compatriot, Eustache de Saint-Pierre, but he was so much younger than the famous Calais-

93

ian at the time of his sacrifice that Rodin was obliged to give up paying him this compliment. His son Auguste was the model for certain portions of the figure of *Le Bourgeois à la clef* and one perceives in it the sloping forehead and firmly rooted nose of the Rodins.

M. Dewavrin became uneasy again at delays which were so hard for a layman to understand, but his friendly objections did not disturb the slow prudent progress of the work. To these the sculptor replied with the confident assurance of a man who has discovered the correct method:

I am working simultaneously at the monument and my *Porte;* therefore the monument moves slowly, but the quality of the work will be good. I sent one of *Les Bourgeois* to Brussels where it had great success, and it will probably go to the *Exposition Universelle.* The group will not be ready until the end of the year.

Sculptors who are commissioned to execute monuments nowadays are not given enough time and their work is without exception bad. Many of them cast from life: that is, they produce photographic work; that kind goes quickly, but it is not art.

Your devoted sculptor,

Rodin

Fresh obstacles emerged to hinder the completion of the monument. The subscriptions had already reached half the necessary amount when, in 1886, a financial calamity overtook the city of Calais and swallowed up part of the funds. Rodin slowed down his work on the group and pushed ahead with other things, but he did not consider abandoning the monument for a moment; he proceeded with determination and fortitude, and wrote to M. Dewavrin on October 18, 1890:

"I have begun to hope again, though I never despaired. Even the most successful ventures take time and are all the better for that reason. I often look at my group and ponder over small improvements in its execution."

He was full of discretion and moderation in his financial requirements, asking for very modest sums and almost apologizing for doing so: "You know that the admirable art of sculpture always overwhelms the artist with expenses." In nine years he had received only a little over eleven thousand francs.

In 1888, two of *Les Bourgeois* were shown in plaster at the Georges Petit Gallery; and in the spring of 1889, before the first showing of a part of the finished ensemble was over, he was able to put the whole group before the public in the same gallery. It created a sensation; the press was full of exalted praise for an extraordinary work of art which seemed to have sprung from the ages. "It is impossible," wrote Mirbeau in *L'Echo de Paris,* "for me to give any idea of *Les Bourgeois de Calais* here; the group has too much feeling, too much thought symbolized in too many sublime forms; I could not, in the space of an article, do justice to this human drama, this mighty historical evocation, for the group is more than the work of a sculptor of genius—it is a superb intellectual achievement."

But Calais was still without the funds necessary for the casting and the erection of *Les Bourgeois.* In view of this lack of money, several Calaisians suggested that a monument be erected using only the figure of Eustache de Saint-Pierre. I can still see and hear Rodin as he sat stiffly erect at our table in his best frock coat, replying to my father's question about the final placing of the famous work. He calmly recounted his difficulties in a cautiously scornful voice: "The Calais Municipal Council would like to have one *Bourgeois,* but it doesn't want six. . . . The group got in my way at the studio and I had to rent a stable for it in the rue Saint-Jacques. . . . *Les Bourgeois de Calais* must wait in a stable till their fate is decided . . . ."

Finally, in September of 1893, upon the determined insistence of M. Dewavrin, the subscription was resumed, though only the smallest contributions were made. Rodin was informed of these efforts and in reply to inquiries of the Mayor, who was harassed by matters of municipal finance and worried at not receiving news of the monument's completion, he wrote:

Dear Monsieur Dewavrin,

Thank you for telling me that you will be able to raise the money for our work at Calais.

You think I have lost the divine fire. This is not so; it is only that I have several other things in hand that must be done.

Since beginning the Calais monument I have given it more of my time than any other work, but it is a huge affair and has very little connection with the current idea of fast working.

I don't want to make any promises, for I might not be able to keep them, but please believe that I am strongly attached to the monument and to you who have honoured me with your friendship; and that is a good reason for remaining worthy of it.

My salutations to you and to Madame Dewavrin,

Yours,

Rodin

Could you write to M. Thiébaut, the founder, whose proposals showed him to be such an artist?

In December of 1894, ten years after the project took form, the Minister of the Interior authorized a lottery of 45,000 tickets at one franc. Local manufacturers and merchants, and even some in Paris, furnished the various knickknacks generally used for charitable affairs of the sort: boxes of chocolates, watches, cases of soap, vases, lamps, flower-stands, etc. . . . But there was difficulty in selling the tickets; the Mayor asked Rodin to help in disposing of them and he took a hundred without promising to get rid of them because of his preoccupations. Finally the Minister of Fine Arts arranged a grant of 5,350 francs.

After negotiating with several founders, Rodin settled with the last one consulted for each of his figures to be cast in one piece, which he felt to be of great importance. The firm of Leblanc-Barbedienne undertook this delicate commission at a low price.

Conflict arose again between the Municipal Council and the

William Ernest Henley (*Henley*). COURTESY OF THE MUSEE RODIN

Spring (*Le Printemps*). COURTESY OF THE MUSÉE RODIN

sculptor, and this time Rodin lost. He wanted his work placed either upon a lofty pylon in imitation of the ancient Breton and Flemish Crucifixions—it would thus have an isolated appearance and the triumphal atmosphere of which he wrote to Cazin—or else, and this is what he would have greatly preferred, in the centre of the city, very low, almost on the ground. He gave his reasons in a letter:

"In the confusion of leave-taking in the Place du Marché, I at first imagined Saint-Pierre beginning to walk away in order to put an end to a painful scene, and I thought that if the group were placed very low it would be more intimate and the public could enter more easily into the drama of suffering and sacrifice.

"It would perhaps be well to have the architect make another design for the setting, but an imposing one all the same.

"I may be mistaken, for my judgment is better when I see things in place. Since I am uncertain, I shall rely upon the committee of which you are chairman.

"In your sketch the monument will be seen against the sky with the Hôtel de Ville on its right and the square on its left, and that will be right—much better than if it were placed in front of the trees and could not be seen in profile; in that case I would prefer my other scheme of having it very low, in order that the public may see into the heart of the subject, as with burial groups in churches where the figures are close to the floor."

The following spring he went to Calais to examine the chosen site. M. and Mme Dewavrin gave him a warm welcome in their little villa at Wimereux at the seaside, but despite the efforts of the Mayor the Council could not comprehend Rodin's arguments and placed the monument in the Place Richelieu, at the edge of a public garden; the base supporting the figures was not high enough and a surrounding grill added a suggestion of banality which distressed the great sculptor. *Les Bourgeois de Calais* had occupied ten years of his life.

Finally, on June 3, 1895, came the official unveiling, for which the City had voted a sum of 25,000 francs. Accompanied by three of his dearest friends: Octave Mirbeau, Gustave Geffroy, Eugène Carrière, and by Léon Maillard, Rodin was given official recognition. The Minister of the Colonies referred to him as the master of modern sculpture; Roger Marx, Inspector of Museums, representing M. Poincaré, Minister of Fine Arts, who was indisposed, delivered a short address full of reverence for the Calaisian heroes and of emotion evoked by the monument erected to their memory.

Describing "this amazing spiritual celebration," Léon Maillard said: "An inspired harmony pervaded the official rejoicings; the noble words spoken and the high thoughts evoked by the monument expressed the very soul of the gathered crowds." The city of Calais issued a "Golden Book," commemorative of these solemnities and of the monument itself, in which were praised both the skill and the unselfishness of Rodin.

Comprehension of the sculptor's intention ripened slowly in the minds of the Calaisians and they grew proud of their monument. Their anxiety to give it protection during the tragic days of March, 1918, added a new episode to its long history.[8] This occurred while the English army was retreating; Calais was bombarded and the figure of Eustache de Saint-Pierre was struck in the leg by a fragment of shell. The Municipal Council resolved immediately to put the group in a safe place, and on the 13th and 14th of March, under the supervision of an officer of the *Protection des Œuvres d'Art* and in the presence of an architect representing the *Monuments Historiques,* the huge mass of bronze weighing over two tons was moved on a lorry to the Hôtel de Ville and placed in one of its cellars. In November of 1919, two years after Rodin's death, it was brought up again and exhibited for a time in front of the ancient communal edifice with its superb Renaissance bell-tower. A close friend of Rodin's had been in Calais, for, in 1914 in the early days of the war, Jules Desbois had finished two large figures which he had been commissioned to execute for the new Hôtel de Ville, representing the city's two industries: fishing

[8] V. A. Chatelle et G. Tison: *Calais pendant la guerre.*

and lace-making. During his stay in Calais he had convinced M. Dewavrin's successor that the best site for Rodin's group was in front of the old building which would provide a background in keeping with its austere dignity; but the time had not yet come. *Les Bourgeois* were taken back to the Place Richelieu. Nevertheless, five years later, in May of 1925, Desbois's advice was remembered, and the group was again transferred to the Place d'Armes in front of the old Hôtel de Ville where it was placed almost on the level of the ground.

There is one more thing to be accomplished by the aldermen of Calais in behalf of this magnificent tragedy in bronze which has today achieved enormous popularity and is constantly visited and praised by foreigners: to free it from the absurdly symmetrical accompaniment of the busts, not without merit in themselves, of the Duc de Guise and Richelieu. Their smallness and slimness, and the meagreness of their pedestals are entirely out of proportion to the monument. It should also be freed of the encumbrance of the iron grill which, though a fine piece of workmanship, is too isolating. The Calais children could then scramble over the base and climb up on the figures, thus giving them the natural glaze which they lack and which adds so much to the charm of old bronzes. In this way Rodin's desire would be completely fulfilled and would further, in his own phrase, "the best interests of art."

The English, in sportsmanlike manner, fond of honouring their adversaries when no longer in conflict with them, and anxious also, doubtless, to pay respect to the memory of the woman Froissart called "England's Noble Queen," who persuaded her husband Edward III to pardon the six condemned Calaisians, formed a committee in London to collect funds for the purchase of a replica of *Les Bourgeois de Calais*. In 1913, His Britannic Majesty's government resolved to give Rodin's work a splendid position and the sculptor went to London where a whole morning with Sir Lionel Earle from the Home Office was devoted to the selection of a site. They both agreed that the bronze should be placed in the public gardens surrounding the Houses of Parliament. Rodin was happy and told the eminent official that for the first time in his life he had been consulted as to the placing of one of his statues. Upon a lofty pylon, the group has the appearance its creator originally desired for it in Calais, except that the base is too narrow and somewhat disproportionate to the weight it has to support.

Whatever may have been said of Rodin's arrogance, he was never satisfied and severely criticized his own work, even when finished. He had a mental reservation about the group: "I should have clothed them in sackcloth and not in smocks," he said to me during one of our many talks. "Sackcloth is more beautiful; it would have simplified the composition and helped the unity of the ensemble . . . but I didn't dare."

IV. THE VICTOR HUGO
MONUMENT – THE MONET-
RODIN EXHIBITION

RODIN was a revolutionary in art, simply because he followed a perfectly authentic tradition at a time when its meaning had been lost; each of his new works provoked, unavoidably, a storm of adverse criticism—not so much from the public as from other sculptors and their adherents—which soon formed itself into a spiteful opposition.

During the affair of *Les Bourgeois,* fresh troubles were brewing. In 1889, a committee was formed at Nancy for the purpose of erecting a monument to the memory of a man whose fame was national as well as local: Claude Gellée, called *Le Lorrain.* Another committee in Paris, seconding the one at Nancy, with the painter Louis Français—himself from Lorraine—as chairman, was entrusted with the organizing of a competition and the judging of the competitors' maquettes. Two important men from Nancy, Gallé, the master glass-stainer, and Roger Marx were members of it. The latter was a clever writer, very young and sensitive, whose admiration and friendship for Rodin showed no signs of diminishing. He was at one time secretary to Castagnary, who had been in the Ministry of Fine Arts, was an eminent critic and one of Rodin's staunchest supporters; and he had acquired an influence with the administration, a prestige which he exercised in the service of the master whose work he praised throughout the next twenty years or more, by means of intelligent monographs dealing with its various forms: sculpture, ceramics, engraving, and drawing. In a pleasantly ironical mood Rodin once wrote to Roger Marx: "My friend Gauchez wants me to get some of my things into the houses of the rich, but there's nothing in my studio that he would like. It's a pity my talents are not pleasing to wealthy collectors. Writers and artists like you, my friend, are the only people who would not be afraid to put the kind of sculpture I prefer on their chimney-pieces."

Rodin finally hit upon an idea for the Claude Gellée monument. One day, on his way from an official call, with his mind full of his project, he went into Jules Desbois's studio in the rue des Plantes to explain it to him and arrange for its execution which was to be twice the size of the rough model he intended to give him. Whereupon, in a fever of creation and without putting down his coat or removing his hat, he amazed Desbois, despite the latter's familiarity with these masterly performances, by producing it then and there in three quarters of an hour. It was two feet high, very complete, and vibrating with intellectual vitality; and the sculptor accompanied his work by spoken directions far less precise than those of his hands. Claude, *Le Lorrain,* "the painter of light," was represented walking, palette in hand, toward the landscape he is about to paint. With a spirited gesture he faces the rising sun, and as an accompanying comment upon his vigorous attitude the horses of Apollo are seen springing up from the stone base, urged on by the young god who, like them, is intoxicated with his task of bringing light to the earth.

His model had difficulty in obtaining a majority of the jury's votes. Out of thirteen, including those of Chapu and Paul Dubois, Rodin received six and Falguière four—there were ten competitors —but he was "asked to make certain alterations in the attitude of the figure of Claude Gellée." The committee at Nancy also criticized it, and Roger Marx and Gallé expended much energy in their efforts to convince their compatriots of the excellence of the work. Meanwhile Louis Français of the Paris committee visited Rodin's studio from time to time during the execution of the monument and the sculptor wrote Roger Marx that the chairman had declared himself to be "pleased, very much pleased."

However, the work did not achieve success when it was unveiled on June 6, 1892, beneath the spreading trees of the Jardin de la Pepinière. The presence of M. Sadi-Carnot, President of the French Republic who was making a gala tour of the Eastern provinces, and of Léon Bourgeois, Minister of Public Instruction and the Fine Arts, retarded the proceedings, but as soon as the official party had departed the crowds began to laugh and make fun of the statute, particularly the pedestal which represented an innovation upsetting to their routine ideas and bad taste. They were unaware of Rodin's careful studies in his youth, and they roared at Apollo's coursers which, naturally, bore no resemblance to bus horses and declared therefore that the sculptor was unable to model a horse. There was even talk of doing away with the monument, and without the patient explanations of Roger Marx and Gallé popular opinion might have triumphed.

Rodin was, however, obliged to remodel his horses, that is, to bring them further out of the marble from which he had wanted them to emerge, as the poet in him had imagined them emerging from the clouds. Ten years later he still felt the injury to his conscience: "I agreed to rework my horses, but it was wrong of me to do it," he said to me contritely. He had not forgiven himself for making this concession to a lack of respect for an artist's knowledge. He was his own best and severest critic. When, in 1907, the State wanted to acquire a bronze copy of *Ugolin,* he himself had the order cancelled because he had become dissatisfied with the group.

A magnificent compensation for his troubles in Nancy came in the spring of 1889. In May and June a large double exhibition was arranged at the Georges Petit Gallery to include most of his work since 1864, and that of Claude Monet. It was a revelation, finally establishing the reputations of both artists and, though people were preoccupied by the *Exposition Universelle* and the centenary of the French Revolution, it achieved the deserved importance of a real event.

Auguste Rodin and Claude Monet were within forty-eight hours of the same age; they were reaching maturity, each with a rich harvest of masterpieces. Both of them, being innovators, had gone through the same inevitable ordeals, the same anxieties; both had experienced the ardent enthusiasms and the hopeless depressions that come to creative artists. They had both endured the wrath of those to whom, according to Baudelaire, "beauty is a personal affront." Endowed with the same strength of character, they had magnificently refused to yield an inch before the attacks of the pontiffs and the sarcasms of the public which for twenty-five years had made just as much fun of Monet's "pictures of nothing" as it had of Rodin's "unfinished" sculpture. As Gustave Geffroy says, "it took Monet that many years (and Rodin too) to obtain respect and admiration for his art." [1]

The history of genius is monotonous and repeats itself, save for a few details. The sculptor, in a revengeful spirit, might have inscribed on the pedestal of *L'Homme au Nez Cassé* the words: "refused by the Salon of 1864" and "claimed to have been cast from life by the Salon of 1887" on that of *L'Age d'Airain;* and the painter could have inscribed his *Le Port d'Honfleur* "refused in 1864" and *Les Femmes au Jardin,* bought fifty years later by the *Musées Nationaux,* "refused in 1867," another "refused in 1870," and finally *Les Glaçons* "refused in 1882."

The catalogue of the seventy paintings shown by Monet was prefaced by Octave Mirbeau and the one listing Rodin's thirty-six groups, figures, busts, and bas-reliefs by Geffroy, the author of *La Vie Artistique,* who since has said: "We indulged in an extraordinary rivalry and I believe our exaggeratedly long comments, especially mine, made the catalogues rather ponderous. If we had not been given a limit our unfailing enthusiasm would have enabled each of us to write a book."

[1] Gustave Geffroy: *Claude Monet,* Paris, 1922.

People of taste and discrimination stood before Rodin's busts and spoke the name of Donatello and they were reminded of Michael Angelo by the *Victor Hugo* and *Les Bourgeois de Calais* which seemed to have been taken from a cathedral portico and evoked aesthetic ecstasies never before experienced. And it was clearly not literature—an influence upon him which has been constantly deplored—that prejudiced people in his favour, for he had been incredibly naïve in naming his works: *Groupe des Bourgeois de Calais* (ils partent de la place du marché); *Deux vieilles femmes assises* (L'une d'elles est à modifier); *Bas-relief; Groupe; Etude; Torse; Masque; Grosse femme*—these are some of the titles he was satisfied to use. One charming figure, half life-size, was called simply *Plein Air;* it was the maquette for the *Bastien-Lepage* which was to be unveiled that year at Damvilliers, the landscape painter's native town. Their shared love of nature had produced a close friendship between the two artists, now strengthened by Rodin's fondness for Roger Marx, himself an intimate of the painter from the Meuse. Death had cruelly separated Rodin from this young companion of his and he strove to recapture his finest qualities for the monument: his love of nature and of art.

Mirbeau celebrated the Monet-Rodin triumph in *L'Echo de Paris* of June 25: "The exhibition just opened at M. Georges Petit's Gallery has been an overwhelming success for the two magnificent artists whose work we are privileged to see there. . . . It ranks them far above other artists. . . . They have produced the most decisively brilliant painting and sculpture of the century."

Rodin and Monet were both very much attached to Mirbeau and Geffroy in spite of the difference in their ages. The man who produced *le Calvaire* excited them by his impassioned and sarcastic manner of talking, and it was at his apartment that Rodin and Monet discovered, in some punctilious argument as to who should enter a door first, that they had both been born on the same day of the same year—at least Rodin thought so, confusing his actual birthday (November 12) with the day when his father went to the Mairie to make his declaration, followed shortly by

Monet senior. Other valued friendships brought them closer: with Renoir, with Clemenceau, with Rollinat. In Monet's house at Giverny they witnessed an unusual scene. Cézanne, who had come to see his friend Monet, confided to Mirbeau and Geffroy with tears in his eyes: "He's not proud, M. Rodin; he shook my hand— a man who's been decorated!" And after lunch he even got down on his knees before Rodin on one of the garden paths to thank him for the friendly gesture.[2]

In that same year, 1889, the sculptor was represented at the *Exposition Universelle* by three of his most important works: *L'Age d'Airain, Le Saint Jean-Baptiste,* and one of *Les Bourgeois* in plaster, as well as by the busts of Dalou, Antonin Proust, and Victor Hugo. It was an imposing selection due to the perfect understanding that existed between Rodin and his friend Proust who was a special representative of the Ministry of Fine Arts at the Exposition. The press was unanimous in its praises. "I didn't think an artist in Paris could have such a good one," he said in a letter to the Mayor of Calais.

So he became a celebrity; from that time every step in his career caused agitation in the newspapers and periodicals. Happily, but without undue excitement, he carried on his work; it had become a kind of mission. Wagner dreamed of keeping his art free from insincerity and facility which he called "musical cholera," and Rodin strove to save his from the same infections: "the phylloxera of sculpture." And he believed that the writers who stood by him were not merely dispensers of praise, but the disseminators of sound artistic doctrine. When they touched on his qualities as a human being he was disconcerted and would joke about it uneasily. When Frederic Lawton, the English critic, in one of the first books devoted to Rodin, attempted a biographical essay, the sculptor said to me with a laugh: "It's written like a life of Charles-Quint!" And he postponed for a time the publication of his views on sculpture, which I edited, because he feared it might be regarded as presumptuous and conceited.

[2] Gustave Geffroy: *Claude Monet*, Paris, 1922.

The writers who supported him were nevertheless of the greatest benefit. Without these solid friendships among men of letters—"swords that never get rusty"—without their vigorous intervention how easily he might have been suffocated, overwhelmed by official committees and articles in the orthodox periodicals! Once when speaking of the ill-will and anger he caused without ever quitting his studio, he said, "When the public gets to like my kind of sculpture and that of the young artists who have adopted my principles, it will have no more to do with the sickly stuff produced under Scholastic instruction."

In spite of his growing fame and his final emergence from the poverty of his young days, he still lacked material security. He lived the life of a workman, without luxuries and even without comfort. Henri Cheffer congratulated him at the Georges Petit Gallery opening and Rodin thanked him, adding: "You know, I'm just as poor as I ever was." A year later he sent his modest contribution to the fund raised by Claude Monet to present Manet's *Olympia* to the *Musées Nationaux,* with this note: "Put me down for twenty-five francs, so that my name will be on the list. I am in financial difficulties and this is all I can afford."

Meanwhile his studios were full of groups and statues. In 1886 he was commissioned to execute the *Monument à Victor Hugo* destined for the Panthéon. Dalou wanted the order himself, even at the price of his friendship with Rodin, but the huge complicated model, flanked by allegorical figures which he exhibited in the Salon of 1886, was a failure according to the critics and did not satisfy the Ministry of Fine Arts. By a curious turn of events the order was given to Rodin.

For people of that generation, Hugo was the bard of the nineteenth century, a legendary figure even in his lifetime; in verbal authority he was descended from the Prophets; he was the superman of Guernsey, holding familiar converse with the sea and the stars. Therefore Rodin, who saw divinity wherever possible, represented him seated upon a rock, naked. Naked because one did not clothe a god in an overcoat; one did not dress Elijah or

Isaiah in modern garments. From the superb bust of 1881, he modelled the head, with certain alterations in expression, and it is not known who posed for the muscular body which resembled that of an ageing Apollo. Three entwined female figures as vivid and powerful as the waves that had cast them at the hero's feet, veritable Rhine-daughters in their rhythmical movement, were murmuring songs to him from the world that he was to re-create in his poetry. Why did Rodin want to change it? Was he afraid it would be reminiscent of the amazing garland of sirens with which Rubens encircled his *Débarquement de Marie de Médicis?* He replaced his sea-nymphs with two figures which were more intimately symbolic: *La Muse Tragique* and *La Voix Intérieure,* embodiments of Hugo's thought; one of them was bending over his shoulder—an eagle flown there in the storm—wresting from him with an imperious gesture the secret of his meditations; the other stood beside him, enfolded in dreams and surrounding him with the calm ecstasy of evocation.

This composition, which suggested Hugo's romanticism at its best, had been preceded by a dozen other projects. In 1890, Rodin offered it to the *Commission des Travaux d'Arts.* Though the jury did not say so frankly, it was shocked by the audacity of the conception and particularly by the sight of this Olympian nudity. It wished to consider the group in the place reserved for it in the Panthéon, but since it was difficult to move, these experts conceived the singular idea of having a rough reproduction of it painted on a huge canvas. Victor Hugo was represented sitting upon a great mass of rocks which had nothing to do with Rodin's model. These efforts could not accomplish anything except perhaps the unanimous rejection of the project. The sculptor, said the committee, had lost sight of the essential condition that Hugo should be standing, in order to be symmetrical with the statue of Mirabeau being executed by Injalbert. What connection was there between the subtle orator and the author of *Les Châtiments?* None, obviously, in any artistic sense.

This was a blow to Rodin. From Touraine where the state of

his health had obliged him to go for a rest, he wrote of his disappointment to Rose who had remained in Paris:

"I'll have to work hard this winter; it frightens me to think of my unfinished things and of the *Victor Hugo* which I must begin all over again after working at it the whole of last winter."

Failing vigorous protests from the art critics and the powerful intervention of a member of the Fine Arts Ministry, his magnificent statue would be left on his hands. Gustave Larroumet, who had for some other reason a profound admiration for the sculptor, realized that any error of this sort would be forever his administration's responsibility. After two years of argument he persuaded the Commission to authorize Rodin's execution of the *Victor Hugo assis* for the Luxembourg Gardens and to order from him another figure of the poet, standing this time and dressed conventionally, according to the fashion of the day, for the Panthéon.

The significance of this gesture by a high official in behalf of an artist scorned and hated by the School had to be extenuated; the official had to get back the good opinion of the Institute, a powerful body in which the politicians—totally lacking in artistic knowledge—put all their faith, and with which they never failed to reckon. When Renoir was made an officer of the *Legion d'Honneur* at the solicitation of his friends, the government so dreaded the hostility of the Institute that he was granted the distinction not by the Fine Arts Ministry but by the Department of Commerce in connection with an industrial exposition in South America.

Thus M. Gustave Larroumet, of the Fine Arts Ministry, deemed it necessary to depreciate the favour he had accorded, not ungracefully, to Rodin by the arrogant of the estimates from the pen of M. Gustave Larroumet, art critic and ex-lecturer at the Sorbonne. In January of 1890 the eminent chronicler wrote a long article in the literary supplement of *Le Figaro,* replying indirectly to Rodin's supporters and brandishing with unusual cleverness that curious weapon familiar to certain pontiffs of journalism, which resembles both the cat o' nine tails and the asperser. The great sculptor was fifty-five and he had been working for no less than forty years—M. Larroumet was no doubt unaware of this; and it was astonishing to read the following, especially the part concerning *L'Age d'Airain*, his most authoritative work:

"Mediocre and ephemeral criticism has very nearly ruined an artist who deserves to last [clearly a reference to the criticism of Mirbeau, Geffroy, Roger Marx, and even a Goncourt]. . . . *L'Age d'Airain* was a powerful but uneven piece of work; it resembled nothing. It had an awkwardness and a harshness which could have been avoided by any student at the *Beaux-Arts*. The whole bore the mysterious and forceful imprint of genius. . . . His works are full of serious faults, so evident that they seem to be intentional. They were intentional, but also unavoidable. The artist realized what he lacked and where he did not know how to be clever he was audacious. What he found himself incapable of rendering correctly he presented in broken, twisted, and knotted form. . . . His work was intentionally ugly and warped; it was also intentionally awkward and clumsy, but its awkwardness and clumsiness was merely exasperating, while its ugliness and its striving after vitality broadened and enriched the influence of art in general. . . . [M. Larroumet, however, recognized that] *La Porte de l'Enfer* might become one of the great works of the century, if the annoyances and the heavy fumes of rich incense periodically burned in their honour would only clear away and give him a chance to finish it."

In the 1897 *Salon de la Société Nationale des Beaux-Arts*, the *Victor Hugo et les deux Muses* was greeted by mingled praise and condemnation. M. Georges Lafenestre, professor at the *Ecole du Louvre* and curator of that museum, critic of *La Revue des Deux-Mondes* and of undisputed authority—the man of whom Rodin said: "Though a friend, he is too Scholastic and of the Administration"—generously felicitated the official sculptors: Mercié, Denys Puech, Verlet, Fremiet, Sicard, et al., and then delivered himself of the following diatribe against a work which had amazed all the artists:

"We shall speak but briefly of the group in plaster: *Victor Hugo* by M. Rodin. In its present state, the work is no more than an incoherent disjointed maquette, upon which it is too soon to pronounce judgment. The catalogue, rather optimistically, calls our attention to the fact that in the huge project there is one incompleted arm. Actually, only one figure is sufficiently advanced— that of the poet sitting naked by the seashore—for one to recognize in its hasty though vigorous and passionately expressive modelling the powerful quality for which M. Rodin has already been praised in some of his single pieces."

Rodin worked at the maquette for his second Hugo monument just as scrupulously as on the original which had been refused for the Panthéon: first the nude; later the clothed figure, lost in mournful meditation; then the addition of the two Muses and *Iris, messagère des Dieux*. But the monument was never finished. Other experimental work absorbed the indefatigable sculptor, to say nothing of the innumerable orders he was obliged to fill so as to meet his heavy professional expenses.

The first Hugo monument remained for ten years in the studio in the rue de l'Université where Rodin went every day: he wished to supervise the work done on the marble block and he would indicate almost hourly with imperious pencil marks the contours to be kept, the depressions to be deepened, the portions to be modelled carefully in high relief. What a sight for those who frequented the studio during those years: that slow logical accomplishment, as of some natural phenomenon, that emergence out of the shapeless block of a god from the snows of some mountain summit.

A site was chosen for the monument, not in the Luxembourg Gardens but in those of the Palais-Royal. The unveiling took place in the spring of 1909. Early in that year, Rodin was still unable to set a date for the delivery of his work. Late one afternoon I found him greatly preoccupied, his face too red, absorbed by the task of placing the two figures with that of the poet. *La Voix Intérieure* and *La Muse Tragique* had been executed separately, and now for the first time I saw the three figures together. The two Muses were of considerable stature, but they lost importance surprisingly when placed next to the *Victor Hugo,* and this inequality seemed to me to weaken their own significance without increasing that of the poet's figure. As soon as his assistants had gone, Rodin turned to me without uttering a word, but with that piercing look which extracted one's most secret opinions. However, I lacked the courage to speak.

"Say what you think," he urged. "You aren't saturated with this piece of sculpture, and I've been looking at it for ten years."

"Well," I managed to say, after a few words as to my incompetence, "the *Victor Hugo* is so complete in itself and its attitude says everything so perfectly that the Muses seem to me to add nothing. He is poetry itself and poetry is unexplainable."

His perplexity vanished and his expression suddenly brightened; doubtless my hesitating words had clarified a hitherto unformulated opinion of his own.

"You're absolutely right," he replied, looking again at his group. "Yes, you're right; I'm going to tell them that my *Victor Hugo* is finished." And despite my efforts to get him to consult other artists whom he trusted, he sat down at his table, pushed aside a pile of papers coated with fine plaster dust, and announced the news at once in his neat round engraver's handwriting to his devoted friend M. Dujardin-Beaumetz at the Ministry of Fine Arts.

To compensate for the absence of the two Muses which the State had paid for, he offered the *Musées Nationaux* a collection of his finest busts: those of Dalou, Puvis de Chavannes, Falguière, and Berthelot. Various European and American museums bought replicas of *La Muse Tragique* and *La Voix Intérieure.* The latter, now titled *La Méditation,* had an adventure of its own. In 1897, Sweden organized an international exposition at Stockholm, with

Mme Vicuña. COURTESY OF THE MUSEE RODIN

The Old Courtesan (*Celle qui fut la Belle Heaulmière*).
COURTESY OF THE METROPOLITAN MUSEUM OF ART

a Fine Arts section under the supervision of Prince Eugène of Norway and Sweden; Rodin was invited to exhibit and sent his bust of Dalou and *La Voix Intérieure* in plaster. . . . Prince Eugène had been brought to his studio the preceding year by the Norwegian painter Fritz Thaulow. When the exposition was over, the committee in charge of purchasing for the museums decided, after endless discussions, against the bronze of Dalou. Norway, less pervaded by the academic spirit, asked for it and another figure. Before these incidents took place, Rodin had offered to present *La Voix Intérieure* in plaster to the Stockholm Museum; the gift was unanimously refused by the committee at the very moment when Prince Eugène sent the sculptor the cross of the Royal Order with his grateful thanks. Twenty Swedish artists immediately drew up and signed an open letter expressing their indignation with the committee for its behaviour and their profound admiration for the great artist. Rodin had told me of these incidents with his usual quiet irony, and several months later he wrote from Belgium that King Oscar was furious about this unseemly treatment and had asked that *La Voix Intérieure* be placed in his own private gallery.

A similar event occurred that same year in Switzerland. Mathias Morhardt who was anxious to spread the fame of three great French artists—Puvis de Chavannes, Rodin, and Eugène Carrière—in his own country, had arranged an exhibition of their work at the Rath Museum in Geneva. To commemorate this event, Rodin presented the Museum with the mask of *L'Homme au Nez Cassé;* then, at the request of Morhardt, he gave the city of Geneva a copy of *La Muse Tragique,* then called *La Femme Accroupie,* for the cost of its casting in bronze. But the time had not yet come for a universal admission and exaltation of his genius; the work remained for several years in the cellars of the Museum before being given the position it occupies today.

Preceding the great success which came to him in Germany, his work aroused the same official hostility as elsewhere, including

113

that of the Emperor until the day when he changed his mind and decided to let the sculptor do a bust of him.

In Italy, so dear to him for its masterpieces and for its contribution to his artistic development, he suffered a disappointment. At first his sculpture was regarded there with indifference; several years later it aroused serious discussion. In 1902, some of his important works having been sent to Venice, violent disputations flamed up. Vittorio Picca, ardent patron of art and letters, warmly supported Rodin. What a magnificent revenge was his ten years later when Italy hailed him as the artistic descendant of the great Michael Angelo.

To judge from their letters, Rodin and my father became friends in 1882 or 1883. They were introduced to one another by the sculptor Dalou whose fine gifts Léon Cladel greatly admired. Among the memories of my young days is that of Rodin's Sunday visits when my father kept open house at Sèvres. A varied group of writers, poets, painters, sculptors, and musicians gathered there, including the engraver Bracquemond, Arthur d'Echerac whose articles signed "Dargenty" in *L'Art* and *La Justice* were among the first to mention Rodin's gifts, Henry Cros, the painter on pottery, poor and almost unknown, Stéphane Mallarmé, Maurice Rollinat, Clovis Hugues, J. H. Rosny aîné, Henri de Régnier, and many others. Sitting apart from the loquacious circle, silently stroking his long red beard which was beginning to silver with the approach of his fiftieth year, Rodin had the air of a slow, prudent, very shy man. At the slightest emotion his clear complexion would turn dark red. He spoke rarely and timidly, and it was difficult to read his thoughts. But in his greyish-blue eyes, sometimes lit by a subtle smile, sometimes by sharp curiosity, there was the shrewd, almost crafty look of an animal of the forest. The shape of his skull, the fine sloping forehead surmounted by its stiff brush of greying hair betrayed a stubborn force. A superficial observer might have taken him for a canny peasant, keeping his thoughts to himself and purposely chary of words; but, for the perceiving, what acuteness, what penetrating force lay beneath this somewhat ponderously solid exterior! And what charm, born of serenity and infinite gentleness.

Sometimes my parents kept him to dinner. At table his searching eyes would move slowly from one face to another, lingering longer upon those of the five brown-haired children. On one such occasion he was unusually silent, but several days later sent a little note, very personal and full of affection for "that charming family where one actually sees portraits by old masters moving about, talking, eating—in short, living." And he never forgot to send his best wishes on New Year's Day "for that family whose amazing kindness is as true and frank as the look on their faces."

My mother had told me that, under the Empire, the Sappers, a privileged division of the army, chosen from among the handsomest recruits, wore very long beards which they put into bags attached to their chins in order to protect them at night. Rodin's beard was just as long and just as well cared for, and I was fascinated by it, so I asked my mother whether, like the Sappers, he put it in a bag when he slept. Children remember things like this about the famous people they meet.

Rodin often made late departures on those Sunday afternoons; whereupon we were called and my father would go a little way with him, accompanied by his four daughters, his son, and his two spaniels.

"I must go through the Saint-Cloud park," he said on one of these occasions; "my wife is waiting there for me."

We walked through the cool shade and before long could make out the figure of a woman in a wide-brimmed hat, sitting on a grassy bank.

"Why don't you ever bring Mme Rodin with you?" asked Léon Cladel. "We should be happy to make her welcome."

"She's too much of a savage," answered the sculptor with an embarrassed smile.

"Then we'll tame her."

He blushed and conveyed his thanks with a look of grateful affection; then he grasped my father's delicate hand in his and was gone. But he did not bring his wife to visit us; she always waited for him somewhere, and his friends knew nothing of his private life.

The close friendship which had united Jules Dalou and Rodin came unhappily to an end. They were very nearly the same age, both had studied at the *Ecole des Arts Decoratifs,* and each had always held a high opinion of the other's work. Rodin had done a bust of Victor Hugo and though warmly recommended by the poet's friend Edmond Bazire and kindly received by Mme Drouet the task had been fraught with difficulties. Hugo had just sat to a sculptor of mediocre talent, and, wearied by the ordeal, had refused to pose again. Nevertheless, Mme Drouet persuaded him to allow Rodin to study his august features while at work or while receiving his friends. The sculptor was still little known and his determination to do the bust made it possible for him to accept the formidable conditions. He had a modelling stand brought and placed unobtrusively in the little house in the Avenue d'Eylau, and he began a rough model in clay. He made sketches in the poet's study and in his drawing-room, also at meals—he was frequently asked to stay for them—where he sat one day at his host's right, another at his left. Sometimes, he said, he was obliged to make his notes on cigarette papers; then he transferred them to the clay, and finally, laboriously, a bust resulted in which the poet is lost in prophetic thought and full of a force that was Hugo's own; it is the most strikingly true likeness of him that exists. Rodin presented him with a perfect bronze copy inscribed: *A l'illustre Mâitre.*

Victor Hugo's family was responsible for the series of misunderstandings between Rodin and his sitter; they did not appreciate the sculptor, despite the fact that his bust was so greatly admired by his fellow artists, particularly Dalou. He presented Dalou one day to the poet, and this friend and admirer so ingratiated himself with the occupants of the house in the Avenue d'Eylau that when Hugo died he was called in to make the death mask. His acceptance of the honour without telling Rodin, and his desire to obtain the order for the monument to be erected in the Panthéon, put an end to anything like friendship between the two sculptors. Rodin said nothing, but his coldness was immediately understood by Dalou. My father tried to bring them together at his dinner table, but distrust had taken root in Rodin's uncompromising heart and the break was final.

My father died in July of 1892 at the age of fifty-seven, after a long and painful illness. We left Sèvres and went to live in Paris, taking an apartment in a beautiful old house in the rue Christine which runs from the rue Dauphine to the rue des Grands-Augustins.

Léon Deschamps, editor of *La Plume,* undertook the raising of a fund for the erection of a monument to his memory in the Luxembourg Gardens, and, when asked to execute a bust or a medallion, Rodin accepted, and there was a certain generosity in his acceptance, for nothing could have been more uncertain than the success of the subscription.

We lived modestly and industriously in the rue Christine, and our greatest pleasure was to entertain those of our friends who remained devoted to our father's memory. These few were the rare minds, the genuinely gifted; the rest, forgetful or attracted elsewhere, had disappeared. Rodin never failed to attend these little gatherings in our dining-room which had no decoration but its pictures and a few flowers on the table. Once he came with Clovis Hugues, a dear friend of ours and a spirited conversationalist. I brought in a dish which had required a certain amount of careful preparation:

"But Judith, it's a Tanagra!" cried Clovis affectionately.

117

"I didn't know that Tanagra was both poet and chef," Rodin said quietly.

Clovis laughed uproariously, but kindly; he was aware of the gaps in the erudition of the man my father had named *l'Illustre Ingenu*. Rodin was in no way upset at Clovis's delight and when we were having coffee he begged my mother to go to the piano: Mozart, Beethoven . . . he listened with his head resting in his hands, lost in pleasurable meditation. Then, when she had finished, he lifted a large blushing face, got up silently, and went over and kissed her hands.

"You will come again soon?" my mother asked later, when he took his departure.

"If you will let me. But . . . I would like . . .," he hesitated.

"What is it you would like?"

"Couldn't everything be not quite so luxurious?"

Poor innocent man! A clean table-cloth, a few roses in a vase, and perfumed coffee were his idea of luxury; actually it was merely the sort of domestic comfort that he had never been able to achieve at home.

Then came a few weeks during which we saw him but rarely, despite the fact that his apartment was quite close to ours. He lived in an old house at 23 rue des Grands-Augustins—a narrow street, cold in winter and damp in summer—into whose lower windows no sunlight ever penetrated. It had appealed to him because of its eighteenth century elegance. When passing it, I often saw a woman watching me intently from behind the curtains at one of the second storey windows. Sometimes I would meet Rodin himself and listen to a confused apology for something—perhaps for never asking us to visit him. He said he was suffering from neuralgia and could not sleep; he seemed older and there were dark patches on his clear complexion. His reddened eyelids and the tense expression in his eyes betrayed care and anxiety; he smiled rarely and alluded several times to serious trouble, the annoyance of which he seemed to be trying to get rid of by means of involuntary upward thrusts of his shoulders. He was clearly going through a most distressing experience of some sort.

One morning, vans stood in front of the old house. Rodin himself supervised the removal of furniture and numberless pieces of sculpture. He said that his wife's health and his own had made it necessary for him to live permanently in the country. He had decided upon Bellevue and had found a vacant apartment in a lane called the Chemin Scribe in memory of the playwright's visit to the town.

The years 1895 to 1900 were marked by a prodigious amount of work; visitors to Rodin's studio were continually surprised by fresh additions to its company of bronzes and marbles. Thus one day they found themselves unexpectedly in the presence of a full length statue of President Sarmiento, the Argentine statesman and reformer, on a monumental pedestal representing *Apollon vainqueur,* bow in hand and the huge coils of Python beneath his feet. It was a poetical antithesis and also a sculptor's impassioned rendering of contrasting light and shade symbolized by the triumph of the mind over barbarism and ignorance. Sarmiento, exhausted by political conflict, face shrunken and deeply lined, had the appearance of a modern prophet, while the god springing from the bright mass of marble was dazzlingly young and triumphant.

The monument was to be placed in a public square in Buenos Ayres, but intellectual phenomena are to be encountered the world over; men's minds are everywhere subject to the same impulses toward comprehension or foolishness, as in other days people were psychologically inclined toward war-madness or revolutionary violence. The Argentine public proved to be no more appreciative of Rodin's art than the French; it desired the false photographic precision to which the nineteenth century had accustomed it, and not the interpretations of a pioneering genius. When it was unveiled in 1898, the Sarmiento monument was criticized, scoffed at, ridiculed; and, inevitably, when the official proceedings were over and the work had been presented to the city, buffooning crowds formed round it, shouting and hurling insults.

During these years, in addition to the large monuments, were produced groups such as *Bénédictions, Paolo et Francesca, La Jeune Fille et la Parque, Les Illusions, Le Poète et l'Amour, Pan et la Nymphe, Le Christ et la Madeleine, La Mort d'Alceste, Les Mauvais Génies, Confidence, La Source;* such subjects as *L'Adieu, Orphée, Génie bénissant, La Main de Dieu,* the famous *Génie* destined for the Puvis de Chavannes monument, *Psyché portant la lampe;* and the busts of Octave Mirbeau, of *Pallas au Parthénon,* of *Minerve casquée,* of Mme F——, of A. J. Eddy. Throughout this productive period Rodin had a terrific battle to fight, and, as one of his biographers has said, it was the most extraordinary of all his experiences.[3] It nearly cost him his health and his creative power, which meant life itself.

[3] Léon Riotor: *Rodin,* 1927.

V. THE BALZAC AFFAIR

SINCE 1883 the *Société des Gens de Lettres de France* had been preoccupied with the idea of erecting a monument to Honoré de Balzac. Thirty-five years after his death, the author of *La Comédie Humaine* still awaited the homage of his country and in particular of the *Société des Gens de Lettres,* of which he was the founder and the second president. The city of Paris had promised a site worthy of its illustrious son in the very centre of the capital, and it had now chosen the Place du Palais-Royal, in front of the Théâtre Français.

The *Société des Gens de Lettres* was merely taking up a very old project which had been promoted by none other than Alexandre Dumas, *père.* The day after Balzac's death, Dumas enthusiastically set about arranging a national subscription for the monument. Famous people are usually storm-centres; if Rodin had known or considered the circumstances of this first project he would perhaps have had some warning of the ordeal in store for him.

The subscription instituted by Dumas in 1851 with the help of the press had poor results. More success was obtained three years later with a gala performance at the Porte Saint-Martin theatre and a concert at the Ambigu, arranged by the young composer Ernest Reyer. The Court, artists, and the general public responded to his appeal and the receipts were excellent. Then, to the astonishment of everyone, the rumour spread that Mme de Balzac was preparing to institute legal proceedings for the suspension of the public subscription. Dumas, however, had been able to deal with that sensitive lady by announcing the fact that she had just set aside out of her own fortune the sum necessary to pay for her husband's tomb.

In a nobly and cleverly phrased letter which appeared in the press, the author of *Les Trois Mousquetaires* strove to soothe the widow's middle-class anxieties: "Tombs are family affairs, but it is the privilege of posterity to undertake the raising of monuments; and happy are those for whom a posterity exists within the space of three years." Mme de Balzac, whose pride prevented her from foreseeing the consequences of her action, replied with a summons.

The case was to be tried before the *tribunal de la Seine,* and on the day of the hearing the court-room was filled with people curious to see how the strange suit would go. But the judge interrupted Alexandre Dumas's counsel in the midst of his speech and declared that Mme de Balzac had no case. Nevertheless, due to the legal proceedings, there was a falling off in the contributions. Dumas had to go to Italy where he made a long stay, so long in fact that he died there without accomplishing his scheme, and his own monument, executed by Gustave Doré, was raised before Balzac's. At its unveiling in November of 1885, the *Société des Gens de Lettres* resolved to put through the project which Dumas had so warmly supported. Thirty-six thousand francs were subscribed and the execution fell to the lot of Chapu, a member of the Institute, who received the sum of six thousand francs in advance. Rodin was not considered, being then little known and, as Octave Mirbeau had written three years before in *La France,* "had not one quarter of Chapu's renown." Actually, Rodin's reputation did not begin to grow until the exhibition at the Georges Petit Gallery in 1889.

Chapu died in 1891. He left a maquette which satisfied Falguière, Antonin Mercié, and Paul Dubois, whose advice had been sought; and they agreed that it was far enough advanced to be carried out in marble. Falguière generously offered to undertake this work and turn over the amount of the subscriptions to the sculptor's widow. The special committee appointed by the *Société des Gens des Lettres* rejected this solution of the matter, and in the course of weekly meetings held at the poet Goeneutte's apartment and attended by the journalist Charles Chincholle, the art critic Paul Eudel, and the popular novelist Arthur Arnould—one of Rodin's greatest admirers—these three proposed the creator of *La Porte de l'Enfer* whose fame had by that time become widely recognized. A report was drawn up and sent to Emile Zola, then president of the *Société*.

Zola, once a supporter of Monet, Cézanne, and all independent art, in addressing the committee, exclaimed: "There is no reason to hesitate; the special committee has proposed two sculptors; one is Rodin. His name is a guarantee. He is one of the best sculptors of our time." And Rodin received the majority of the votes, with Frantz-Jourdain as collaborator for the architectural portion of the monument. Both declared themselves satisfied with the thirty thousand francs, and the six thousand paid in advance to Chapu went to his widow.

At the suggestion of his friends, Rodin wrote a formal letter to Zola. He undertook to execute the statue of Balzac in eighteen months, that is, to deliver it in January of 1893. What a short-sighted flight of fancy! What naïve optimism! What forgetfulness of the slow deliberation with which he carried all his important works through to completion! In this case the intensity of his desire wiped out the memory of his inevitable temporizations.

The committee's choice could not help offending the three sculptors whose advice had been sought in the first instance. Two of them, Dubois and Falguière, were Rodin's friends. It also ended by annoying the numerous other competitors and with them all the official sculptors who were conscious of the irresistibly soaring development of an artist on whom they had mercilessly turned their backs. It stirred up jealousy, malice, and anger which needed only an excuse to burst forth. This excuse was soon provided.

The date set by the sculptor arrived, and the work was not ready. Did this mean that Rodin had not been working? On the contrary—but according to his accustomed routine: idea conceived with lightning rapidity; execution worked out with the utmost precision after tireless fresh beginnings. In February of 1892, "a maquette exists, very finished, superb; Balzac is standing, clad in his Dominican frock." So wrote Roger Marx in *Le Voltaire*. Hostility flamed up immediately among Rodin's opponents and already, less than a year after he had received the commission, his supporters were obliged to come forward.

He had been absorbed from the beginning by the endless pondering which always prefaced the composition of his important works. This time he was faced with some formidable aesthetic problems. The Balzac iconography was limited and somewhat inexact; no death mask had been taken and the indications and measurements so precious to those who were to paint or model his features did not exist. And there was also the seemingly insurmountable difficulty of faithfully producing a full length figure of the novelist, with his admirable head and his thick short body deformed by a long sedentary life: sixteen hours a day bent over his writing table. The sculptor had to represent not merely the familiar appearance of the author of *La Comédie Humaine*, but also the spiritual emanations from one of the most prodigious brains of the century, the outer evidence of a mind in ceaseless gestation—the features of a visionary that were moulded and elaborated from within; he had in short to represent a literary giant in the act of creating his world.

In order to render these well-nigh inexpressible qualities, Rodin sought the guidance of a poet, as he had sought that of a historian for his conception of *Les Bourgeois de Calais:* he read Lamartine, steeped himself in the passage devoted to Balzac and in the even more famous phrase: "He was the embodiment of an elemental force." That was the watchword he obeyed, for it corresponded with his own realistic lyricism, it confirmed his own ideas of spiritual greatness and nobility.

As he wrote Zola, he had, two years before being entrusted with the execution of the statue, visited Balzac's native Tours—drawn there by the beauty of the architecture; he had spent many hours wandering along the banks of the Indre, and in the evenings, sitting in his hotel bedroom, he had re-read *Le Lys dans la Vallée* and the pages in which the writer had described the country of his birth. His artistic sensibilities had been heightened by this account in which passion and a caressing tenderness were mingled. He was already conscious of a fraternal love for this genius, and he dreamed of the figure in stone or bronze which some sculptor would one day consecrate to his memory. Now this stupendous task was his own, but the exigencies of art compelled him to free its accomplishment from the inaccuracies of his dreaming, to work from a solid foundation of reality, to attain the utmost precision of morphology and documentation. The decorative and characterless bust by David d'Angers, a few lithographs and sketches, and an oil portrait by Louis Boulanger were the only aids at Rodin's disposal. Except for the bust, these were of no use to him in his task of recomposing a human figure. He was obliged to turn to human beings. In a given period of time, humanity varied little and repeated itself; these repetitions formed a regional type and Rodin remembered with a certain amusement a phrase that had gone the rounds of the studios: "It's no use doing his bust; you can find him in the museums." He therefore tried to find Balzac, or rather his double, among the people of Touraine.

In August of 1891, he revisited the valley of the Indre, making Tours his headquarters. He did not concern himself with Balzac's true origins. Did he, or did he not know that the great author's father was of Albigian peasant stock and his mother of Parisian? Fate sometimes works miracles for the strong-willed: Rodin soon picked out several people who resembled Balzac and modelled their features. He met a young commercial traveller, got him to pose, and made a large carefully detailed bust of him, animating the frank open features with the novelist's Rabelaisian joviality and the spiritual fire that blazed in his eyes. This was a smiling, delightfully young Balzac, full of self-confidence, but it was not the Balzac of *La Comédie Humaine*.

Rodin returned to Paris at the end of October. He read and re-read everything connected with Balzac, following the advice of his friends, particularly that of Octave Mirbeau. Someone told him of an old tailor of Balzac's, who had moved out of Paris. He ordered a pair of trousers and a waistcoat made to the great man's measurements, put them on the tailor and modelled a new figure. Then one day, to his great joy, Mathias Morhardt brought him the recently discovered reproduction of a superb daguerreotype that belonged to Nadar. "It is Balzac toward the end of his life, grave, ill, his hand on his chest as if to call attention to the malady of which he was to die and the immensity of the work that would thus be cut short." [1]

This moving likeness enabled Rodin to come to definite conclusions. But the sculptural problem was still unsolved. Victor Hugo, though advanced in years, still had the noble figure of an athlete which made possible his deification in marble; but what of Balzac's similarity to a short thick-set monk with a protruding stomach? Obviously he would have to be represented in the monk's gown which he had worn during his long hours of work. Thus the deformity of the heroic torso, set upon a gnome's legs, could be concealed. If he were standing with arms crossed, the cavity above his stomach might be filled out. Nevertheless, to avoid the appearance of an empty envelope, the nude figure had to be present beneath the folds of the cloth; the palpitating presence of the huge suffering body was essential.

As he had done in the case of *Les Bourgeois de Calais* and the *Victor Hugo,* Rodin got someone to pose for the nude and modelled a figure with one foot forward in the attitude of a warrior marching into battle; but he was not satisfied. Its overflowing vitality did not evoke the great thinker, lost in meditation, immobilized by his work. Rodin experimented again, altered the attitude to that of an older man whose face was lined by years of arduous toiling. Finally there were seven nudes encumbering the

[1] Gustave Geffroy: *L'Imaginaire. Le Figaro,* August 29, 1893.

126

studio with their aggressive presence, giving it the fantastic appearance of some haunted chamber, some witches' cavern.

The place chosen for the statue was long and carefully studied by the sculptor. From each corner of the Place du Palais-Royal, his eye measured the space that was to be occupied by the massive sculptured cube. The broken lines of the surrounding edifices required a scheme of the greatest sobriety; the figure, apart from the pedestal, was to be ten feet high so that it would not be dwarfed by its setting. Balzac must proudly dominate the multitude which had supplied him with the material for his works. . . . Rodin again made drastic transformations in one of his figures. Balzac, this time, stood undraped with feet together, arms crossed, head held high: in such an attitude, Jupiter brought forth Minerva.

Rodin's casters draped the seven figures in cloth, each one differently, and threw wet plaster at them, which as it dried, clothed them in rigid robes. Of these seven spectres he was to choose one for his final working model. In order to solve this complex enigma, he had been obliged to model no less than seventeen figures.

Early in 1893, several subscribers to the fund, roused perhaps by secret intrigue, became worried by the non-appearance of the statue and sent in a complaint to the committee of the *Société des Gens de Lettres*. The committee was divided: Rodin's admirers argued angrily with his opponents at its meetings. From the beginning, Alfred Duquet had shown himself to be antagonistic. He was an able man and of value to the committee, but he was also brusque and impulsive; he declared that the statue would never be completed. Why was this remarkable military historian so resolutely hostile to Rodin? Did he think a statue could be executed in a few days, in a few hours, like the winning or losing of battles in history? Even if the sculptor had been a paragon of subtlety and diplomatic craftiness he would have flatly refused to sacrifice his time or his dignity in pulling wires; he even neglected to invite the committee to come to his studio, which, perhaps, would have appeased M. Alfred Duquet and others. In July, however, he arranged this visit; he must have shown the model so enthusiastically described by Roger Marx eighteen months before, but it seems not to have been noticed. The committee was merely stunned by "a strange Balzac in the posture of a wrestler defying all comers, legs apart, stomach enormous, shocking, distorted. It was respectfully intimated to Rodin that he could have represented the author at another time in his life." Thus said Charles Chincholle who had established himself as the chronicler of the affair in *Le Figaro*. What was responsible for the misunderstanding? Was it that Rodin had not sufficiently explained what he was doing? Had he retired into silence when he felt that they had lost confidence in him? Or was it that the majority of the committee was maliciously inclined to believe in the sculptor's intention to put a naked, big-bellied wrestler in the Place du Palais-Royal?

Whatever its origins, the conflict was now fully launched. At first Emile Zola used his powerful influence to calm the most aggressive among his colleagues who were already talking of a lawsuit against Rodin. He persuaded them to give him time to finish the statue according to the dictates of his artistic conscience, and he himself visited the studio where he learned of the sculptor's hope of completing the maquette in the course of the winter. Then would come the execution of the full-size figure and the casting in bronze; the delivery would thus be delayed another year, until the spring of 1895. This fresh postponement was allowed.

In April of 1894, Zola's term as president of the *Société des Gens de Lettres* came to an end. He was succeeded by the poet and novelist Jean Aicard, also an admiring friend of Rodin's. Before his departure to Rome, where he went to collect material for his next novel, Zola frankly and amicably advised his successor: "There is a stormy question which I have had to leave for the *Société* to decide—the Balzac statue. Between ourselves, it is likely to be a frightful annoyance to you. I am devoted to Rodin—you have heard me exert myself in his favour—but I don't want you to feel obliged to adopt my opinions. The best thing for everyone

Dawn (*L'Aurore*). COURTESY OF THE MUSEE RODIN

Falling (*Mouvement de Chute*). COURTESY OF THE MUSEE RODIN

would be for you to establish relations with Rodin's friends. Be conciliatory, and try for some mutually satisfactory understanding. A suit would waste the sculptor's time and do harm to the *Société*. . . . I fear the squall is about to strike."[2]

Actually, the feeling was running high in the committee. Half of its members, who were in close touch with the Institute—that secret power fanning the flames of discord—were on Alfred Duquet's side against Rodin. At the end of May, the committee paid a second visit to the studio and declared the project "artistically inadequate." It was dumbfounded by what some of its members considered "a formless mass, a nameless thing, a gigantic foetus." Furthermore, these gentlemen stated unsympathetically that the sculptor's health was such that he could do no work and they forced him to postpone the completion of the statue indefinitely. Though his physical exhaustion did not excite their sympathy, it did make them apprehensive. Would Rodin have the statue ready in time for the Balzac Centenary in 1899 which the *Société* wished to celebrate with suitable splendour? They believed the time had come to demand that he either deliver the statue or return the signed agreement. MM. Henry de Braisne, Pierre Sales, and Pierre Maël protested vigorously against the severity of this proposal. Jean Aicard declared that an artist could not be treated as a manufacturer and that Rodin's physical and mental condition made it necessary for the committee to be extremely lenient. He obtained a short respite. At the end of October, M. Edmond Tarbé, the former editor of *Le Gaulois* and the author of several so-called Parisian novels, proposed that Rodin should be forced to deliver his statue within twenty-four hours or cancel his agreement and repay the ten thousand francs received in advance, plus one franc damages. To the painful astonishment of Jean Aicard, this proposal was unanimously approved. The poet controlled his indignation and strove to pacify the angriest members, but all he accomplished was to postpone the enforcement of the action for a week or two. In that time he hoped to persuade Rodin to re-

[2] Jean Aicard: *L'Art au-dessus de l'Argent. Le Figaro,* December 3, 1894.

linquish the execution of the statue of his own accord, and, following Zola's advice, he besought Rodin's friends to try to convince him of the wisdom of this course. It was a cruel concession for the president of the *Société* to have to make, but he felt bound to act impartially and loyally toward those who had placed their confidence in him by making him their president.

Early in November, he again advised and exhorted them with the utmost firmness; was it necessary in their opinion "to treat Rodin as an artist with freedom to proceed according to his inspiration, or as a common labourer with a date set for the accomplishment of his work? What will the *Société* gain in bringing suit against M. Rodin—a suit whose outcome is more than doubtful? It behooves the committee of the distinguished *Société des Gens de Lettres* to act with the greatest courtesy, with the highest and the noblest motives." Jean Aicard did not seek to excuse Rodin, but in speaking thus he felt sure he was considering the best interests of the *Société*. He had had a visit from Rodin whose health had improved, and that morning he had received a letter from him which he considered splendid and very moving; he would read it to his colleagues and they could then reply to it according to the dictates of their conscience:

Dear Mr. President:

I beg you to believe that I fully appreciate your asking my friend Geffroy to approach me about the statue. My best reply is to tell you again of my joy when I accepted the task your great Society entrusted me with. What I desire above all is that neither you nor your colleagues should misunderstand my intention. It is to complete the Balzac monument to your satisfaction, to give you a work that I am striving to make worthy of its subject, of you, and of your conception of the manner in which Balzac should be honoured.

I ask you to admit that the progress of a work of art which is to be produced under the best conditions and to the satisfaction of those who have commissioned its execution, must not be interfered with and subjected to fixed time limits. All those who have struggled to produce such works know that calm untroubled reflection is absolutely necessary. This is what I would like you to grant me, in order that I may bring mine to a prompt and satisfactory completion.

You can and you must admit this, for these are the anxieties of all creators in the field of art and letters.

I have been conscious continually of my responsibility as an artist and that is what has filled my mind since the few weeks' rest I was obliged to take. I ask you to allow me to do honour, with all my power and determination, to the great man whose example must be an inspiration to you all. I think continually of his relentless labours, the difficulties of his existence, the incessant conflict in which he was forced to involve himself, and of his splendid courage. I want to express it all. Put your faith and your trust in me, and believe me to be

yours sincerely and devotedly,

Auguste Rodin

Some of the sculptor's friends, perhaps with Gustave Geffroy, must have helped in the writing of this letter which contained none of Rodin's imperious precision and none of his pungent stylistic shortcomings. But it was nevertheless difficult to answer a communication of such perfect restraint and moderation by coercive measures. This, however, was not the opinion of M. Alfred Duquet who vigorously opposed the conciliatory impulses of certain of his colleagues; he stressed the fact of their responsibility as to the financial phase of the matter. Actually, that was the fundamental cause of their anxiety. Rodin might die before the completion of the statue. How then could the *Société* recover the money it had paid him in advance which his heirs would consider to be legally theirs? When Rodin heard of these fears he immediately let it be known that he was ready to return the ten thousand francs, or rather, that he would place this amount in the government deposit and consignment office, until the delivery of his statue; and he asked for a year's grace. Upon receiving this offer the members of the committee were reassured, even pleased, and they made no objection to the further delay.

It seemed now as though these new arrangements might provide Rodin with the tranquillity he needed for the re-establishment of his health and the completion of his statue. But the opposing group, outside the *Société,* was far from satisfied; it was consumed by spite against the sculptor and refused to let pass this unique opportunity to attack him, to destroy his prestige, and, perhaps, due to the low state of his health, to get rid of him permanently.

The committee was secretly worked upon by these outside influences. At its next meeting, to Jean Aicard's disgust, there was a violent flaming up of anger, again concerning the financial aspect of the question. The government deposit and consignment office did not receive conditional deposits subject to change of ownership and refused to accept Rodin's. The sculptor then announced that he would put the money into the hands of the notary employed by the *Société.* But anger soon arose again and the committee, against the advice of its president who was opposed to the proceeding, decided forthwith to summon its legal advisers and Maître Ausoux, Rodin's attorney and friend.

On November 26, to the profound astonishment of the *Société,* Jean Aicard, whose dignity as president had been insulted by the opposition of his colleagues, handed in his resignation; and in order to explain fully his motives for this action he read a long letter couched in terms of unexpected severity and vehemence. He then withdrew, followed by six members of the committee: MM. Henry de Braisne, Pierre Maël, Henri Malo, Marcel Prevost, Raoul de Saint-Arroman, and Gustave Toudouze.

"The squall is about to strike," Zola had said. It had struck, and it was raging with tempest-like fury throughout the press and literary circles. In crises of this sort, it is never possible to conceal what is going on. That evening, in editorial rooms, at gatherings of writers and artists, there was talk of nothing else. The words of Aicard's stern rebuke to his colleagues spread rapidly; it was incredible that this tender poet of the soil who had always been criticized for his lack of vigour and realism should have enunciated in such reproachful terms his opinion of the committee's unseemly attitude. He was attacked by several newspapers and arrogantly defended himself in *Le Figaro*.

There was great anxiety in the rooms of the *Société* in the cité Rougemont. The committee, dismayed by the noisy withdrawal of seven of its members, feared serious complications—perhaps a collective resignation and a general meeting of the *Société*. There was a unanimous vote against the acceptance of the resignations, but Jean Aicard, Gustave Toudouze, Henry de Braisne, and Raoul de Saint-Arroman held to their intention.

Aurélien Scholl saved the situation by accepting the presidency. Léon Deschamps, editor of *La Plume,* at once arranged a conference in his office, which was kept a secret till the end of the conflict, between Scholl and Rodin who were embarrassingly polite to each other. The intelligent and generous editor offered to hold himself personally responsible for Rodin's expenses in case the *Société* should be obliged to default.[3] Upon this satisfactory solution no difficulty remained but that of coping with the daily avalanche of newspaper protests against the committee.

From that time until its final flare-up in 1898, the Balzac affair was a daily feature throughout the entire press. It invaded drawing-rooms, and soon became the catch-word of all Paris. Even the Dreyfus Affair, which was throwing the country into confusion, failed to obscure it. Amid this uproar which penetrated into his studio—endless visits, interviews, fifty press-cuttings in every morning's post—Rodin, ill, worried, and anxious above all not to commit any artistic blunders, was labouring hard to finish his statue, to complete other work, to be present at the unveilings of the *Monument Claude Lorrain* and *Les Bourgeois de Calais*. It was an unrelenting struggle, and Rodin might easily have succumbed. An attack of influenza had left him sleepless, subject to headaches, easily fatigued, and he was also going through a distressing private

[3] *La Plume,* May, 1898.

crisis. During this troubled period, Edmond de Goncourt met him in a train carrying them both into the country to dine with Octave Mirbeau and wrote in his *Journal* that he found him "greatly changed, very gloomy and worried about his fatigue after working." To the Mayor of Calais who had been urging him to put the final touches on his group, the persecuted sculptor had written: "I am resting now and will not be back in Paris for two months. I was at the end of my strength—worn out." This was when he left the dreary apartment in the rue des Grands-Augustins and went to live at Bellevue. He expected the peace and the fresh air of the suburb, with its shady trees and cool gardens, to revive his exhausted mind and body, but his retirement to Bellevue did not deliver him from the torments of his private life.

During the autumn of 1894 he travelled in the south of France, visited Auvergne, Dauphiné and the Engadine, stopping at Saint-Moritz. The journey was beneficial; he partially re-established himself and went to work. One the 16th of January, 1895, he presided with his usual serenity and grace at a banquet arranged at his own request by Mathias Morhardt to celebrate the seventieth birthday of his great friend Puvis de Chavannes. But Morhardt had another purpose in mind: to create an opportunity for the artists who attended to offer their sympathy and their allegiance to Rodin at that particular moment.[4] Also the conspiracy to keep Rodin from being made head of the sculpture section of the *Société Nationale des Beaux-Arts* might be forestalled.

Each guest was given a small bronze plaque showing a reproduction of Rodin's bust of Puvis. The sculptor read an excellent speech, plentifully edited and revised by Jean Marras, then curator of the Dêpot des Marbres, and polished up by Gustave Geffroy, but no one heard a word, for he muttered it timidly into his beard.

Thanks to a constitution inherited from peasant forebears and the ardent support of his friends, Rodin was not yet "finished,"

[4] Mathias Morhardt: *Le Banquet Puvis de Chavannes, Mercure de France,* August 1, 1935.

despite the rumors maliciously spread abroad by the hack sculptors. Thus the campaign against him had to be reopened. His defenders saw clearly what was going on: "The cut-price sculptors are always there, waiting for the chance to deposit statues along the public thoroughfares," wrote Jean Aicard. "They make their deliveries in forty-eight hours."

In *Le Voltaire*, Edouard Conte was still more explicit: "It is an open secret," he declared in January of 1896, "that there is a conspiracy to take the commission for the *Balzac* from Rodin and give it to someone else. M. Marquet de Vasselot has already offered to execute it rapidly. M. Marquet de Vasselot is a skilful dabbler" not only in sculpture, but, the editor added, "in social publicity"; Conte did not neglect to sound the political note, "and he managed to get himself papal orders in return for making a bust of His Holiness."

M. Marquet de Vasselot had done a bust of Balzac in 1872 for the Théâtre Français. In his anxiety to realize a recently formulated ambition, he had invited the committee of the *Société des Gens de Lettres* to inspect the monument he was getting ready for the writer's centenary, the model for which had been shown in the Salon of 1896. The great man looked like a crouching sphinx; it was Balzac with a head as empty as an unlit lantern and a body more nearly resembling a cow's than a lion's. This absurdity was laughed at by all intelligent Parisians; it dumbfounded the rest. Up to that time only the supporters of Rodin had made public the old grudges against him. But now one of his pretended friends who had joined the opposite camp suddenly exposed the hack sculptors' sham reserve. From Academic and Government corridors he gathered up a fifteen years' accumulation of spite and malice, and he condensed it into a newspaper article of three columns. Even Rodin's rivals were appalled by what they read in *Gil Blas* of September 13, 1896 under the title: "A Would-be Genius." They themselves had inspired this article by M. Félicien Champsaur without realizing that they would be so crudely unmasked. To

135

speak of him at all gives him an unmerited importance, but he is the most plain-spoken of all Rodin's detractors.

M. Champsaur dedicated his article to "Honoré de Balzac, powerful creator of immortal characters: the man-to-whom-through-the-fault-of-M. Rodin-Paris-has-not-yet-raised-a-monument." Excusing himself for his article ten years before in which he said of *La Porte de l'Enfer:* "It is a veritable epic, both complex and harmonious, grandly conceived and perfect in execution. Why not compensate the creator of this masterpiece with a little glory?" M. Champsaur now changed sides completely and, exasperated by the advent of this glory for which he had once made appeal, he wrote:

"It is forbidden to speak Rodin's name in any but the most reverential terms. The snobs of literature, journalism, the drawing-rooms, and the boulevards think themselves clever when they set up these more or less harmless ephemeral gods: Mallarmé, the prince of poets, a literary puppet; Rodin, famous for a *Porte de l'Enfer* which will never be finished; which, indeed, no longer exists because it sprang from a magnificent dream only to be absorbed into it again; and now this statue of Balzac which he cannot execute. . . . MM. Dalou, Falguière, Boucher, Desbois, Injalbert, and the rest, you do not exist. I tell you no one exists but Rodin. Nevertheless Dalou is a master; his *Mirabeau* and *Monument Delacroix* are superb. But for the last ten years it's been all Rodin—Rodin alone and all-sufficient. . . . As for the Balzac statue, it is fashionable among Rodin's satellites to be contemptuous of M. Marquet de Vasselot, but the marble bust in the Théâtre Français is evocative, excellent beyond all dispute, almost the living features of the great writer."

M. Champsaur, like Goncourt, then describes with sadistic delight the sculptor's mental and physical exhaustion, his "dreamer's impotence." He advises him to "give it up" and suggests calling in another sculptor to execute the Balzac monument: Dalou, for instance, or Bartholomé; then, in conclusion:

"Rodin never got beyond the modelling of rough sketches; he never had a place among the great, the geniuses, the masters of all time. He is the failure of Rodin, which may, after all, be fame—in memoriam."

We shall never know what enraged vanity, what frustrated pretentions to talent and notoriety released this flood of hatred, for Rodin did not allow himself to break his scornful silence and reply to these flunkeys of literature who strove to spatter his statues with ink and mud. . . . It must have wounded his feelings to discover Dalou once again among the hostile forces, Dalou, the friend of his youth, his admired fellow sculptor who had never reached greatness and had never forgiven Rodin for leaving him so far behind. The loyal Desbois was in a fury at being slanderously spoken of as one of the envious antagonists.

In 1897, Rodin had not yet delivered his statue and hostilities were revived in the committee of the *Société*. Henri Houssaye was then president. The opposition group was again roused by Alfred Duquet to the point of suggesting legal action, for it had no clear idea of the actual intention of the sculptor. M. Henri Malo had questioned him eighteen months ago: "Well, what about the *Balzac?*" and Rodin had replied: "It's getting on." But M. Albert Cim had seen him two months ago and had also asked: "What about the *Balzac?*" And this time: "It's not getting on," had been the evasive answer.

Every weekly meeting of the committee was devoted to discussing the irritating question. In March, Henri Houssaye saw the maquette and was assured that the statue would be ready in October. In May, Rodin asked for a short delay in order to make some slight changes. . . . At last, toward the end of March, 1898, the chairman announced that the statue had been completed and asked the committee whether they deemed it advisable to have it exhibited at the next Salon. He received a favourable reply to this singular question which actually concerned no one but the sculptor.

Emile Zola knew better than anyone else what a decisive battle would be fought round the statue. He courageously reasserted his opinion of Rodin, and, with no other significance than that of the date of his letter, he wrote these few lines to a representative of the *Société des Gens de Lettres* the day before the Salon *vernissage*:

25 April, 1898

My dear Colleague,

When I appealed eight years ago in *Le Figaro* for a statue for Balzac, I said I would give a thousand francs. Here they are.

Cordially yours,
Emile Zola

The *Balzac* was sent to the *Salon de la Société Nationale des Beaux-Arts*. Rodin had been a member of it since 1890 when the *Société des Artists Français* had split into two groups, and he had taken Dalou's place in 1893 as head of the sculpture section. The Salon was held in the *Galerie des Machines* in the Champ de Mars, built ten years previously for the *Exposition Universelle*. Several sensational works were to be shown: the *Sainte-Geneviève* of Puvis de Chavannes; Besnard's enchanting *Portrait de Réjane*, which the great actress did not accept; Carrière's huge decorative canvas for the *Salle de l'Enseignement* at the Sorbonne. But critics and public were more curious to see the Balzac statue than any of these, and to form their judgment of this work, famous before being exhibited.

Rodin was fully aware of the magnitude of the conflict into which fate was drawing him. With the approach of old age he had come to dread noisy controversy and the attacks of the smaller periodicals which concealed treacherous self-interest. But he was careful not to confuse these with the regular press which had supported him magnificently for twenty years. He resigned himself to the consequences of his proudly held opinions and he entered the battle courageously; he was fighting for something greater than personal advancement; he was fighting for art, and destiny had endowed him with the power to reinstate it among the virtues of his race. He was seriously and resolutely determined to let nothing interfere with the full accomplishment of this duty.

One morning late in April of that year, I found him in the vast court-yard of the Dépôt des Marbres in the rue de l'Université. He had had his statue brought out into the daylight and was submitting it to a rigorous examination, with unaccustomed indifference to the warm spring air and the tender young leaves on the chestnut trees. It was a painful ordeal; the bright daylight diminished the importance of the volumes, flattened the planes, and played havoc with the modelling. Could the statue survive this pitiless illumination? Rodin looked old; his complexion was bad and his eyelids inflamed. After anxiously appraising his work he turned to me and took off his hat, passing his hand across his brow as though trying to rid himself of the obsession which had pressed down upon him for ten years. I did not know what to say, for I was overcome by the strange figure and had a presentiment of the fury that would be roused by such an unusual technique.

"They're taking away my statue," he muttered complainingly. "Sculpture requires a lot of time; the artist ought to be able to forget his work, to go for months without seeing it, and then return to judge it as though it were someone else's. But try to get the bureaucrats to understand that!"

He kept rubbing his forehead and told me he was having bad neuralgia, giving me the impression that he was in great mental distress.

However, on the day of the opening of the Salon, he had got back his composure and his colour was good. In the huge ship-like building in the Champ de Mars he stood, close to *Le Baiser* which, with a touch of artistic vanity, he had determined to exhibit along with the *Balzac;* it was an exquisite piece of work, produced fifteen years before. A few yards away, against the high windows of the nave, the towering phantom, sheathed in its robe of white plaster, raised its magnificent grief-stricken head almost seventeen feet above the crowds—its mouth twisted with irony and pity, its "eyes seek-

139

ing the sun and already invaded by darkness."[5] Its strange aspect produced in some a wordless astonishment, and in others indignation, or laughter, and for the most part a complete misunderstanding. People gathered round this druidical stone with human countenance; then with naïve indiscretion they walked over to inspect Rodin. Amazed by the placid demeanour of this man whose features were almost hidden by the brim of his hat and his beard, some turned away to hide their sudden bursts of laughter—they wondered whether he was a lunatic or a practical joker; others gazed eagerly at him, grinning with malicious curiosity. Some of his fellow sculptors pretended to or actually did believe that Rodin had become too literary and, exceeding his customary medium, had wanted to produce a symbol, to represent, not a man of genius realistically conceived in flesh and spirit, but the quintessence of his mind and his work—a metaphysical dream in which the weaklings and the eccentrics of art often lose themselves. To these platitudes one might have replied with a single gesture, that of breaking the frock in which Balzac was clad and thereby revealing the ruthlessly exact modelling of the pulsating figure beneath, a human being whose heart beats were soon to cease.

Motionless and preoccupied, Rodin talked with a few friends, unaware of the curious circle forming and re-forming round him. By four o'clock the building was crowded; more than two thousand spectators gazed upon the "phenomenon," declaring their opinions defiantly and authoritatively. One sculptor exclaimed that "if Balzac were to return to this earth he would disclaim the statue." The painter Harpignies said: "One cannot criticize a work which is incomprehensible." The journalist M. Alphonse Humbert, former deputy and President of the Municipal Council, complained: "Is this all he could make of a man so gifted?" And the great poet Léon Dierx emerged from his mood of tender musing to say bluntly: "For ten years this unbelievable humbug has lasted!"

French artists and those of other countries went from *Le Baiser*

[5] Léon Daudet: *Rodin* (*L'Action française*), November 19, 1917.

to the *Balzac*, voicing their admiration. Those who had been present the day before when the President of the Republic had visited the exhibition had plenty to say regarding the chief executive's attitude. As head of the sculpture section, Rodin had himself shown M. Félix Faure the exhibits of his fellow sculptors. After complimenting him upon *Le Baiser*, the President had walked past the *Balzac* without looking at it, his attention fixed upon a row of busts across the aisle. [6] Thus in two minutes M. Félix Faure had decreed what good sculpture should be, when Rodin, after forty years of tireless labour and experiment, hardly dared to commit himself.

Emile Bourdelle spoke for one group of artists: "That is delightful," he said, referring to *Le Baiser*, "but it hardly exists beside the other. The *Balzac* is a hundred times finer. What sculpture! Rodin is showing us all the road to follow."

Full of confidence, as in his young days, "in the power of truth," he held himself aloof from the conflict. At closing time, Georges Montorgueil, the well-known journalist, asked him deferentially: "How do you think the battle is going?"

"I think I've won, and it's been a good day's work," he answered calmly.

The next morning the press was loud with the voices of angry critics. Scholastic enmity seemed to have lost none of its violence since the romantic days of *Hernani*, of Wagner and *Tannhäuser*, of Manet and his *Olympia*. A flood of stupidities, commonplaces, and malice was released. M. Oliver Merson, father of the painter, member of the Institute, and professor at the Beaux-Arts wrote, in his rôle of art critic for *Le Monde Illustré:*

"I will say nothing of the *Balzac* by which we have been so horribly bored, for some of our 'intellectuals,' who imagine they

[6] Mathias Morhardt: *La Bataille du Balzac* (*Mercure de France*), December 15, 1934.

know about such things because they are in the habit of discussing them, have poured forth endless verbiage to prove *urbi et orbi* that a work which went wrong almost before it was begun—that is, a work which is artistically a piece of absolute nothingness— is a miraculous accomplishment, a masterpiece without equal today or in the past. No wonder people shrugged their shoulders! Indeed, no one with a grain of sense could fail to recognize in this lump of plaster, thrown or kicked together by a lunatic or some hopeless weakling, the work of a mind in complete confusion, or if you will, the impudent act of some Master in the Art of Humbug."

M. Gaston Migeon lumped all of Rodin's work together and condemned it pityingly: "Poor man! Does one need to recall his misfortunes? *Les Bourgeois de Calais, La Porte de l'Enfer,* the *Monument Victor Hugo."* M. André Pératé wrote in *Le Correspondant,* a periodical purveying current opinion:

"Never was known such a stupendous misunderstanding between the arts of writing and modelling. The advance-guards of criticism attacked the ancient fortress of French good sense and calmly declared that it was not the distinctive features of the man, but his great work: *La Comédie Humaine* in all its complexity and symbolism, that was represented for us by the big sarcastic mouth and the deeply furrowed face rising above the famous dressing gown so stiffly and comically as to give the impression of a puppet in a gigantic Punch and Judy Show."

Without realizing that the two works exhibited by Rodin marked a departure and a final arrival, Benjamin Constant exclaimed in *Le Figaro:*

"*Le Baiser!* What a masterful piece of work! Never before has marble lived so vividly. Never has a kiss joined two human beings in such a beautiful, such a sculptural caress. This is the expression of an artist's inmost heart. Truly a masterpiece! . . . The statue of Balzac . . . is painful to look upon. . . ."

Henri Rochefort, forgetful of the splendid bust Rodin had done of him which perhaps in any case he had never understood, delivered himself of some school-boy humour in *L'Intransigeant:*

"Balzac is now explained for us! George Sand, Hugo, and Sainte-Beuve were dazzled by his intellect; Rodin alone, by virtue of goodness knows what sort of X-rays, has pierced the great writer's skull; and he probably felt that there was something God-like in his divination. No one has ever thought of extracting a man's brain and putting it upon his face. Let Rodin give us Balzac's nose, his mouth, his brow and the structure of his powerful head; then we will be able to distinguish Balzac's genius. But for the love of art, may the sculptor spare us his private commentaries!"

In *Le Gaulois,* M. Jean Rameau devoted a long article to the dispute, entitled "The Victory of M. Rodin":

"It is generally thought that we should do our utmost to persuade the *Société des Gens de Lettres* to see to it that M. Rodin's *Balzac* is not placed in the Place du Palais-Royal to horrify all who must look at it. My humble opinion is that this stupendous statue should be erected there at once upon a high pedestal so that it may be seen from afar, and that it should be cast of indestructible bronze so that people of the centuries to come may know what mental aberrations were current at the end of this one. But I ask that upon the base of the statue be inscribed the names of the eminent artists who have praised it. This would be their punishment and our revenge."

Why did M. Jean Rameau desire revenge? Because he was a man of no importance and still less genius?

The newspaper editors left their critics free, except in political pronouncements, and personally responsible for their opinions. *Le Figaro* published a splendid analysis by Georges Rodenbach, concluding with, "the last manner of this great artist is his highest achievement," and the following day in the same place there were three columns by M. Philippe Gille demonstrating that Rodin had committed a grave blunder; in *La Fronde,* as a reply to what I had written the day before, our editor, Mme Marguerite Durand, published an exasperated article by Mme Daniel Lesueur, entitled "A Bankrupt Imagination." Two years later the celebrated Feminist paper was to publish a superb article by Mme Harlor under the prophetic title of "The Rodin Museum." [7] Naturally Rodin's supporters all took up their pens. Among the first of these were Camille Mauclair, Louis de Fourcaud, Gustave Kahn, Raymond Bouyer, Jean Dolent, Fagus, Gabriel Mourey, Roinard, Paul Gsell and twenty others; and their less talented adversaries were subjected to some unpardonable berating.

The affair turned into a public scandal. Groups of friends gathered at the Salon to make fun of the statue, "the snow-man," "the sack-race" as Rochefort had called it. The man in the street took it up and the so-called comic press was filled with caricatures; little white lumps of imitation snow, bags of flour, and plaster figurines representing penguins or seals standing on their tails were sold everywhere. The streets echoed with "Buy Rodin's Balzac!" A picture dealer gave a masked ball and greeted his guests disguised as the *Balzac;* he had had an enlargement of one of the little plaster seals made in pasteboard and in this ludicrous shell achieved a huge success.

A rumour began to spread that Rodin had tried to mystify the public and a journalist had the impudence to question him regarding his intentions. Without losing his temper the great man replied:

"I no longer have to fight for my sculpture; it has been able to defend itself for a long time. To say that my *Balzac* was executed in order to hoax the public is an insult that would once have infuriated me. Today I pay no attention to such things and keep on working. My life is one long course of study. To scoff at others would be to scoff at myself. If truth must die, my *Balzac* will be

[7] *La Fronde:* June 1, 1900.

144

broken in pieces by future generations; but if truth is eternal, *I predict that my statue will make its way alone.*

"While we are talking of this spiteful affair which will probably last a long time, I want to say something that needs to be said clearly. My statue which people are making fun of because they cannot destroy it is the result of a whole lifetime of effort; it is the mainspring of my aesthetic theory. From the day of its conception I was a changed man. My development was along fundamental lines. I had forged a link between the great traditions of the past and my own time which each day became stronger.

"Aesthetic law-makers are against my *Balzac,* also the majority of the public and the press. What does it matter? The statue will make its own way into people's minds, either by force or persuasion. There are young sculptors who go to see it and who think about it while searching for their ideals." [8]

The committee of the *Société des Gens de Lettres* was now in the predicament so long hoped for by the majority of its members. The time had come for a definite decision and the affair was a delicate one from every point of view: the moral, the legal, and the financial.

Henri Houssaye was president of the *Société;* Alfred Duquet and Henri Demesse were its vice presidents. On May 2, after a noisy argument, Alfred Duquet addressed his colleagues; first he read some of the unfavourable newspaper criticisms of the statue. The work in no way came up to the expectations of the committee. Was the *Société* obliged to accept it? . . . In signing the agreement with the sculptor the *Société* had undertaken to do so and not to give the order to anyone else. How, under these conditions, was the knot to be cut? M. Duquet was of the opinion that at least a protest should be made, and he proposed this astounding resolution: "The committee of the *Société des Gens de Lettres* forbids M. Rodin to have a bronze cast made of the plaster statue exhibited at the *Palais des Machines;* the committee refuses to accept a work which has no connection with the statue ordered."

[8] *Les Arts Français:* February, 1918.

The president approved the text and proposed to add that the committee would leave M. Rodin free to execute a new statue!

There were violent protests against M. Duquet's phrasing. M. Rodocanachi drafted another letter which was no more satisfactory and which was not approved by their legal advisers. M. Henri Houssaye craftily suggested that the Municipal Council's refusal to grant permission to use the site originally assigned to the monument would solve the difficulty; the gentlemen of the committee had friends in the Council and would make use of them. Briefly, no agreement could be reached, and, as several of the members had still to visit the Salon, the decision was postponed until the following week when everyone would have been able to view the monster.

On the 9th of May the committee was more numerous and more determined. Henri Houssaye was in the chair and the following members were present: MM. Léon Barracand, Ernest Benjamin, Louis Collas, Henri Demesse, Alfred Duquet, Léonce de Larmandie, Henri Lavedan, Marc Mario, Jules Mary, Charles de Mouy, François de Nion, Georges Pradel, Jean Rameau, and Raoul de Saint-Arroman. MM. Demesse, Saint-Arroman, Mary, and de Nion asked that a different sort of letter be addressed to Rodin. The others preferred an immediate break with him. M. Pradel declared that the statue of Balzac was the work of an imbecile; M. Jean Rameau read the draft of a letter so insulting to the artist that his colleagues begged him to withdraw it.

The committee voted unanimously in favour of a protest and then took up the several motions. Jules Mary's was considered too conciliatory and Henri Lavedan's was passed by a vote of eleven to four. During the noisy discussion following this vote, MM. Houssaye, Demesse, Larmandie, Mary, and de Nion declared that Rodin should be unofficially communicated with before the publication of the resolution, but the majority decided to dispense with this courtesy and instructed M. Edouard Montagne to send an official letter immediately, in M. Lavedan's phrasing, acquainting Rodin with the committee's resolution, and to notify the press at the same time. The resolution was as follows: "The committee of the *Société des Gens de Lettres* finds itself regretfully obliged to protest against the unfinished work exhibited by M. Rodin at the Salon; it cannot regard this as a statue of Balzac."

It is difficult now to understand how a group of writers (of secondary importance, to be sure, but representing a society whose membership included the majority of France's men of letters) could have committed such a grave blunder. Artistic and literary circles were stupefied, but the insulting resolution found sympathetic echoes in the Paris Municipal Council. The Municipal Works of Art Commission exceeded the committee of the *Gens de Lettres* in impertinence; incredible declarations were made at its meetings. According to the official reports gathered together and summarized by Léon Riotor,[9] "certain members of the commission defied their colleagues to grant a site for Rodin's monstrosity." "In spite of my high opinion of Rodin's gifts," wrote M. Lampué, "I feel this time that he has blundered badly." M. Grebauval went further, declaring that "it would be absurd to award a place of honour to this shapeless mass," and M. Labusquière outdid himself, concluding with: "the statue does indeed require a refuge—a refuge from itself." Poor souls! They would have similarly discarded the statues of Thothmes III or Rameses II.

The resolution of the *Société des Gens de Lettres* was a windfall of a sort greatly relished by the press. Rodin had never supplied it with such dramatic news. The committee congratulated itself upon the action it had taken. Nothing remained now but to gather up the shower of protests that each day filled its offices. Camille Mauclair, Arsène Alexandre in *L'Eclaire*, Charles Frémine in *Le Rappel*, Maurice Hamel in *La Revue de Paris*, Roger Marx in *Le Voltaire*, Rodenbach in *Le Figaro*, Robert de la Sizeranne in *La Revue des Deux Mondes*, Gaston Stiegler in *L'Echo de Paris*—all voiced their opinions of this strange group of writers. Several months before, Emile Bergerat had severely taken them to task, prophesying, in one of his "Caliban" articles in *L'Echo de Paris* entitled "Word

[9] Léon Riotor: *Rodin*, 1927.

Hawkers": "Rodin will continue his work for himself and at his own expense, and it will be exhibited; whereas you will be left staring stupidly at the lifeless absurdity with which you have replaced it."

Charles Chincholle went immediately to see Rodin and wrote vividly of his visit in *Le Figaro*.[10] The sculptor had just arrived from Meudon and Chincholle found him in his studio with the committee's letter still in his hand. Its phrasing was so unusual that he did not at first understand it.

"Do you think it means they don't want my statue," he asked simply.

"I'm afraid it does," said Chincholle.

"But you were on the committee; you know my agreement is perfectly clear. There was to be no discussion of my statue. How can I waste my time going to law about it? I want peace; I want to forget everything but my work."

In the afternoon there were hordes of visitors, telegrams, letters —one bearing the signature of Albert Besnard to which was added that of Mme Besnard: "A sad day for art," wrote the great painter, "when a man of genius is only credited with talent."

Some of Rodin's friends besought him not to surrender, urged him to have the rights of art publicly proclaimed and to insist upon the purchase and erection of the statue by the *Société des Gens de Lettres*.

"But I want to work in peace," he sighed apologetically.

Nevertheless the Dépôt des Marbres was soon the busiest spot in Paris. In one of his studios, curious visitors watched his skilled marble-cutters at work; in the other, where his friends gathered to discuss the question of a formal protest, a waiting-room had to be improvised with screens. The son of M. Bernheim jeune brought an offer to purchase the *Balzac;* it came from a rich manufacturer and collector, M. Auguste Pellerin. Rodin was gratified by the offer, but asked for time in which to consider it. The next day M. Bernheim brought a letter from M. Pellerin: "Sir, the *Société*

[10] *Le Figaro:* May 12, 13, and 17, 1898.

des Gens de Lettres has refused the Balzac statue. My opinion of it being absolutely the reverse, I ask you to sell it to me. The statue will be in good company, for it will be placed beside Manet's *L'Artiste* which was refused by the Salon of 1876." M. Pellerin offered twenty thousand francs for a bronze casting; he did not need the pedestal.

The same day another offer came from Belgium. Representing a group of Rodin's admirers there, Edmond Picard wrote: "Our enthusiasm for your statue leads us to hope sincerely that the *Société des Gens de Lettres* will refuse it. We beg you in that case to let us buy it. Balzac is greatly admired in Brussels and the statue would be placed in one of our public squares."

Rodin had scarcely finished reading this communication when a dealer called upon him with a proposal to purchase all his future work, and, following him, a lady made her way into the studio and bought then and there a group in marble.

Before making any decision Rodin telegraphed for his lawyer, Maître Chéramy, in whom he had perfect confidence: "You have a good case," Chéramy told him. "You can compel the *Société* to abide by its agreement. However, you must wait until it forces you to bring action. You cannot help winning, but it will take a long time. I advise you not to listen to your artist friends; don't let a lawsuit waste your valuable time. It would be much better to write the *Société* a carefully phrased letter, merely stating that you renounce your rights and thereby authorize the withdrawal of the ten thousand francs that are being held for you, and that you will keep your statue."

This advice was obviously sound, for if, after the lengthy proceedings, Rodin won his suit, would the Municipal Council grant the promised site? If it did not, the *Société* would probably put the statue in some dark corner of the house in the cité Rougemont. The course advised by Maître Chéramy did not provide for any compensation for the serious injury, both financial and otherwise, which had been done to Rodin—he was far from well off and his works were still selling at relatively low prices. But his artist friends were to see that he was given this compensation.

Upon the publication of the committee's resolution, the great painter Eugène Carrière wrote to Mathias Morhardt:

"The *Société des Gens de Lettres* has refused Rodin's *Balzac*. Are we to disregard this insult to an artist in whom our country takes such pride and who has repeatedly stirred our emotions so deeply? Should we not protest against the atrocious action of these ignorant men? My dear friend, you are a courageous man; you have already fought for Rodin. We are at your service whenever you need us." [11]

Mathias Morhardt immediately summoned a few of Rodin's most intimate friends—Carrière, Mirbeau, Geffroy, Georges Lecomte—to one of the studios in the rue de l'Université. "We were all of us trembling with anger," said the eminent writer. A protest was at once outlined and, as soon as it could be printed, sent out for the signatures of all those who it was thought would resent the shameful insult to the great man:

"The friends and admirers of Rodin, believing the resolution passed by the *Société des Gens de Lettres* to be without significance from an artistic point of view, urge the artist to complete his work without allowing the unfortunate circumstances which have arisen to hinder him; and they sincerely hope that the people of our noble country will always accord him the high esteem to which his integrity and his admirable achievements entitle him."

The protest was sent out bearing the signatures of Arsène Alexandre, Eugène Carrière, Charles Frémine, Gustave Geffroy, Georges Lecomte, Octave Mirbeau, Mathias Morhardt, Francis de Pressensé, and, at Rodin's request, that of J. L. Forain. It caused a splendid disturbance: a display of fireworks let off by Toulouse-

[11] From Mathias Morhardt's long and remarkable article in *Le Mercure de France* of December 15, 1934, dealing with this phase of the affair, I have borrowed innumerable details for the rest of this chapter. [Author's note.]

Lautrec, Albert Besnard, Vincent d'Indy, Paul Adam, Henry Becque, Paul Signac, Maximilien Luce, Catulle Mendès, Courteline, Paul Fort, Alfred Valette, Aristide Maillol, Bourdelle, Georges Clemenceau, Henry Cros, Lucien Guitry, Claude Debussy, Camille Mauclair, Jules Renard, André Berthelot, Claude Monet, Alfred Bruneau, Mme J. B. Carpeaux, Lugné-Poë, Georges Rodenbach, J. E. Blanche, Constantin Meunier, Jules Desbois, J. P. Toulet, Jean Moréas, Henri de Régnier, Frantz-Jourdain, Séverine, Pierre Louys, Anatole France. . . .

Pierre Louys declared that he had been delighted to sign, adding: "Of all Rodin's works, I particularly admire the *Balzac*—a prodigious conception."

Others withheld their signatures because, as they said, they did not understand the statue. MM. Charles Maurras and Raymond Poincaré argued and made reservations; Jules Dalou let fly a Parthian arrow at his former friend and reproached those who were supporting him: "My memory of the great friendship that once existed between Rodin and myself prevents me from taking part in this further manifestation of his blundering friends." And finally there was an imperious admonition from M. Alidor Delzant who, notwithstanding his high opinion of the sculptor, advised him to destroy the *Balzac* which was not his work.

The success of the protest "induced its sponsors to give it a more positive character." On the 20th of May they instituted a subscription for the purpose of buying the statue and erecting it in a public square; the sum to be collected was thirty thousand francs, and Rodin expressed the desire that the great Stéphane Mallarmé should be a member of the committee. Funds poured into Mathias Morhardt's hands, accompanied by enthusiastic letters. New and important names were added to the original list; newspapers, magazines, and publishers sent their contributions. François de Nion, in sending his, mentioned the fact that he was a member of the *Gens de Lettres* committee. Edmond Turquet, who had been responsible for commissioning *La Porte de l'Enfer* twenty years before, wrote: "You are a brave and powerful man; keep on calmly following your path and pay no attention to the attacks of envious people." René Quinton, the young and already famous naturalist, subscribed a thousand francs and, though of moderate means, promised a further contribution if it were needed. "The general public," he wrote to Rodin, "must be made familiar with your statue which is one of the most majestic conceptions of the human mind." Alfred Sisley, ill and very poor—he died several months later—sent a touching contribution of five francs.

The object of this homage, which might have turned the head of a weaker person, did not accept it for himself, as was intended, but regarded it rather as the pledged love and gratitude offered to his predecessors, the unappreciated artists of the past who formed the long chain of which he was, he said, merely one of the links. One of these pledges, perhaps the one which moved his sculptor's heart the most deeply, bore the cherished name of the preceding link in that chain: on May 24, Mme Jean-Baptiste Carpeaux, the great sculptor's widow, wrote this simple and touching letter to Mathias Morhardt:

Sir,

I wish to put at your disposal for the Rodin Subscription either the half-life-size plaster model for the Ugolin group or a terra cotta bust of one of the dancers from the Opera group. You may choose between these two works of Carpeaux: one is an especially interesting composition; the other is purely decorative. Kindly tell me which one you prefer and I will send it.

A. Carpeaux

The malignant fever which attacked France at that time further complicated the *Balzac* quarrel; in the summer of 1898 the Dreyfus Affair reached an acute stage, with the Esterhazy trial, the condemnation of Emile Zola and his exile in England, the forgery and suicide of Colonel Henry, and the elections during which the two factions clashed. In *Le Temps,* as elsewhere, disputes and controversies were carried on. Two editors, MM. Thiébault-Sisson and Morhardt, who had hitherto used no other weapon but the pen, fought a duel—fashionable procedure in those agitated times— which resulted oddly enough in a subsequent happy reconciliation. Rodin found his friend setting forth with two swords under his arm and insisted on accompanying him to the duelling ground. What did the peace-loving sculptor make of this behaviour? He had the good sense—and the shrewdness—to pay no attention to the Dreyfus Affair and refused to become involved in politics: "How could I possibly undertake anything more? My fight for sculpture uses up all my time and strength, and even then I lose!"

But the majority of the contributors to the purchase of the Balzac monument were supporters of Captain Dreyfus, and Rodin was greatly disturbed to find that one of the best known of these, Francis de Pressensé, was a member of the committee. Fearing that he might be drawn into the conflict in spite of himself, he asked that several men of the opposing faction be made members, particularly Forain and Rochefort. But this was a vain precaution: Rochefort's behaviour is already known and Forain scratched him cruelly with the point of his unsparing pencil. These scruples irritated the Dreyfusards: "My dear colleague," Georges Clemenceau wrote to Morhardt, "M. Rodin told a member of the staff of *L'Aurore* that he was afraid of having too many of Zola's friends among the contributors to the *Balzac* fund. Kindly remove my name from the list in your possession."

Despite the fact that the necessary thirty thousand francs might have been rapidly collected, Rodin was tempted to accept M. Pellerin's offer and thus avoid trouble with the Dreyfusards and their opponents. Carrière, Mirbeau, and Geffroy failed to allay his fears, but Morhardt convinced him that he ought not to deprive his friends and admirers of the *Balzac* by selling it to a private individual. While listening to these perfectly reasonable objections, he came to his final decision: he would not sell his statue to anyone, but would keep it himself. On the 9th of June he wrote the following letter to the subscription committee and the next day it appeared in the press:

My dear friends,

I have a strong desire to retain possession of my statue. During the interruptions to my work I have thought the matter out and I must keep it. All I ask of the generous contributors is a list of their names; that will be a sufficient reward for my efforts.

And you who are even more enthusiastic, you who have always been my friends and who have perhaps made it possible for me to do sculpture—to you I say thanks with all my heart.

A. Rodin

This decision did not procure him the peace he longed for. Indecencies were still being committed at the Salon: the *Balzac* continued to be scoffed at, and *Le Baiser,* which had been called a masterpiece and the honour of the Salon of 1898, was scarcely noticed, despite its style being far more accessible to the public. When Rodin told me of his decision there was an afflicted look on his face, not on account of these personal insults but because he was oppressed by the boundlessness of human stupidity. He showed me the brief letter he was sending to the press: "I am primarily concerned with my self-respect as an artist and I beg you to announce that I am withdrawing my monument from the Salon; it will not be erected anywhere."

The events of 1898 produced a situation quite contrary to the expectations of Rodin's enemies: wide-spread publicity; among foreigners, deep interest in the artist and lively curiosity as to the man. His smallest doings were of importance now, because he was a celebrity; his opinions on various subjects were sought by writers and journalists; several times a week an interview was requested. As soon as he had gone back to his infallible healers, nature and work, his bodily fatigue and mental lassitude vanished and he recovered his poise. Sometimes he referred to the crisis that was past with as little bitterness and as much coolness as a doctor making a diagnosis: "That Balzac business was a defeat just the same," he wrote to his friend, Captain Bigand-Kaire, and on the 7th of July he replied to a letter from Monet:

My dear friend,

You make me happy with your opinion of the *Balzac*. Thanks for it. Your appreciation is among those that give me strength. I've had a mass of letters like the ones you had when it was the fashion to laugh at your invention of putting breezes in landscapes.

Please thank Mme Monet for her kindness in telling me her opinion; I appreciate it very much.

Your triumphant exhibition gives courage to all artists who are being persecuted as I am now. . . .[12]

The conflict with the *Société des Gens de Lettres* was terminated by Rodin with great dignity. The committee, unaware at first of his intentions, was apprehensive as to what the aftermath might be, and it had had a very bad press. There was further anxiety lest the sculptor should claim an indemnity and the committee was determined not to grant it. To the intense relief of that body, a letter was received on June 13 from Maître Chéramy informing it of Rodin's renunciation without demanding the indemnity to which he was entitled. It remained for them to obtain the sculptor's signature which alone could release the funds deposited.

The committee congratulated itself upon the fortunate conclusion of the affair and was delighted to receive a letter from Falguière to say that he would execute a statue of Balzac if his name were mentioned in this connection by a member of the committee. Finally, Maître Chéramy telephoned just before the adjournment of the July 18 meeting to say that M. Rodin had just signed his release and an authorization by virtue of which the *Société* could repossess itself of the ten thousand francs, plus three hundred and twenty francs interest. Frantz-Jourdain also renounced his commission to execute the architectural portion of the monument.

[12] Gustave Geffroy: *Claude Monet.*

Eight days later the committee unanimously availed itself of Falguière's offer to produce a statue in time for the Balzac Centenary in the spring of 1899. Falguière thought and worked more rapidly than Rodin.

The Balzac statue was taken to Meudon, where Rodin had established himself several years before, and placed in the open air upon an improvised pedestal in a large paddock adjoining the Villa des Brillants and its small garden. Thus isolated, its magnificence became frightening; it seemed possessed of an unearthly quality. On moonlit nights it rose up white and phosphorescent from the dark surface of the meadow, its strange head like that of some huge nocturnal bird in the silvery light—a phantom from a hidden world, the astral body of the immortal writer, visible to profane eyes, and, like the ghost of Hamlet's father on the ramparts at Elsinore, invading the soul with fear.

Rodin himself was struck by the strangeness of his work; he often studied it in this insidious illumination and verified the precision of the planes which were somehow clarified in this unusual distribution of light and shade.

Edward Steichen and some other young American photographers spent several nights in the meadow to wait for the right moment in which to make their exposures. The results were fantastically beautiful and have been reproduced in *Camera Work*.

It was not long before the prophecy which Emile Bergerat flung at the *Société des Gens de Lettres* came true.

As soon as Falguière received the commission to execute the statue, he paid a visit of courtesy to Rodin. The two sculptors had been friends since the affair of *L'Age d'Airain*, and had become more intimate after Falguière's defence of the Saint Jean-Baptiste in 1881. Rodin received his friend with smiling amiability, which concealed some shrewd reflections.

I found him at his studio one afternoon in the spring of 1899, working at a bust. The sitter had just departed and he was imprinting his "observations" upon the obedient clay. His features had recovered their calm, but I could detect a mischievous look in his eye.

"Who is it?" he asked me, pointing to the bust.

"I don't know the face," I replied fearlessly, for his likenesses were always excellent.

"It's Falguière," he said gleefully, "and he's going to do one of me." He was careful not to spoil the effect of this piece of news by commenting further upon it. The two friends had hit upon this exchange as a token of their mutual understanding.

Shortly afterwards Rodin showed me the bust which Falguière had done, and it was without intention to flatter him that I said I did not like this flabby reproduction of his powerful head. He had a great liking for Falguière's painting and told me of a large and very beautiful canvas his old friend had given him—nymphs with bodies like mother-of-pearl disporting themselves in the depths of a green forest—which he had been delighted to hang in his drawing room at Meudon. Later, he wrote with his customary reticence to his friend Captain Bigand-Kaire in Marseilles: "When you come to Paris I will show you Falguière's bust of me —it's very odd."

The new *Balzac* was exhibited in the Salon of 1899. No public demonstration took place before this big lumpish man sitting on a bench with the famous cloak drawn awkwardly about him, like a comfortable middle-class citizen after his bath. Falguière was sensitive and adroit in his rough models and many of his medium-sized figures, but he was unable to endow his large ones with the necessary vigour and depth. No one realized this better than he did towards the end of his career. His pupils remember his moving words to them one day after he had criticized their work. He was speaking of Rodin: "I was mistaken! I've made mistakes all my

157

life. He was right!" and there were tears in his eyes. Whatever may have been the conscious feeling of casual observers about the other *Balzac,* something of its magnetic power had entered into their inner beings. If it had been shown to them again they would perhaps have been astonished to recall that they had laughed at it the previous year. To the hastily composed woollen bundle now put before them, they were coldly indifferent.

Rodin also exhibited in the Salon of 1899. He had—let me repeat it—his artistic affectations. By way of revenge he could have shown some brilliant piece of sculpture, but Falguière's bust cast in bronze was all he sent. Though only a head, it was as compact as a bomb—a work of great intensity despite the slight bending forward of the brow and the slackened muscles that revealed the man's illness. "Falguière is like a little bull," Rodin said of him, "a wounded bull." Falguière was indeed ill; he died before the unveiling of his statue which the municipal authorities preferred to erect at the intersection of the rue Balzac and the Avenue de Friedland, instead of in the Place du Palais-Royal. In loyalty to his old friend, Rodin attended the unveiling. "He sat modestly in his seat listening to the long official speeches until he was recognized, whereupon the crowds rose as one person and gave him a protracted and noisy ovation." [13]

The *Balzac* was not cast in bronze during Rodin's life. Just before the War he considered having the statue reproduced in stone. Remembering certain Egyptian and Chaldean figures, he thought of using a dark granite, almost black, and Charles Despiau, his youngest and perhaps his favourite assistant was to have been entrusted with the work. The War came; then illness; then death carried off the sculptor and his project.

In 1912, the city of Mannheim wanted to buy a bronze casting of the *Balzac* for its Municipal Museum, but Rodin refused the offer with thanks, for he wished the first casting of the statue to be kept for France. A few years ago, the curator of the Rodin Museum, M. Georges Grappe, received a similar request from

[13] *La Bataille du Balzac:* Mathias Morhardt.

the Antwerp Museum; two castings were made: the first to be reserved for France, and the second to go to Antwerp.

The *Balzac* affair is not yet ended. Public opinion changes; it accepts today what it rejected yesterday; it enjoys righting the wrongs done by preceding generations, which is called doing justice. This change has been felt by the *Société des Gens de Lettres*. The ageing members of the committee of Rodin's day have been replaced by vigorous young men fully conversant with matters of art. A noble task remains to be accomplished by this great association: the destiny of the heroic bronze figure must be fulfilled; Rodin's *Balzac* must soon be erected in the heart of Paris in order that the statue of the most French of all our novelists may have a place among the people of whom he wrote and whose hearts he so ardently probed. This beacon light of intelligence must shine brightly for the guidance of these people. The president of the *Société des Gens de Lettres* and the Minister of Fine Arts responsible for this accomplishment will win the gratitude of all who are convinced that, in a country such as ours, art is at all times the most effective means of development—a power greater, actually, than the force of arms.

VI. A *GRANDE PASSION*

D URING our long talks while strolling in the park at Saint-Cloud, Rodin sometimes referred briefly to the *Balzac* affair, and one afternoon he became extremely confidential, telling me of the ordeal he had undergone in his private life during the course of the conflict just ended.

She was very beautiful, an artist of great talent, and fifteen years ago she had become his pupil and his favourite model. He had often made use of her finely bred features in works whose mellowness recalled certain figures at Chartres. His poetic imagination had transferred them to *La Pensée, La France, La Jeune Guerrière*, and *L'Aurore*. Her youth had been spent away from Paris. As a child she had modelled, and at eighteen she was painting remarkable portraits; later she devoted herself completely to sculpture. Alfred Boucher, a neighbour in the country, visited her studio and spoke of her exceptional qualities to Paul Dubois who had been made director of the *Ecole des Beaux-Arts*. Dubois himself went to her studio and was struck by the vigour of her technique: "Have you been studying with M. Rodin?" he asked her. But she had never heard his name spoken before.

About 1880, the family moved to Paris and she was obliged to contend with her middle-class parents' prejudice against the idea of one of their daughters embarking upon the career of an artist. She was obstinate and high-spirited, and she finally succeeded in installing herself in a small studio in the rue Notre-Dame-des-Champs, from which she soon began to send her sculpture to the

Salon. She took the studio with several other young women who helped with the rent and the models' fees. Alfred Boucher had been supervising their work, and on his departure to Italy he asked Rodin to take his place. Again, and this time without knowing it, Boucher played an important rôle in the life of his fellow-sculptor. So Rodin taught this group of students, and, at first, he arranged for his son to join them, hoping thus to develop the habit of work in him. From the beginning he had recognized the brilliant gifts of the young woman whose magnificent dark blue eyes soon enslaved him. She came to his studio in the rue de l'Université and worked with him on his own statues; she was his valued assistant for four or five years. He consulted her constantly and entrusted her with the task of modelling, under the most exigent directions, the hands and feet of many of the figures he produced. This work was difficult but it brought results. "Do hands and feet," was his invariable advice to the beginners who came to him at the height of his career. When she first worked with him he was finishing *Les Bourgeois de Calais* and the *Claude Lorrain;* he had begun the *Balzac* when she left him. She went to live alone in a remote quarter of Paris, which in those days had more the atmosphere of the country than of the city. She saw no one and devoted herself exclusively to work, modelling all day long with her strong unerring hands, and exhibiting each spring, at the Salon, works which caused the astonished admiration of the connoisseurs who saw them. The catalogue listed her as a pupil of Paul Dubois, Alfred Boucher, and Rodin. Several years later she claimed Rodin alone as her master.

She rapidly made a name for herself. Mirbeau, praising her, wrote: "She is clearly a great artist—a unique person, one of nature's rebels: a woman of genius." Morhardt published a splendid article about her, and Maillol spoke of her as one of the few sculptors who cut their own works in marble; when she was accused of excessive subservience to the influence of Rodin, the master replied: "I showed her where the gold was; she found it, but it was her own gold, not mine." Naturally he gave her his support and would allow no doubts to be cast upon his artistic judgment of her rank as a sculptor. Carolus Duran, who had been made head of the painting section of the *Société Nationale* during Rodin's occupancy of the same office in the sculpture section, told of the committee meeting during which Rodin insisted that his pupil's work be given a place of honour in the approaching Salon. Some of the members protested, but he remained firm.

"Well, Rodin," said Carolus Duran, half angrily and half in fun, "do you want us to retire and leave you to deliberate alone?"

"Yes," replied the sculptor, calmly.

The spirited sculptress was not satisfied with her position of beloved and admired disciple. Her heart was set upon becoming the sole object of Rodin's affection and the intimate companion of his private life. Then came a period of anguish for three people. Rodin felt that he was bound forever to the woman who had lived with him for almost thirty years, to the Rose of his young days who had courageously shared his poverty and his endless waiting for success. Suddenly his life became cruelly divided: in Paris at his studio, from which he had excluded Rose, he belonged to his youthful assistant; at the evening meal at Meudon and during the walks which were necessary to his night's rest, he gave himself up to Rose's tender solicitude and her childish conversation.

As always happens in such cases, both women suffered agonies, and, since both of them were uncompromising and strong-willed, Rodin was overwhelmed by reproaches, tears, and even threats. If he was late in arriving from Paris, Rose, crazed by jealousy and burning with revengeful schemes, would prowl round the dark garden like a lunatic, listening for the footsteps of the man she both loved and hated. His strength began to fail him with the multiplication of these stormy scenes. Work became difficult; everything tired him. Finally there was nothing for it but to make

162

his choice, and he decided to leave things as they were. He chose not to abandon his life-long companion, his "humble servant."

"But," I ventured, during a moment of dreaming silence, "if you . . . it is rumoured . . . that you and she have . . . four children."

"If that were true," he answered simply, "my duty would have been only too clear."

The young woman did not accept his decision at first, but after a succession of agonizing scenes, she concluded that a complete break would be best, and he was left in solitary despair.

She still lived alone, but was then occupying a bare-walled apartment in an old house on the Ile Saint-Louis; plaster casts, a few exquisite bronzes, and some unfinished clay figures enveloped in linen cloths, resting upon upturned packing cases, a bed and several chairs, were the only furnishings. I had gone to see her there, without any knowledge of the drama which was being enacted, for I wanted to do an article on her work. Rodin had urged me on, undoubtedly because he hoped that I would be able to bring him news of her. She received me with warmth and sincerity, and I admired her *Sirènes* and her *Faunesses*. We did not mention the great man whom she now hated as deeply as she had once loved him, but her clear blue eyes were full of unspoken thoughts.

La Fronde, for which my article was destined, fostered ideas that were opposed to the conservative convictions of the lonely sculptress. In those days the Dreyfus Affair had upset everyone, and shortly after my visit I received a letter asking that my article be published only in a paper or magazine whose political opinions were similar to her own.

Rodin could not endure the thought of her precarious situation and of the low prices at which she was still obliged to sell her work. His connection with the Ministry of Fine Arts had enabled him to get the State to buy several of her best pieces for various museums. He sent mutual friends to propose assistance, but she always angrily refused, wilfully misconstruing his intentions. She could not believe in his protective affection which had naturally been strengthened by the separation, and she imagined that he was determined to perscute her.

Such exaggerated fury foretold the eventual collapse of a disorganized mentality. Before long, her behaviour exceeded all bounds; love and admiration gave way completely to savage hatred; talent, intelligence, and beauty were soon obscured by the most hopeless neurasthenia. Rodin, despite the congenital egotism of the superman, never got over this calamity. He had been tortured by the separation, and the suffering it caused lasted for many years.

When the project of establishing a museum in the rue de Varenne seemed on the point of materializing, Rodin spoke to Mathias Morhardt of his desire to keep one of the rooms in the Hôtel Biron for the work of his pupil, but his death occurred before he saw his museum and had the satisfaction of knowing that his disciple would share his fame.

At the end of our walk, the low-voiced confession came to a close; the candour of genius was alone responsible for its communication to me, his very young friend. "Lovers are besotted idiots," he said; "they can never keep their heads. Virtue, according to the ancients, meant taste and moderation. Moderation is not necessarily abstinence; real love occurs when a man gets the exact amount of pleasure and emotion he is capable of enjoying, no more. Love, like art, results from a perfect balance."

Rose's apprehension was doubled because the ties that bound her to Rodin were not legal ones. Throughout these long years she had been desperately afraid he would leave her. She was never to forget that despairing vigil. Other ordeals followed and the terror of abandonment was always in her mind. Rodin loved her, but his love was that of a matured being for one who had remained artlessly simple. Intellectually, they were strangers, but their hearts were united forever.

"Why did X—— want a divorce?" he asked the unhappy wife of a fellow-sculptor upon her telling him of their final break.

"Because he loves someone else."

"That's no reason. I've loved other women, but I did not leave Rose."

During his periods of unfaithfulness, the cruelty of which he never fully realized, a deep affection kept her in his mind. This from England in 1886, after more than twenty years of life together:

My darling Rose,

I dreamed of you last night, and if I had written immediately this morning I would have said many tender things to you. You must love me a great deal to put up with all my whims. I am, dear Rose,

Your affectionate

Auguste Rodin

Rose never accompanied him on his journeys, because it was her duty to supervise the studios, also because, for the outside world, he did not concede her the rank of wife. But he worried about her health and her well-being. When he was absent she lived a lonely existence, poor thing; she had no one else; no relatives in Paris and but few friends except the wives of Rodin's casters. Once she fell ill and sent for a doctor whose address had been given her by his laundress. Vivier was his name and after Rose's recovery he and his wife came constantly to the sculptor's apartment. Then Doctor Vivier left Paris and settled at Le Châtelet-en-Brie where, one day, he received an agonized summons from Rodin. Rose had had a heart attack which appeared serious, and a local doctor was giving her caffeine. She was delirious when Doctor Vivier arrived and "railing against Rodin's mistresses." The sculptor had also called in Professor Huchard and both doctors concluded that the caffeine had poisoned her and produced the disorders which, owing to her highly nervous organism, had been so frightening. Morphine calmed her and in several days Doctor Vivier took her to Le Châtelet-en-Brie for her convalescence; Rodin joined her there later.

Mme Vivier was a woman of great kindness and simplicity, middle-aged and of a physique in no way likely to rouse Rose's ever-watchful jealousy. The doctor, several years younger than Rodin, was a native of Rouergue, and his southern vivacity and intelligence made him a delightful companion. Le Châtelet-en-Brie now became a refuge to which Rodin could escape when overworked and mentally exhausted. No one bothered him there, and when he was obliged to return to his studios or impelled to embark on some amorous adventure, Rose could wait for him there and pour out her troubles to the sympathetic Mme Vivier.

During a journey through Touraine and Anjou in September of 1890, he wrote:

My dear Rose,

Don't be impatient. Stay a little longer with the Viviers. I am more and more fascinated by my studies here. I feel as though I had come to life in another century. Surely there is something in me of the past; the sight of this architecture awakens hidden knowledge in the back of my mind. I'm turning into an architect; I must, because there are things to be done about my *Porte*. Write to me at Saumur, Maine-et-Loire, "to be called for." My love to you and please get all the good you can from the country air, so that you'll be able to stand this winter better than last when you suffered so much from the cold.

Your

Rodin

Several months before this, Rose had lost her mother and had gone to Vecqueville for the funeral. There she received this firm but affectionate admonition:

Madame Rodin,
care of Madame Beuret,
Vecqueville, near Joinville
Haute-Marne

My dear Rose,

I share your sorrow at your mother's death, but y
not very well; please take good care of yourself. If y
more money, send me a telegram.

Your poor mother has been a splendid example to her ch

                                        Your

                                              Rodin

Tell me what train you will be taking and I'll come to meet you.

Enchanted by the churches and chateaux of Touraine and Anjou, and by the Loire, "this indolent river," Rodin prolonged the luxury of his visit, his only anxiety being Rose's condition. He wrote to her from Saumur on September 10:

My dear Rose,

Vivier tells me you are not very well. You mustn't give in to your foolish notions. Take advantage of this fine weather and build up your strength. I must do the same, for Gonet's cold studio chilled me to the bone and brought back those pains. But a little outdoor exercise has done me good and I feel better. . . . Don't make me worry so much about you that I can't work properly at my architecture.

Stay with the Viviers longer than the 20th if you can and if it suits them. You'll need strength for our moving which is going to tire you more than me; so try to stay longer.

We'll be near Notre-Dame and the Louvre this winter, and I'm going to keep Sundays for you so that you won't get bored.

                                        Love from your

                                              Auguste

I'm glad Vivier liked the bronze group.

Writing was difficult for Rose and she sometimes failed to mention a recent letter from Rodin in the course of her complaints about his silence:

Loches: 19, September

My dear Rose,

My letter from Saumur must have got lost. Write to Tours immediately, "to be called for." I'm very anxious about you. You know, dear Rose, how much I love and admire you. Write to me and put my mind at rest. I will be so glad when we are together again in our little apartment in the rue des Augustins and can go on Sundays to Notre-Dame and stroll along the quais.

Much love from your

Rodin

They often made eleventh-hour visits to Le Châtelet, taking a cab from the station at Melun or Bois-le-Roi and filling it with provisions: fresh fish, ham, sausages, choice fruit, chestnuts. . . . This country existence was for them both a renewal of their youth, but without the continual anxiety about money: leisurely walks to Fontaine-le-Port or Sivry by the upland road, stopping at an inn on the way for an omelet with bacon and a bottle of white wine. If there was a gentle rain, which he loved, he bought sabots and socks for both, and they wandered beneath the trees delighting in the cool fresh air and the pattering rain-drops on the leaves.

In the mornings he would study the flowers in the garden closely, or pick up pebbles whose shape and iridescence pleased him. Nothing was too insignificant to be recorded by his sensitive eye. He often made notes: "A snail crossed the path, leaving its moist track, and I watched the insect [sic] as it sketched a superb moulding. This made me think that what we call chance is just as much a law as the one which regulates the functions of our bodies without consulting us."

If the doctor proposed a drive in his carriage and asked Rodin where he would like to go, the reply was frequently: "To Champeaux." He had an extreme fondness for the church in that village, as evidenced by the notes and sketches in his book, *Les Cathédrales de France*: "It is not a church but a perfume—a thing of sheer delight. These graceful French masterpieces are at the mercy of Historical Committees as dogs are at the mercy of the pound." The little crouching figure of a man supporting the springer of a vaulted arch appealed to him particularly:

"Look at that," he exclaimed to his friend. "No sculptor of our day could have done that marvellous little figure. What feeling! What colour!"

"What colour do you mean? It's all white."

"You make the usual mistake. Colour exists in sculpture as well as in painting and drawing."

A momentary coolness interrupted the friendly relations between Rodin and Doctor Vivier. The sculptor's love of nature included a perfect understanding of animals and he could not endure cruelty to them. The doctor's old horse had an infirmity which caused great amusement among the boys of the neighbourhood. The valiant beast's tongue was six inches too long and the extra length hung out of its mouth. The effect was extremely comic and produced roars of merriment from the youthful spectators who gathered to watch the "laughing horse." One day when the crowd was larger and noisier than usual, the doctor lost his temper, took a scalpel from his case, and cut off the offending six inches. When Rodin heard of this, he was filled with horror and could not conceal his wrathful indignation. [1]

The secret of the Le Châtelet retreat was finally discovered by a number of people. Loie Fuller, the dancer, whom Rodin and his wife greatly liked, turned up several times, volubly and exuberantly American.

In 1891, Rodin spent two or three months in Touraine, deeply preoccupied with the Balzac statue. Rose stayed in Paris and the sculptor was anxious that she should get some country air:

[1] Anthony L. Ludovici: *Personal Reminiscences of Auguste Rodin*. London, 1926.

Rose dear,

Write me at Tours, "to be called for." Keep happy and above all take good care of yourself. You can be very obedient when you want to please me. I would like you to go to the Viviers for a week or two; it will do you good.

Your truly affectionate

Rodin

On October 15, he wrote her again from Tours; he was progressing slowly with his scheme for the *Balzac*:

I may be in Paris as soon as this letter, or possibly a few days after it. In any case the prospect of being with you makes me very happy. It's nice to be taken care of so well.

Always your devoted

Rodin

Luckily I've got a lot of work done.

Shortly before this he had made a bust of Rose which was cast in bronze and exhibited in the Salon much later. He also had it done in marble as a gift to his companion. The features of this bust did not recall the tragic expression of the *Bellone,* executed ten years previously, which Rodin frankly admitted he had produced rapidly, during one of her violent fits of jealousy; they expressed the calm maternal tranquillity of a wife. This bust was bequeathed by Rose to the Rodin Museum.

VII. EXHIBITIONS – MEUDON

RODIN was known in foreign countries for various single pieces of sculpture, but there was little familiarity abroad with his work as a whole; it was still the subject of lively discussion in France. Some friends of mine in Belgium, whose interest I had aroused in his behalf, wanted an exhibition of important statues and drawings in Brussels. Rodin listened attentively to the proposal and was rather tempted; but I was surprised to find him over-prudent, hesitant, and even distrustful. His mental processes seemed in this matter to be as evasive and complicated as they were lucid and determined when it was a question of work. There had been no exhibition since his extraordinary success at the Georges Petit Gallery almost ten years before. Was it not time for foreign countries to be made aware of his genius? He was nearly sixty now and he complained continually of his vast expenses: studio rents, materials, assistants' and casters' wages. Even at the threshold of old age, he still had no financial security.

I went to see him from time to time in order to keep myself informed of the progress the proposal was making in his mind: delays, doubts, and evasions—one day the idea would be given up; the next he would decide to send merely a dozen groups and busts. He was full of apprehension: his works would be lost, broken, or stolen; agreements would not be adhered to. He was given full guarantees and his own man was to be entrusted with the packing, both in Paris and in Brussels. Then, one day, when everything seemed to be moving smoothly, he brought out a fresh scheme:

"Perhaps it would be a good idea to include painting in the exhibition? Monet was with me at the Georges Petit Gallery and each man's work gained accordingly. If only my friend Puvis de Chavannes would agree to show with me! That would be splendid! Will you ask him for me?" His eyes flashed with anticipatory pleasure; then he added with a smile: "But you must not go after eight in the morning; he refuses to be disturbed later than that, on account of his work."

I knocked at the famous painter's door in the Place Pigalle one dark winter's morning and was admitted by a tall elderly man whose features suggested those of an army officer; he wore a bathrobe and was drying his hands on a towel. Rodin's bust enabled me to recognize the painter of *Le Bois Sacré*.

He quickly agreed to do what his friend desired, but was afraid it would be difficult to collect a sufficient number of easel paintings; the murals could not be taken down and sent to Brussels.

"I want to please that great man Rodin whom I love," he said, "and I want to please you too. But what on earth brought you here so early in the morning?"

"Isn't it the time when you receive visitors? Rodin told me it was."

"But not you, not you! Rodin must have been dreaming!" He smiled graciously as he led me to the door.

Rodin was happy at this change of plan, and the important dual exhibition was mapped out. But the project could not be accomplished. Puvis de Chavannes, who had seemed so vigorous when I saw him, died after a short illness. Grief at the death of his wife, Princess Catacuzène, two months before, hastened his end.

Rodin was deeply affected by this tragedy, and, believing him to have relinquished the idea of an exhibition in Belgium completely, I was greatly surprised when, some time later, he declared:

"I suppose you're right after all. I will send fifty pieces of sculpture to Brussels, including the *Victor Hugo, Eve, Les Bourgeois de Calais;* and also a hundred drawings. All that will give the young Belgian artists a lot of studying. But," he added, "I'm going to make a stipulation: you must give a lecture on my sculpture."

If *La Porte de l'Enfer*, towering above me there in the studio, had suddenly crashed at my feet I could not have been more violently startled.

"I—give a lecture! I've never done such a thing in my life. I don't know how to speak."

"You can learn to."

I explained that such Belgian writers as Camille Lemonnier, Edmond Picard, Emile Verhaeren would be only too glad to speak at the opening of such an exhibition, and would do it admirably.

"No doubt they would," he replied, gently obstinate. "I know what they would say. I don't want eloquence; I want the truth about sculpture. The Belgian public would much rather hear a young woman's accurate and straightforward explanation than some well-known man's high-sounding oration that did not get to the root of the thing." I had never heard Rodin speak at such length.

"Thanks to you I have come to love sculpture, but I know nothing of its governing laws and principles."

"All the better. You haven't been spoiled by Scholastic instruction. I will explain sculpture to you myself."

Today, even more than in 1898, his attitude astonishes me. He was so simple and uncalculating; he scorned the support of influential people and was putting his faith in my timid inexperience. An agonizing apprehension nearly lost me the marvellous opportunity this great man had calmly offered, as a tree offers its shade and its fruit. I was at last to learn what I so ardently longed to know.

The subsequent conferences were a revelation; I was fascinated by the new relationship that had sprung up between us. Candles stuck into the mouths of two bottles supplied the only illumination in the vast studio; the bronze and marble figures, the *Victor Hugo* gleaming as though carved out of glacial ice, came alive in the flickering light. . . . Taking off his long linen smock and washing his clay-covered hands, he paid his casters, dismissed his model, dusted off a wicker chair, and sat down near me in the now silent room.

He rested an elbow on his knee and began gently to stroke his beard; in a low distinct voice he started effortlessly to expound his ideas. They rose up from the depths of his mind like the buds of water-flowers to bloom upon the surface of a clear still pool.

He made only the briefest and most casual references to himself, but he enumerated quietly and positively the simple and timeless principles of sculpture; love of nature and continual study, not only of its exterior aspects, but of its innermost composition; the error of slavishly copying it; the necessity for its slow transposition to the clay according to the dictates of the supreme counsellor: Taste. Then he spoke of the artist's duty never to depart from the course indicated by his conscience, never to allow the weakening of his determination to work; he also mentioned the ancient examples in Egyptian, Greek, and Gothic art; of his deep regret for the general decadence of modern art and of the rare emergence of talent which gave reason to hope for French architecture and sculpture—talent which was misunderstood and persecuted. He alluded without bitterness to his own work which had occasioned so much hostility and ridicule, sarcastically touching upon certain academic reputations and the manner in which they had been acquired.

This was splendid instruction. The man who had hitherto been reserved, wrapped up in his own affairs, almost speechless, now revealed himself as an educator—setting forth his knowledge with the precision of a scholar, and in vivid confident phrases which contained no trace of professorial dogma. Nothing could have been less like an arbitrary concept; all was based upon observation and experience. He was a man of things, an artisan who had succeeded in conquering matter through love. Eloquence for its own sake he scorned, casting aside all conventional and bookish terminology, and only using concrete words that sprang from reality—the sheer common sense of his discourse was overwhelming. He borrowed freely from the vocabulary of the artisan, and his smoothly flowing exposition was interspersed not only with popular locutions but with poetic imagery from the classics.

I felt the burden of ignorance falling from my shoulders; my mind was swept clear of its confused notions; doubt and uncertainty were banished and I saw everything in its proper relation. It was the incomparable gift of a master to his pupil: the establishment of clarity and truth.

All difficulties were finally overcome; Rodin's works were packed and sent off to Brussels, and he came himself three days before the opening to supervise their placing in the *Maison d'Art* where the exhibition was to be held. He was pleased that the whole building had been placed at his disposal, for, as he said: "One can never have too much space for showing sculpture." There was a large entrance hall, a gallery, and some well-lit smaller rooms. Rodin cared nothing for symmetry: "cream-tarts of the museum curators"; he did insist on having the right sort of lighting. About sixty pieces had to be placed, of which at least fifteen were of sizeable dimensions: *Eve, Les Bourgeois de Calais, Victor Hugo, La Voix Intérieure, La Muse Tragique, Iris,* etc. . . . They were brought out one by one and, with his glasses on his nose, he carefully considered and settled the positions of them all. He was polite to the ladies present, often seeking their advice; but to the men he spoke harshly and briefly. The young curator of the *Maison d'Art* asked him a question with extreme deference and the inexplicable reply was: "I am master here. I am the one to give orders." I was aware for the first time of the lion's claw.

On May 8, 1899, a select gathering attended the opening of the exhibition, in which the place of honour was given to a bust of Rodin by his favourite pupil, Camille Claudel. That evening I stood among the gleaming statues and delivered my lecture. Immediately afterwards Rodin said, with gentle peremptoriness: "Now we must write it out so that those who did not hear you may read it."

His love of sculpture exceeded all personal considerations. Urged on by his hope of starting a new Renaissance, a new school of realism, and by his desire to combat the disastrous precepts of the Institutes, he eagerly sought converts.

The public did not crowd the rooms of the *Maison d'Art*, but it arrived in larger numbers every day. Belgians are never exuberantly enthusiastic; they are serious, reflective, and inclined to consider thoughtfully the impressions they receive. The press devoted many important articles to the French sculptor's work and the artistically elite were loud in their praises.

A number of people were somewhat embarrassed by this success; certain sculptors, painters, and journalists had bitterly opposed Rodin twenty years previously when he produced *L'Age d'Airain*. In view of his irresistibly growing fame, these gentlemen had to manage an about-face and they did not know how it was to be accomplished. Rodin was happy to resume relationship with his two old friends and ardent supporters: Camille Lemonnier and the sculptor Constantin Meunier; and it was delightful to watch him strolling with the latter through the rooms of the *Maison d'Art*, chatting and gesturing about the various figures and busts. They had the perfect understanding of two powerful animals who had long worked under the same yoke. Rodin had warmly supported Meunier several years before when his work had been exhibited in Paris.

Memories of his young days in Belgium crowded his mind. He had gone to the same little hotel in the Place de l'Hôtel de Ville and would get up early each morning to prowl through the well-remembered streets. Edmond Picard was unaware of his simple tastes and feared for his comfort, so he insisted that the distinguished visitor should move to his own luxurious house in the rue Ducale, and it is more than likely that Rodin longed to be back in his little room in the old part of the town, with its windows giving onto the beautiful old square.

Long ago, when *L'Age d'Airain* had aroused such hostility in official circles, the sculptor Van der Stappen had taken sides with the enemy. He had not openly attacked Rodin, but had maintained a too-prudent reserve. The French sculptor's triumphant return to Belgium was extremely upsetting to Van der Stappen and he made every effort to wipe out the memory of his past behaviour. His social position was excellent, due to his reputation as an artist and a professor, and to the probability that he would be made head of *L'Académie des Beaux-Arts*—a prospect that did not recommend him to Rodin. He was therefore able to have him invited to dine at the house of a rich banker who liked to consider himself a patron of the Arts and who would perhaps buy something from the exhibition. My mother and I were also invited to this luxurious affair. Our host was politeness itself, the wines superb; nothing was lacking. Rodin, at his hostess's right hand, was stonily silent, and Van der Stappen struggled to draw his colleague into the conversation. He was like a fox-terrier pestering a Great Dane.

After dinner we were shown through several reception rooms hung with portraits of members of the family, all of them painted by the banker's wife. Rodin glanced rapidly at them, but his expected words of approbation were not forthcoming. Van der Stappen redoubled his efforts, but they accomplished nothing; Rodin's silence was freezing us all. Then suddenly perceiving a cabinet filled with bibelots, he took out his glasses and made for it.

"What a lovely little Egyptian figure! What miracles of delicacy those great artists could produce! Who are we compared with them?" His fingers itched to hold it in order to enjoy the touch as well as the sight of it. Then silence came down upon him again, and this time it remained unbroken. We felt that it must be very late and took our departure, but it was only nine-thirty when we reached our hotel. Our great Rodin's conception of social diplomacy made us laugh very hard that night before retiring.

On his return to Paris a letter from Holland awaited him. Due to the success of the Brussels exhibition, the *Cercle Artistique* of Rotterdam sought the privilege of arranging a similar one.

"It might be managed," said Rodin in a voice full of caution, "but you would have to go there to do the placing. You saw what the arrangement was in Brussels. Just do the same for me in Rotterdam. And I'm very anxious for you to give your lecture there; some explanation is necessary."

The members of the Rotterdam *Cercle* and their president, Van Stolk, the ship-owner, were men of great simplicity and sincerity. On the day of the opening they had filled the lobby of the gallery with white flowers as though for a wedding: "This ceremony is really," the president told me, "the wedding of the City of Rotterdam and Great Art."

I brought back with me an invitation to Rodin to exhibit at the famous *Arti et Amicitiae* Society of Amsterdam, under the royal patronage of Their Majesties the Queen and the Queen Mother of the Netherlands. I told him of my enthusiasm for Holland which he had never visited, and I made him promise to come there to see the Rembrandts.

"But my friend Carrière says all of Rembrandt is in the Louvre."

"The Louvre has neither *The Syndics* nor *The Jewish Bride*. You must come!"

In spite of his work and his endless anxieties, he joined me in Amsterdam. It was July and the hotels were full; not a room could be had, and it seemed to me that some member of the *Cercle* could have invited the great man to stay with him. But I did not find in Amsterdam the unaffected simplicity and devotion to art that I had encountered in Rotterdam. Had not one of the members of the *Cercle* referred scornfully in my presence to Rembrandt's dissolute old age, saying that he and his cook "had lived together as man and wife"? His cook! Hendrickje Stoffels! That great-hearted woman with the velvety eyes, immortalized in the master's portrait of her in the Louvre!

To these quickly penitent gentlemen I proposed that Rodin should take my room in the vast Amstel-Hotel where I had been lying at night beneath netting imposed by the mosquito-infested canals, and awakened every fifteen minutes by the charming but tyrannical pealing of churchbells. This was arranged and I found myself in a little room under the roof, probably intended for a house-maid. I insisted upon absolute silence as far as Rodin was concerned regarding this sacrifice which was not a sacrifice at all.

We went to the station to meet him in two landaus which were relics of the Second Empire. It was just at sunset: "It's a city out of *The Arabian Nights*," he murmured ecstatically, as we drove to the hotel. Later, as I stood at my narrow window with lights out in order to get a few breaths of cool air, I heard hesitating footsteps in the corridor and a gentle knocking at my door. It was Rodin. He had inexplicably discovered that I had given up my room to him; he was profoundly embarrassed and I had the greatest difficulty in convincing him that I did not want it back and that I could not let him carry my luggage down again upon his shoulders.

The next morning I suggested paying a visit to the *Cercle Artistique,* but he would have none of it:

"I would like to see Rembrandt's house first," he replied, with the impatience of a lover to gaze at his beloved's window. Long and silently he looked at the modest, freshly-painted dwelling in the Joden-Breestraat, as though expecting Rembrandt himself to emerge from its door.

"Let's go to the museum," he said at last.

There, he lost himself in revery again before *The Night Watch,* and he found *The Jewish Bride* "charming with her timid, rather anxious look; obviously Rembrandt's wife, for she is painted with such affection." The *Portrait of Elisabeth Bas*—then believed to be the work of the master, but recently attributed to his pupil Ferdinand Bol—was "admirable in its profound study of detail, but a little colder than the others; the hands and the fabrics are superbly painted, but all the same there is a certain coldness about it."

Suddenly he caught sight of *The Syndics,* and, as he stood gazing at the picture, its light seemed to be reflected in his now suffused complexion and to have kindled his artist's soul.

"Ah, they're getting up; they're going to speak to us."

He examined the canvas closely, passionately, and with a sort of fraternal delight—one master discovering the secret of another master.

Finally he said: "When you look closely at this picture it seems to be more coarsely painted than the others; bold brush-work. And when you stand farther off, it is an absolute masterpiece. How old was he when he painted it?"

"Fifty-two."

"Exactly. It couldn't have been done by a young man; Rembrandt was almost an old man. He had completed his study of detail. In this picture he is freed of all that preoccupation; he knew what to keep and what to let go. People regard it as less finished, less subtle, and it is actually a sublime creation; they imagine he was getting old, that his art suffered on that account, but it was really becoming so stupendous that they couldn't understand it any longer. It retained only the *essentials.*"

He developed his idea further and feasted his eyes upon the great picture.

"I'm sure Rembrandt is still not fully understood; people admire his mediocre things the most. How could the general run of them possibly comprehend such paintings as *The Jewish Bride* or *The Syndics?*"

"Don't you see a similarity," I asked, "between Rembrandt's career and your own? For instance, doesn't *The Syndics* occupy a place among his works somewhat like that of the *Balzac* among yours?"

He turned again towards the painting, visibly moved.

"It's true," he said. "I have worked hard to broaden my art in order to achieve simplicity which is the true test of excellence. Few people will admit that. At this moment I feel more than ever how

Tympanum of the Gates of Hell (*Tympan de la Porte de l'Enfer*).

Pygmalion and Galatea (*Pygmalion et Galathée*).

right I was. I'm glad I've seen Rembrandt. It's as though he had come back to say: 'You made no mistake; you have done well.'"

Rodin returned to Paris before the opening of the exhibition; his refusal to visit the studios of young painters in Amsterdam had offended several members of the committee. Small difficulties arose which he anticipated: "I'm sure that Amsterdam will be less successful than Rotterdam," he wrote. "My visits always cause trouble of some kind."

The opening took place on August 15, 1899. As I stood talking with the committee after delivering my lecture, I noticed a little slender man in a smartly cut dinner jacket walking towards us. His eyes gleamed maliciously, and the make-up on his lips and cheeks made feverish patches upon an otherwise ivory-pale complexion. His features were sharply and deeply carved like those of a Japanese figure.

"How frightfully hot it is!" His voice was thin and metallic. "Has Holland moved into the tropics?" He sat down near the grey-hung walls, crossed his thin legs, and, stretching out his delicately veined hands, rested them upon his knee. Where had I seen those hands, that pose?

"Could that be Whistler?" I asked my neighbour.

"Of course."

"He is very like his mother."

"Do you know her?"

"No, but I've seen his portrait of her in the Luxembourg."

The metallic voice continued: "I counted on seeing Monsieur Rodin here this evening. He's a great friend of mine. I missed him yesterday too, at Dordrecht. Chance has not favoured me."

A few months after that, in the late afternoon—one artist respects another's working hours, especially the short winter ones—Rodin took me to Whistler's studio in the rue Notre-Dame-des-Champs. It was a vast grey-walled room on the sixth floor, out of which a white lacquered staircase led to a gallery. Rodin hoped that he would show us his pictures which were all draped in linen coverings, and also the etchings he had recently done in Holland. The painter cleaned his palette slowly and meticulously, making Rodin laugh at his sarcastic remarks about people, mostly Americans, whom, though a native of the United States, he luxuriated in denouncing. The author of *The Gentle Art of Making Enemies* was at the top of his form. Presently he began to rummage in a dark corner, and we were regaled by the dreadful monotony of a Negro song, played on a very imperfect American phonograph. This was all he did that day for his great friend's entertainment.

Rodin was in his sixtieth year, extremely obdurate in many ways, but with his capacity for admiration unimpaired. He still had a beginner's respect for any real achievement.

I was spending the summer with my family at Fontainebleau, where we were near neighbours of Stéphane Mallarmé. With his wife and daughter, the poet always left Paris at the first sign of warm weather and took up his abode at Valvins on the banks of the Seine. Rodin visited us and went with us to see Mallarmé whom he knew and liked. We were taken into his study where we felt ourselves to be among the privileged few, and the poet showed us the proofs of his latest poem. He then explained, in phrases both affected and spontaneous, his theory of the relationship between writing and musical composition. He maintained that the reader should receive an impression from the printed page similar to that conveyed to the musician on going through a score in order to acquaint himself with the melodic development. The famous though complex poem, *Un coup de dés jamais n'abolira le hasard*, had no punctuation; its phrases were separated into short fragments, single words—some in small letters, others in capitals, others in italics; and they were placed at the top, middle, bottom, and to the left or right of the page.

Rodin looked at the sheets and listened rather uneasily to Mallarmé's persuasive and lucid reasoning. He was familiar only with the poet's simplest poems, those in which the emotion was expressed with perfect clarity. He knew that the author of *L'Après-Midi d'un Faune* was an artist of absolute sincerity; he regarded such experimentation sympathetically—his own after all was unending; but he waited in vain, as did many others, for the revelation.

When we returned to Fontainebleau it was almost seven o'clock. Rodin asked with some embarrassment whether we objected to his paying a visit to a friend. A visit at seven o'clock! He hastily added: "It's quite near—at the Château." This happened several times and my sisters and I twitted him at dinner about the "mystery of the Château"; he seemed not to mind and devoted himself to the food that was set before him—country dishes prepared as he liked them, with pot-herbs and mushrooms. Several days later he wrote: "It exasperates me not to be able to come to see you, and you know what pleasure your friendly invitations give me. The last time I was there I saw and tasted the cooking of angels—not Murillos—but more beautiful, more real; I might say more ideal."

It was not until after his death that the "mystery of the Château" was solved. One of his relatives told me that in his young days he had fallen in love with the sister of J. J. Weiss, the curator of the Château, and had thought of marrying her. At her brother's death, Mlle Weiss continued to live there, and whenever Rodin visited Fontainebleau he paid his tribute to an old love.

The woods, the fields, and the river were aglow with autumn light the next time he came, but there was grief in every heart. Stéphane Mallarmé had died and his friends followed him to his last resting place in the little cemetery at Valvins.

Early in the summer of 1899, Rodin began to occupy himself with another scheme. He was determined to wipe out the memory of the seeming failure of the *Balzac,* and this could be accomplished only by exhibiting to the public the results of almost half a century of superhuman labour. The *Exposition Universelle* which was to take place in 1900 would provide a splendid opportunity. People from every corner of the world were coming to it, including at least several hundred lovers of art who must be urged to voice their opinion of a sculptor still causing great critical commotion in France.

A room in the *Exposition* exclusively devoted to his works was not to be dreamed of. In a democratic country, no living artist could hope for such high consideration. Rodin accordingly proposed to show his work unpretentiously but proudly, outside the *Exposition*. He had found a site and would have a pavilion put up at his own expense; he asked the municipal authorities to allow him to lease the ground. This request was of course refused. He wrote to me in Holland:

28 June 1899

My dear little friend:

Your letter was very comforting. I have just heard that the Commission has voted against my scheme. Now I will have to try some other way and will probably fail again. If only you, my dear, were a member of the Commission, all would be well. It's annoying always to struggle uselessly.

Things move so quickly that I don't know what to do. I could have gone to Rotterdam on Monday if I had known sooner. I would have liked to spend a few days in that beautiful place.

What can I say?

Since the opening is tomorrow, you will have to tell me about it. I have confidence in your good taste; also in your friendship for me. I'm so afraid of your not knowing how grateful I am for all you are doing.

You devote so much of your precious youth to me and my career.

You are very dear to me.

And now I can only read your lecture. You see, you must write it out so that I as well as the others can read it. Choose for us both one of my favourite drawings for the place of honour.

I feel really like an exile from art. I ought to show more draw-

184

ings, but I can't do what a powerful man should do. I've only got a poor man's ability.

I am so anxious to go on reading the results of our conferences.

With respect and affection,

Your servant,

A. Rodin

He was continually using phrases of startling candour like the one about his drawings. On a late summer afternoon we stood on the deck of a river-boat which was taking us to Meudon; some bathers were disporting themselves in the cool water and I asked him if he knew how to swim.

"Do poor people know how to do anything?" he replied a little drearily, thinking of his poverty-stricken youth.

Thanks to the intervention of powerful friends, the Municipal Council finally allowed Rodin to erect a pavilion in the Place de l'Alma at the corner of the Cours la Reine and the Avenue Montaigne, but he was not given any financial assistance. During the *Exposition Universelle* of 1867, Manet and Courbet, two insurgents like himself, two traditional artists wrongly labelled "revolutionaries" had shown some of their works in an improvised gallery almost on the same spot.

"I'm running heavy risks," he said. "My expenses will be very high." Then he went on apologetically: "If my show is not successful I must make up my mind to become a member of the *Institut*."

"The *Institut*—but why?"

"Because that is the only way to obtain big commissions, and I must have them to pay my debts."

I had returned from Belgium and Holland greatly excited by the success of his exhibitions and by the invitations from other European capitals. I assured him that the one in Paris would be a triumph. Was it then the moment to turn traitor to himself and throw in his lot with the men of the *Institut*? What an example

185

for the younger artists! And moreover, was he certain that there would be no opposition to his membership? Had not Rude failed four times, and had not Puvis de Chavannes been advised not to apply because his friends could not guarantee him a majority? The great Marsyas, as his intimates called him, owed it to himself, and to those who had put their faith in his leadership, to maintain his absolute independence.

My imprudent declarations restored his self-confidence, and, with school-boy delight at the revoking of a penalty, he said:

"You're right, my friend; I'll have nothing to do with those Apollos. They would destroy me."

Three financiers who were admirers of Rodin's work, MM. Dorizon, Peytel, and Kahn, each lent him 20,000 francs. To these three parts he added a fourth, and a Louis XVI pavilion, resembling the orangery of a château, was built. In it he placed one hundred and fifty pieces of sculpture, as well as many drawings and water-colours. The catalogue contained a brilliant essay by Arsène Alexandre and was prefaced, not by writers, but by four artists: Eugène Carrière, Jean-Paul Laurens, Claude Monet, and Albert Besnard. Rodin would have preferred prefaces by sculptors, but Rude, Barye, and Carpeaux were dead. Who could have taken their places?

At the end of May, Georges Leygues, the Minister, officially opened the pavilion in the Place de l'Alma. The exhibition lasted until the end of October, and lectures were given by Charles Morice, Camille Mauclair, Léopold Lacour, Edmond Picard. The opening was not a stormy one like that of the Salon of 1898; it was a brilliant gathering of artists and society people, from which resulted exactly what Claude Monet predicted in his preface:

"I am anxious to express my deep admiration for this extraordinary man, this great man among the greatest. This exhibition of his work will be an event; its success will establish the position of a fine artist."

Rodin's reputation was internationally enhanced, and when the exhibition was over he sent a victorious report to his old friend Captain Bigand-Kaire:

I must tell you, friend, that my show helped my reputation wonderfully, and it paid my debts. I sold 200,000 francs' worth, perhaps more. And got some orders too. Almost all the museums bought things: Philadelphia, *La Pensée;* Copenhagen spent 80,000 francs and I am to have a whole room to myself in their museum; Hamburg, Dresden, Budapest, etc. Few Americans, few English, but a great many Germans at the show. Strange how different from what we thought. Entrance fees not numerous, but a lot of buying. Of the 200,000 francs I spent 60,000 on materials: marble, bronze etc.; I have 140,000 left and my debts were 150,000. I'm very well satisfied, friend, and I hope to see you one of these days.

Aug. Rodin

Thus the two-fold peril was averted: debts and the *Institut.* Certain foreigners who could afford it wanted their busts done by the famous sculptor; these orders interfered seriously with his other work and he imagined there would be fewer if he put up his prices, but he was surprised to discover that he could charge 40,000—his protective measures only made his work the more desirable to the rich. A long series of busts resulted, to which he still added from time to time those of his friends. From the evils of success he was immune, and he executed each one as though his reputation were at stake. Between 1900 and 1910 appeared busts of Mme de Nostitz-Hindenburg, a young German artist who has since written her charming *Souvenirs sur Rodin;* of George Wyndham, the English statesman; of Eugène Guillaume, the head of the *Beaux-Arts* and a member of the *Institut,* finally won over to Rodin's art; of Mrs. J. W. K. Simpson, a beautiful American (this marble bust made a sensation in the Salon of 1906). Thanks to Mrs. Simpson and to a friend of hers, Thomas Ryan, a well-known art-lover, a room in the Metropolitan Museum of New York entirely devoted to Rodin's work was opened in 1909. There were also busts of Mrs.

Potter Palmer, another American; of M. d'Estournelles de Constant; of Miss Eve Fairfax, who represented the Anglo-Saxon type so attractive to Rodin; of Gustave Geffroy; of Bernard Shaw, whose pungent wit enlivened the sittings; of Rodin's friend, Mrs. Hunter, and Miss Hunter, a true daughter of Albion; of Lord Howard de Walden, who commanded the British forces in the Transvaal; of the illustrious and learned Berthelot; of the Comtesse de Noailles (unfortunately not finished); of Georges Leygues; of Mme de Goloubeff; of Mme Elisseieff; of Mr. Pulitzer, the owner of an important New York newspaper; of the Japanese actress Hanako; of the Duchesse de Choiseul; of Mr. de Kay, an American; of Lady Warwick, a work which marked a new summit in Rodin's achievement; of the poetess Renée Vivien; of Barbey d'Aurévilly; of the Americans, Mr. Harriman and Mr. Ryan; of the Austrian composer, Gustave Mahler; of the Duc de Rohan. During the execution of this last-mentioned bust, Rodin was ill and deeply involved in a love affair; when he recovered he reproached himself for having inadequately reproduced the delicacy of his sitter's aristocratic features—he had not, he said, fully appreciated it until too late.

His genius and his fame caused many young men to indulge in fantastic dreaming. One of them, realizing that he had an incurable disease, set aside a large sum in his will for a tomb by Rodin, and his monument at Amiens is adorned by a touching adolescent figure in marble.

The unpretentious *Monument à Maurice Rollinat* must not be forgotten. Its place among Rodin's works is unimportant, but it represents a curious experiment in synthesis for which the two-fold influence of Carrière and Medardo Rosso was responsible; it was an experiment which Rodin did not repeat. [1]

The creation of this gallery of contemporary portraiture did not delay the progress of his other work. Some of the latter was im-

[1] Aurel: *Rodin devant la Femme*, Paris, 1919. An essay of great interest, in which the author brilliantly develops the thesis of Rosso's influence upon Rodin, but gives it an importance which chronological study of the latter's work does not justify. [Author's note.]

Sleep (*Le Sommeil*). COURTESY OF THE MUSEE RODIN

Rodin's Wife (*Mme Auguste Rodin*). COURTESY OF THE MUSEE RODIN

portant; for instance, the decorative sculpture for Baron Vitta's villa at Evian, exhibited in the Luxembourg in 1905. For the three lofty stone pediments, representing the Seasons, and the two large jardinieres, encircled by groups of infants, Rodin made use of Halou's vivid talent. In order to execute the commissions that poured in, he was obliged to employ numerous assistants from among the best-known modellers and cutters. His first assistants were Jules Desbois and Camille Claudel; to these he added Turcan, Escoula, Halou, Peter, Pézieux, Mathet, Alexandre Charpentier, the Schneeg brothers, Rousaud, Dejean, Despiau, Pompon Soudbinine, and Drivier—in short a whole school of fine sculptors was created under his direct influence. These young artists were all happy to receive his instruction, but many trembled at the strictness of his never fully satisfied demands. "He made me weep," Despiau said in affectionate recollection; "he made me weep, but what a master to work for!"

Rodin's influence upon young French sculptors, and later, upon those of other countries, caused further irritation and envy at the *Beaux-Arts,* but this hostility only heightened the existing enthusiasm and increased the number of his followers.

This phase of superabundant production might be called Rodin's second career, his career as a draughtsman; and his fame could easily have rested upon his accomplishments during this period alone. Those first ten years of his powerful old age represented one of the noblest periods of his whole life.

He had been obliged to leave Paris for Bellevue in 1893. In 1897 he bought the now famous little house called the Villa des Brillants on a hill-side near Meudon at Val Fleury. It has been described a hundred times: brick, edged with white stone, almost Louis XIII in style, but actually pure "Paris suburban" despite its long avenue of chestnuts. It has a splendid situation, overlooking the Seine as it winds luxuriously among the slopes dominated by Mont Valérien. In Rodin's time the house was surrounded by meadows and orchards; today this peaceful country scene has changed; its seclusion has been destroyed by a flock of untidy little hovels and cafés—the encroaching Parisian fringe.

As soon as Rodin bought the place, its appearance was altered; successive additions were made which conformed to no particular scheme. After 1900, the pavilion from the Place de l'Alma was rebuilt in the garden. Later, on a hillock at the edge of his property, Rodin erected the façade of the Château d'Issy, designed by Mansart; this he had rescued from the company which was tearing it down, "the abode of Gods now departed, with beauty condemned for the crime of nobility." In the morning mists and the fading gold of evening, the pediment and the columns (discovered in a ditch) and the sash-less window frames took on the aspect of a temple.

The house was almost hidden behind a screen of trees and hedges. Fragments of Greek and Roman sculpture, nymphs and goddesses, a statue, *L'Amour Endormi,* "that little antique that might be Louis XIV," a pool containing two carved swans, produced the atmosphere of a Roman villa.

The rooms were painted in bright colours. The tiny dining-room and the vast studio-drawing-room on the ground floor were unpretentiously furnished with straight-backed lacquered chairs; no carpet, no comfortable arm-chairs; at that time Rodin rested in bed only. Later on, the drawing-room was filled by a somewhat strange collection of cabinets, Empire arm-chairs, and some useless pieces—especially a Renaissance bedstead without spring or mattress which served no other purpose than to protect some fragile objects placed within its framework.

In fine weather Rodin would rise soon after dawn to occupy himself with his world of statues and busts. It had overflowed into the outbuildings and even into the poultry house, from which the hens had gradually been excluded to the great sorrow of Mme Rose who liked to remember that she had once been something of a farmer in her native Marne village. Two hours later they would set forth, on foot or in a little horse-drawn victoria, to Saint-Cloud or Versailles. Mme Rose, with the sharp eye of a country woman, would point out wild rabbits, pheasants, magpies, and turtle doves when their way led through the forest. On Sundays they lunched at Bas Meudon or Pont de Billancourt at some little river restaurant; the caster who was employed at the time accompanied them, and he, as well as the cab-driver, would be asked to sit at their table. After this relaxation Rodin returned to the Villa des Brillants to work till eight or nine in the evening. They also greatly enjoyed entertaining their friends at dinner with good food and wine, and Mme Rose would labour indefatigably to make these dinners excellent. When her guests thanked her, she replied: "I'm only a peasant with no education, but I was properly brought up." She did not seem in any way to resemble "a peasant with no education," I thought, one winter afternoon as she drove me to the station at Meudon, shrouded in an otter-skin cloak and wearing a toque upon her handsome head. She seemed also to have conquered her jealousy and to be happily tranquil.

One morning I brought out a photographer from the office of the publisher Van Oest who was to issue my book: *Rodin, L'Homme et L'oeuvre*. We met the sculptor in the vestibule, on the point of leaving for Paris; he spoke to us briefly and went off to catch the eleven o'clock train. The photographer, a rather crabbed little German, conscientious and expert, worked hard until about three o'clock; neither he nor I had even thought of lunch. When we were ready to leave, Mme Rose had disappeared, but I discovered her finally in the house, sitting on the lowest step of the staircase. With head bent forward and hair dishevelled, she looked like one of the Furies. In this dark corner she sat sewing and when I appeared she asked me rather sharply whether Monsieur Rodin had finished.

"Monsieur Rodin!" I exclaimed, guessing the reason for her mood. "But we scarcely saw him; he took the eleven o'clock train." Whereupon she apologized for not having insisted on my eating lunch and hurried me into the dining-room, feverishly busying herself on my behalf in order to atone for her jealous imaginings.

She even wanted to call back the photographer who had by that time made his escape. "If you only knew what Monsieur Rodin makes me go through!" she cried. "He lets me get lunch all ready and goes off without telling me, without even saying good-bye." I spoke of the endless indulgence one had to show towards men of genius, how incurably absent-minded they were, but she proceeded as though I had said nothing, admitting that there was "someone" (probably the wife of one of Rodin's casters) who kept her informed as to the visitors who came to his Paris studio, and insisting again and again upon her companion's tyranny. "You see, Madame," she once said to Mme Emile Verhaeren, unconsciously corroborating the final scene in Shakespeare's *Taming of the Shrew,* when the two were discussing their respective husbands' despotism, "I've always got to think as he does. I don't even dare to say the weather's hot, or the weather's cold."

Meudon was soon the Bayreuth of sculpture. French and foreign notables, artists, politicians, ambassadors, sovereigns, and kings of industry regarded it an honour to be received at the famous studio. Delegations arrived from several foreign countries, including Japan. Remembering, in the latter case, a national love of flowers, Rodin had caused pale pink roses, white peonies, and white carnations to be strewn about the pedestals of his statues. The Ambassador was touched by this special courtesy and asked if he might pay his respects to Mme Rodin. She was sent for and appeared in a blue apron with sleeves rolled up and arms covered with soap-suds; she had been doing the washing in the back premises.

In 1908, the King of England visited Meudon. Edward VII did not want his own bust done, but shortly afterwards Rodin executed that of a great lady of the English aristocracy whom His Majesty honoured with his affectionate friendship. During the King's visit, Mme Rose sat with a faithful servant waiting for a sight of him from behind lowered Venetian blinds. This time she had been ordered not to leave her room.

The King of Greece invited the creator of *L'Age d'Airain* to visit the native land of Phidias—Rodin in the presence of his forefathers! What a meeting! What marvellous things he would have to say! The prospect of recording them was irresistible and I asked boldly if I could go with him. He promised willingly, but, alas, his scheme of life began then to deviate from its admirable course —also, he was afraid of sea voyages. He never saw Greece.

About 1912, through the Under Secretary at the Ministry of Fine Arts, Dujardin-Baumetz, an extraordinary proposal was presented. The Emperor William II, antagonistic to Rodin at the time of his exhibition in Germany, had now made known his desire for the French sculptor to execute his bust—a desire with perhaps more of a political motive than personal inclination. Representatives of high standing came to Meudon; the number of sittings, their dates, and the terms were discussed. Among these Imperial messengers there was one whom Rodin thought he recognized as the Kaiser himself, who, it was said, occasionally came incognito to Paris; "in any case it was someone who looked very much like him." After all the arrangements had been completed, Rodin began to reflect. Dignity and prudence, fundamental in his character, gradually brought him to the point of feeling that it was not fitting for a French artist to model the features of a monarch who could not with assurance be counted among the sincere friends of France. Perhaps too, he thought, such a client would rouse the sort of controversy with which he was surfeited. He made a pretext of ill health—he was actually far from well—and let it be known that he would be obliged for the moment to deny himself the honour of complying with the Emperor's request. This was greatly to be regretted. At the height of his powers of psychological penetration his portrait of William II would have been—as was that of Clemenceau several years later—a prophecy.

The day following King Edward's visit, Rodin said to me, with the air of one who has arranged a surprise: "Come out to Meudon and look at my studio." This invitation astonished me. What could be there that was new?

There was something that will never be seen again.

The great room, bright with May sunlight, was like an extension of the enchanting flower-filled garden. In it there was nothing but the pure whiteness of marble and plaster—an orchard in early spring blooming. *Le Baiser* in the centre flashed its domination over a group of mythological figures: *Pygmalion et Galathée, Psyché, Adonis, Ariane; Ugolin* was below them; the *Balzac* rose up Druid-like in the background, and the snowy visages of a hundred tenderly entwined figures were haloed with light. What music! What poetry! Whence had come this dazzling multitude? I could not tell, and the great magician only smiled and kept the secret of his display.

Official honours came to him from every quarter. He had been awarded the cross of knighthood in the Legion of Honour in 1888; the rosette in 1892, and the scarf in 1903. Foreign countries sent ribbons and badges. England overwhelmed him with tokens of her esteem; a bronze casting of the *Saint Jean-Baptiste* was publicly subscribed for, and he crossed the Channel in 1912 for its presentation to the South Kensington Museum. He was received like a statesman or a victorious general, and the banquet presided over by the handsome Chief Secretary for Ireland, George Wyndham, was an ovation. After it the great Frenchman's carriage was drawn through the streets by students from South Kensington and the Slade School. There were like demonstrations at Prague during the exhibition suggested by his former pupil Maratka and organized by the *Manes* Society, and the municipality bought *L'Age d'Airain;* whereupon Rodin presented the city with a copy of *Les Bourgeois de Calais.*

Upon the death of Whistler, Rodin was asked to replace him as president of The International Society of Sculptors, Painters, and Gravers. He crossed the Channel again and was once more warmly acclaimed. After the speeches in his honour he remained, to the surprise of everyone, in an embarrassed silence, but he made repeated gestures of gratitude to his hosts. A ceremonial chair had been arranged for him, a sort of throne with a high back, but when the moment came for the company to sit down he became uneasy at the excessive pomp, possessed himself of an ordinary chair and sat down quietly beside the more elaborate one.

In 1907 he again visited London—this time to participate in a more serious ceremony. W. E. Henley's death had occurred the previous year and his friends had been authorized to place his bust by Rodin in the crypt of St. Paul's Cathedral. He was anxious to supervise this placing and to pay tribute to the memory of the man who had first made his work known in England. Oxford conferred upon him the degree of doctor *honoris causa* along with General Booth, Mark Twain, and Camille Saint-Saëns. As the imposing procession, traditionally costumed, proceeded through the town to the Cathedral, Rodin was astonished to discover that the crowds cheered most, not for the head of the Salvation Army, but for Mark Twain who exchanged rapid fire witticisms with the boys in the streets. This award was followed by a doctor's degree from the University of Jena.

Rodin was of course frequently invited to the *Elysée*. One evening I accompanied him from Meudon to Paris where he was to attend a gala dinner given by the President of the Republic. He had dressed with great care, drenched himself with eau de Cologne, and had been to the hairdresser; his white hair clung closely to his head like a cap of silver. The great Marsyas was disguised as a government official. He took it in good part when I told him that an old man had to be over-careful about his appearance, in order not to be repulsive. We were alone in the compartment and he drew from his pocket a collection of little leather cases containing badges and beribboned crosses, asking me to pin them in their proper places. I knew nothing of masculine decorations and advised him to get a footman at the *Elysée* to help him. I fixed the red scarf about his neck, but his beard, though fairly short in those days, concealed it completely. Then he gathered up the little cases, complaining that a man who had decorations should bring with him a pretty woman who could wear them.

To these official functions he greatly preferred intimate gatherings of his friends and disciples; such a gathering was the banquet in the Vélizy forest arranged by Jean Baffier, Emile Bourdelle, and Lucien Schneeg, on the occasion of his being made a Commander of the Legion of Honour. The weather was fine, everyone was happy, and Mme Rose was of the company. A half-life-size copy of *L'Homme qui marche* had been placed on a column in the centre of the lawn in front of the Inn, and Isadora Duncan, young, shy, and exquisitely graceful, danced with bare feet to the music of Thaulow's 'cello and Bourdelle's violin.

A very different ceremony was enacted before the peristyle of the Panthéon in 1906. Two years previously Rodin had exhibited at the Salon an enlargement of the figure of the *Poète* taken from *La Porte de l'Enfer*, calling it *Le Penseur*. This statue was so severely criticized that the writer Gabriel Mourey organized a public subscription as a protest. The sum of 15,000 francs was collected and a bronze casting of *Le Penseur* was acquired and presented to the city of Paris. At the unveiling, to the surprise of those gathered to witness the ceremony, Mme Segond-Weber, very like a woman of ancient Greece with her noble gestures and her floating veils, appeared among the lofty columns and recited a poem by Victor Hugo.

The Municipal Council which had not yet recovered from its annoyance over the *Balzac* affair was far from unanimous in its approval of the position accorded to *Le Penseur*, and when the city was considering the acquisition of several copies of *Les Cathédrales de France* M. Lampué, one of the Councillors, found an opportunity to air his opinion of the statue which was on its way to gaining international fame: "The most undistinguished student in our drawing courses would hesitate to publish such sketches, but the sculptor of the ape-man that disgraces the portico of the Panthéon obviously has no objection to imposing further upon the credulity of the public."

The Councillors who shared Lampué's opinion held firmly to it. In 1922, on the pretext that its bulk interfered with official ceremonies, *Le Penseur* was removed from the Panthéon and placed in the Hôtel Biron. In withdrawing this great work from a public place, the municipal authorities deprived the man in the street of a work of art which, without his realizing it, had exerted a powerful influence upon him.

Rodin travelled extensively in 1906; he went to Spain with Zuloaga, visiting Madrid, Toledo, Cordova, and Seville. In the summer he spent several weeks in Belgium, perhaps to please his wife. The Ostend *Centre d'Art* was holding an exhibition of painting and sculpture which included Rodin's *Saint Jean-Baptiste* in bronze. This casting had been purchased by a Belgian collector who intended to leave it to the Brussels Museum. I helped with the arrangements for the exhibition at the *Centre d'Art,* and before going to Ostend I took a short vacation with my mother at Groenendaël in the Soignes forest. Rodin joined us there with Mme Rose; she was in high spirits and recounted vividly and happily many episodes of their poverty-stricken youth. Long hours were spent among those majestic beech trees and every day a visit was paid to the little forest chapel of Notre-Dame-de-Bonne-Odeur. Rose, as usual, carried Rodin's overcoat and he took notes continually: "Beloved forest of Groenendaël! . . . It was there, perhaps, that I discovered my shy muse. . . . That wavering light, that moist air in a country of mist. . . . Green trunks mingling with yellowish and reddish leaves. Notre-Dame in the heart of the forest, hiding among the trees like a little peasant girl—but it marks the path for travellers." And after a day in Brussels, he wrote: "I used to find fault with *Sainte-Gudule*—such was my ignorance—but it seems to me now as perfect as *La Joconde.*"

He came to Ostend in the midst of a particularly brilliant season. Georges Marquet, a curious, rather Balzacian individual, who was managing the Kursaal with great pomp and magnificence, had inaugurated a series of very special intellectual entertainments under the supervision of Edmond Picard: concerts, theatrical productions, lectures, and exhibitions. Actors, musicians, and scholars —for the most part French—were invited to the Kursaal. At a sumptuous dinner one evening, Rodin and Paul Doumer who had just given a lecture on Indo-China were among the guests. The restaurant occupied the vast entrance hall of the Kursaal which, on gala evenings, held as many as eight thousand people. This arrangement permitted the diners to watch the endless stream of gorgeously attired foreigners from every corner of the world flowing toward the gaming rooms, while from a lofty dais the famous François Ruhlmann orchestra poured down music upon the gay throng.

Mme Rose had never in her life seen anything like it and laughed quietly in her enjoyment of the scene: "My old Marie [her cook] will never believe me when I tell her about this." She apologized for the simplicity of her gown and Edmond Picard reassured her: "But, Madame, what does it matter? Are you not clothed in the name of Auguste Rodin?"

But the sculptor felt—and not without reason—that this mundane atmosphere had little connection with his austere art. He wrote to me on his return to Paris:

August 1906

My friend,

Thanks for all you did for me at Ostend, and please thank M. Picard too; he was delightful.

My instinct is right; I do not want to show my work at the Kursaal. In fact I am a little ashamed at the possibility that people may think I sold my *Saint-Jean* there.

Affectionately,

A. Rodin

By 1908 I had left Saint-Cloud and was living in the Batignolles quarter of Paris; in the spring of that year a monument to Henry Becque whose death had occurred ten years before was to be unveiled in the Place Prosper Goubeaux at the intersection of the

Boulevard de Courcelles and the Avenue de Villiers. Rodin had known this vigorous follower of Molière very well and had done his bust in 1883, also the now famous etching. The monument was an enlargement in marble of this early bust.

I had neither seen Rodin nor heard from him for several months; he appeared at my apartment a half-hour before the unveiling, looking older, his hair in disorder, but with flashing eyes and his customary air of having just arrived from another planet. After a glance at my apartment which was small but comfortable, he offered to do a little marble figure for my chimney-piece. Then he took me off to the rather uninteresting ceremony at which Clemenceau, then Minister of the Interior, drowsily listened to a savourless oration by the Prefect of the Seine. When the official party had withdrawn, Rodin, declining an invitation to lunch with Octave Mirbeau and some friends, turned to me: "If you like, we'll lunch at the *Rocher de Cancale* where I used to go with Becque." There, he sat in Becque's favourite corner seat and entertained me with stories about the famous dramatist.

After lunch we went to the Georges Petit Gallery to see the *Cent Pastels,* a remarkable collection of eighteenth-century works. Those of Perronneau, La Tour, Falconnet, and Clodion received his homage, especially Clodion's marble bust of a woman which, according to the press, had fetched an enormous price. "Its weight in gold was paid," said Rodin, "but even that wasn't enough for it. A masterpiece is priceless because it cannot be duplicated." Then he said in a low voice full of emotion, "I am a pupil of the eighteenth century."

Even those most appreciative of his gifts had little knowledge of the eloquence of his intimate conversation. Some of these only knew the Rodin who appeared at official dinners and ceremonies, the man of great reserve and few words. "He couldn't have said all those things!" exclaimed Léon Bourgeois on reading the book in which I had recorded some of the sculptor's conversations. When I assured him of their authenticity, he said: "You must arrange for us to meet again." An informal evening was arranged. Bourgeois talked delightfully and brilliantly all through dinner. Rodin was enchanted by the grace and clarity with which he expressed himself, but he contributed little to the conversation beyond a few words in praise of Pierre Loti whose books he had been reading; then he leaned toward a bowl of Christmas roses and relapsed into a pregnant silence. "You see," exclaimed Bourgeois when the sculptor had departed for Meudon, "he said nothing!"

"Of course not; weren't you talking all the time?"

A huge banquet organized by Bourdelle took place on the 15th of June, 1910, in the Bois, celebrating Rodin's promotion to the rank of *grand officer* in the Legion of Honour. Willette designed the menu with the dedication: "To Rodin—pupil of God," and Jean Aicard presided. Dujardin-Baumetz was present, also Edmond Picard who had come from Belgium for the occasion. When the repast was over, a group of young men amused themselves by making fun of the officials; inexplicably, one of the objects of their derision was Jean Aicard. In their cruel ignorance they ridiculed the poet who, fifteen years before, had fought courageously for the *Balzac,* and it required the efforts of Edmond Picard to smooth things over: "I am greatly disturbed," said the famous Belgian at the beginning of his address, "by this cruelly unjust treatment of a great poet and man of letters—one of your own countrymen. What is to happen to me—a foreigner?" The young men applauded him loudly and favoured poor Jean Aicard with a few cheers.

VIII. THE RODIN MUSEUM – RODIN AND RILKE – EGERIA

T HE years now passing were the most glorious in Rodin's whole career—years of apotheosis. Those who loved him, particularly those engaged in the bitter exhausting struggle for existence, were happy at the thought of his success, his relative affluence, and his god-like serenity.

His influence upon his contemporaries was more like that of a great writer or a scholar than of an artist. The robust simplicity of his philosophy gave them strength; by his example they were made to realize the benefits of hard work and endless study; his sculpture exalted them; his pantheism showed them the real sources of happiness. Nature, his spiritual helpmate, afforded him unlimited joy, and he made amorous protestations of his devotion: "My soul is a circle of lighted candles round a bier. . . . Surrounded by light, I feel beauty in all its emanations . . . the wonder of it overwhelms me afresh every day. I am going to die—I must die—but I am like a tree in full flowering."

In his garden at Meudon, enjoying, as he alone could, the fresh air, the silence, the shape and colour of the flowers and the trees, he seemed like one of the blest, one who, arrived at the culmination of his tranquil raptures, would melt away upon Nature's breast, vanish into the great blue spaces and be borne to Heaven like a prophet.

It was impossible not to ascribe his extraordinary poise and his fundamentally robust constitution to an inherited mysticism and to the influence of his early up-bringing. "I am essentially a very religious person, but today I have no formal belief. I deny nothing because I am certain of nothing. I am filled with wonder at my surroundings, and, without great understanding, I freely admit that there is a Mind above me which has ordained the existence of Nature and which has my adoration."

All who knew him received the impress of his serene power, felt the dominating spell of his deep understanding. Though fully aware of all this I was continually being surprised and enslaved. No one has written of this side of Rodin with as much perception as Rainer Maria Rilke:

"You have an abounding and pulsating strength; you are invaded by a joyful vigour which I have never conceived of till now. . . .

"What of all our hours of self-satisfaction—hours spent in the woods, at the seaside—what of our endeavours to live a healthy life, of our confident dreaming? What does all this amount to in the presence of one who is the forest and the sea himself, of the indescribable serenity and frankness of his steady gaze, of the edifice of his mental sanity and stability? He is everything, absolutely everything." [1]

A spark in that forest, a squall upon that sea, a crevice in that structure—the chain of his incomparable existence was going to be broken and he to be caught in the most banal of snares.

The studios in the Dépôt des Marbres had been for some time inadequate; they were too small to hold the accumulation of statues, and unpleasantly like rebuilt stables. In 1908 an important event occurred in Rodin's life: he moved to the famous Biron mansion, lured there by Rilke, then a young poet little known in France and filled with dreams of a closer acquaintance with the superman whom he passionately admired. He had been commissioned by a German publisher to write a book about Rodin, and had come to

[1] Rainer Maria Rilke: *Lettres, 1901-1911.* (Translated by Zylberberg and Nougayrol, Paris, 1934.)

Paris to talk with him and study his work. Captivated by the young man's charming personality, Rodin had invited him to live at Meudon in a little house on his property and to participate in his simple existence at the Villa des Brillants. Later, he made the young man his secretary. It was an odd choice, for Rilke had at that time a very imperfect knowledge of French; but Rodin's distrust of his young compatriots and his preference for foreigners were responsible for this irrational appointment. So after Ludovici, the Englishman, came Rilke, the Czeck. But the two artists' congeniality was of short duration. Rodin's disposition had begun to change; he was impatient and despotic, and his commands fell like swords upon innocent necks. His warmest friends turned from him in dismay. Rilke was brutally and unjustly dismissed.

Several months later, Rilke's wife, the sculptress Clara Westhoff rented an apartment on the premises occupied for the sixty years previous to 1904 by the convent school of Sacré Cœur. Since the beginning of the eighteenth century it had been lived in by famous people, including the Maréchal de Biron whose name it now bore. When the convent had been obliged to close its school the courts took over the management of the buildings and let the pavilion and the chapel as apartments while waiting for the fate of the property to be decided. Clara Westhoff, and then Rilke, lived at the Hôtel Biron simultaneously with Jean Cocteau, Henry Matisse, De Max, the actor, and several American and Russian women-writers. Isadora Duncan rented a long gallery built at the beginning of the nineteenth century but not in existence today, which she used for dancing rehearsals. To their credit, foreigners in Paris have a way of discovering and making use of our beautiful old houses.

In 1908, Rilke, having generously forgotten Rodin's unjust treatment, took him to the Hôtel Biron. The sculptor was captivated by the surrounding trees and bushes, and by the proportions of the vast Regency rooms; he at once rented the ground floor of the pavilion for 5,900 francs a year, put some furniture in it, and set happily to work. How amazingly well this lordly dwelling suited him! After a day's work he would wander beneath the fruit trees in the garden, enclosed by masses of shrubbery—it was a delight to watch him, alone, enchanted, in that Eden, above which rose the golden tiara of the Invalides; and when I visualized the essential harmony of his sculpture with Gabriel's vivid and graceful architecture, these words sprang to my lips: "Master, here is where your museum must be."

His brows went up, causing a strange deepening of his eye-sockets:

"It's a dream, and one that is too beautiful," was his only response.

Since the exhibitions in Belgium and Holland, and especially the one in Paris in 1900, I had a burning desire for Rodin's works to be assembled for the glory of our country and for the education of young artists. In 1907 I had appealed, in *Le Matin de Bruxelles,* for the establishment of a Rodin Museum in France and a Constantin Meunier Museum in Belgium. The idea was taken up in *Le Figaro* and *Le Journal* by Gustave Coquiot in 1911, and it was making its way in Rodin's mind; but he did not know how it was to be accomplished. In fact a day soon came when all hope was destroyed: he informed me despairingly in November, 1909, that the property was to be sold; it would be divided into lots, and he produced a map showing how the lots were divided and a catalogue of the sale, already distributed among the speculators. These gentlemen had long been looking forward to the profits to be made in this transaction; they expected to buy for five or six millions a property of 63,000 square yards which was easily worth fifteen. There were forty-five lots; the mansion itself which occupied only three or four of these was priced at 160,000 francs and merely regarded as old lumber. New streets would be cut through the desecrated gardens and apartment houses would soon lift their dismal façades in the rue de Varenne and the Boulevard des Invalides. The 18th of December was the date fixed for the sale.

Rodin was not discouraged for long. A few comforting words

and his young enthusiasm returned. I told him the Hôtel Biron had to be saved; he must at once inform his influential friends in legislative circles. It might be necessary for him to put his name at the head of a public petition. He was convinced of the need for immediate action and went to see Clemenceau, Aristide Briand, and Gabriel Hanotaux; a helping hand, as effective as it was unexpected, came from the opposing political group: on December 14, 1909, four days before the date fixed for the sale, at the pressing request of M. Gaudin de Villaine, the Senate had the sale postponed and asked the government to consider the question of acquiring the property. The legal proceedings took two years and on the 13th of October, 1911, the State purchased the Hôtel Biron for six millions. The buildings and gardens were appropriated by the Ministries of Public Instruction and Fine Arts, pending a decision as to their ultimate fate.

Rodin had installed himself simply and unostentatiously, but the setting, his taste in arrangement, and the presence of his works created an intimate luxury pervaded by the atmosphere of work, meditation, and the emanations of genius. Several pieces of polished mahogany and chestnut, a secretaire, five or six arm-chairs, a wide table covered with some Persian material—that was all; but gleaming white statues rose up among the furniture and baskets of ripe fruit were placed here and there. Many of his precious water-colours were on the walls; on a chest stood an exquisite *kwanine* which he called his Chinese virgin, and above it hung one of Renoir's loveliest paintings; there was also the torso of a young woman, worthy of the Greeks. Here, one heard Rodin's clear voice speaking of eternal things, a voice which was like the voice of eternity itself.

After his three years' occupancy, Rodin imagined that he would spend the rest of his life in the Hôtel Biron, and that his works would perhaps be finally collected there. He was nearly seventy-one and greatly concerned as to their fate. Further complications developed which shook his faith in this eventuality.

At the time of the State's decision to appropriate the property, public opinion created something of a crisis. The resentment caused in certain political circles when the Convent school had been obliged to move out was still alive, and there was much complaining in the press. Several of the subsequent tenants supplied it with excellent material. The presence of Mme Jeanne Bloch, a music-hall singer, in the holy precincts of the former school, among whose aristocratic pupils had been Eugénie de Montijo, Comtesse de Teba and future Empress of France, seemed an offence. [2] De Max, the actor, had had the bad taste to turn the sacristy of the chapel into his bathroom, and several newspapers, delighted to be able to reiterate their attacks on Rodin, declared that he had filled the old dormitories with statues and drawings which bordered on the obscene. This was sacrilege, and the occupants of the Hôtel Biron were turned out; in October of 1911 Rodin received notice to vacate in three months.

His health was not good; he showed signs of lassitude and this bad news affected him profoundly. I went to see the Inspector of State Property, M. Doussot, who was very civil to me and, fortunately, an admirer of Rodin. He advised me to arrange a petition to be widely circulated for the establishment of a Rodin Museum, and I had the great pleasure of taking back to my illustrious friend an eighteen months' extension of his lease with a promise of renewal.

It was imperative to take immediate advantage of this delay, for the Government was hesitating between several projects. The important buildings along the Boulevard des Invalides had been appropriated at once for the future Lycée Duruy, but the Hôtel Biron itself was being considered for five different purposes: it would be used by the Under Secretary of Fine Arts, by the Pensions Office, for the offices of the Mayor of the VII arrondissement, as an annex of the Ministry of Justice, or as a mansion for the entertainment of visiting sovereigns—a scheme enthusiastically supported by Paul Doumer. The Government's hesitation proved that none of these projects was indispensable. Rodin's project was

[2] Georges Grappe: *L'Hôtel Biron* (Catalogue du Musée Rodin).

to spend the rest of his life in the Hôtel Biron and to establish his museum there; for these privileges he would make over all his works to the State, with full rights of reproduction which he had never been willing to grant, and to this gift he added his collection of antiques.

I obtained an interview with the Chancellor, Aristide Briand, who amiably assured me that he was as comfortable in the Place Vendôme as Rodin in the rue de Varenne, and that he would see that this state of affairs was maintained. Paul Doumer, though very sympathetic to Rodin, was more reserved. The great hope of his life was to be President of the Republic, and he saw himself offering the hospitality of the noble dwelling of the Maréchale de Biron to visiting monarchs.

The petition had to be got ready immediately and signed by the people of intelligence who had so often and so powerfully supported Rodin. Léon Bourgeois, though on our side, declared that the State would never grant one of its properties to a living artist, however great. Paul-Boncour shared his opinion, but was kind enough to hand my article on the question to M. Henry de Jouvenel, editor-in-chief of *Le Matin*. M. de Jouvenel gave us his immediate support and the article was published in November of 1911 with headlines, sub-heads, and impressive illustrations. This brought us the adherence of many politicians, writers, and artists. I went to see Georges Clemenceau who received me politely and replied in his well-known nervous staccato:

"Rodin? His museum? . . . At the Hôtel Biron? Why there? Don't understand . . . don't understand. . . ."

Etienne Chichet, manager of the *Paris-Journal* and future editor-in-chief of *L'Homme Libre,* took me to see Raymond Poincaré, President of the Council and Foreign Minister, of whom Rodin said: "He is like a country doctor totally absorbed by his patient's progress."

"I would be happy to see that great Rodin and his works installed permanently in the Hôtel Biron," the statesman said to us, "and I will see that something is done about it, but I've promised the chapel to the Maronites. I hope Rodin won't mind their being there."

"Rodin is a monk himself," I replied, "an artist monk. He will therefore be pleased at their presence."

Poincaré's support was essential. Nevertheless the project depended on the Minister of Fine Arts, and even more on the Minister of Finance whose duty it was to put the proposal before the Chambers. At the Louvre, M. Lucien Klotz was distinctly discouraging, even impatient: "Not a day passes without several more or less qualified people coming to talk to me about Rodin. Great artist though he is, I cannot grant him this huge property worth several millions!" This showed that the minister had been misinformed, and I explained that Rodin knew the Lycée Duruy was to have the larger part; he merely wished to occupy the pavilion in the rue de Varenne, for which privilege he would bequeath all his works to France and establish his museum at his own expense.

M. Klotz replied that this was the first precise statement he had received. Rodin's offer now struck him as being "not only a splendid arrangement, but also an advantageous one." He would see what could be accomplished, and this as quickly as possible, "for it's one of those things that must be done in twenty-four hours or twenty-four days, or not all." He apologized for the rudeness of his first remarks: "Forgive me. I am the keeper of the nation's wealth, the watch-dog of France."

He kept his word. Two committees—one appointed by him and the other by his colleague at the Ministry of Fine Arts—conferred with Rodin in the rue de Varenne. The sculptor was strangely apathetic; he seemed to have little interest in the project which represented his most ardent desire. A woman was now in control at the Hôtel Biron; his life had been completely transformed.

Until then, in spite of the great passion which had lasted almost fifteen years and had ended so tragically, Rodin had fairly successfully avoided the "feminine snare" which he denounced as the most formidable danger to an artist. I do not mean that he was not

208

credited with innumerable affairs. What sordid tales had been concocted about Rodin's women! What an arsenal of slanderous ammunition had been placed at the disposal of his opponents. The public looked upon his works as concentrated passion and sensuality, despite the aura of modesty in which his art had enveloped them, and it ascribed to the sculptor himself the frenzies of the beings he had created. Rodin was the male, crazed with desire for all women, the satyr let loose, the pitiless warrior claiming the rights of victory. Thus the public wished to regard him. No one considered whether this faun-like behaviour was compatible with his prodigious accomplishments and his unquenchable thirst for knowledge. How differently he was portrayed by Jules Desbois who witnessed a revealing incident in the studio in the Boulevard de Vaugirard: "Rodin's sensuality was fastidious. One day, from the scaffolding round *Les Bourgeois de Calais* upon which I was working, I could see him over the top of a screen modelling a nude figure. His model was lying upon a table and when he had finished for the day he leaned over and kissed the young woman tenderly on the stomach—an adoring tribute to Nature for the countless favours he had received from her."

Like Racine, Balzac, and Wagner, Rodin was really a profound worshipper of femininity. He loved women both spiritually and physically; he was an intensely virile man who had moments of sensual impetuosity, perhaps brutality, but his extreme sensitiveness enabled him to recapture these moments and perpetuate them in his works.

A chaste youth; a deep conjugal affection which no one had succeeded in supplanting; a great love which had yielded to this first indestructible emotion; a profound respect for women resulting from his up-bringing and his memories of his mother, his sister, and the other female relatives who had watched over his young years; and, finally, an astounding productiveness due perhaps to the suppression of powerfully erotic instincts ("The man of genius," he said, "is a stallion who does something with Nature.")—these were the elements of his being, and it was within these limitations that he reached the summit of his achievement.

Obviously his fame could not fail to attract innumerable feminine admirers. In the beginning he seemed quite able to perceive the true nature of these tributes and the practical reasons for some of them, but in his old age he persisted in deluding himself and accepted them indiscriminately.

In his studio I sometimes encountered people to whom I was mentioned but not introduced: "My pupil," he would say, simply. Contrary to what one would have expected, these women, mostly foreigners, were not all beautiful—far from it. But with him beauty often became confused with vitality, and he was able to find it where others could not. Sometimes jealousy flamed up, and there are friends of his who remember a certain Salon *vernissage* when violent attacks obliged them to form a protecting circle round him.

I was absorbed for a time by my own concerns, and after two or three months without seeing him I went to his studio to walk with him as far as the river. He at once took up the discussion we had been engaged in at our last meeting, and it was so engrossing that I did not notice the presence of a third person. When we left the studio I was aware of a little thin woman in a wide-brimmed hat, dressed with an elegance that was spoiled by the violent make-up on her faded features (make-up was not fashionable in those days) and a coiffure of thick red curls. During the walk from the studio to the boat landing, Rodin talked exclusively to me, and she came along modestly behind. Then, to my intense surprise, she accompanied him aboard the "Hirondelle." I was accustomed to his "originality" and actually I thought little of this encounter, but I met her soon again at the studio. Rodin was engaged with some other friends and she chatted amiably with me in a very Anglo-Saxon accent. She was an American, belonging to a family whose men were lawyers, and had married a Frenchman with a great name, the Marquis de Ch——. They lived at Versailles and Rodin had several times visited them at their château in Brittany.

During the long months that were taken up with the question of the Hôtel Biron, the influence of the Marquise de Ch——, now become a duchess, had strengthened. I was not greatly surprised. At Meudon, Rodin had never succeeded in achieving the neatness and order which he had learned to appreciate in his mother's tiny apartment long ago. "If those round me had understood me, I would have lived an existence as well-ordered as William II's. Most people are like animals; they break, they soil, they destroy everything." It was quite natural for the Duchesse de Ch——, with plenty of time on her hands, to be lavish with her care for the neatness of his surroundings. His relations with the United States were now numerous and she seemed able to facilitate these for him. She and her husband left Versailles and took an apartment in the Champ de Mars. Believing herself now to be firmly established in Rodin's life, she threw aside her early discretion. She fluttered anxiously about, disturbing and invading, with a manner and a mentality in painful contrast with the dignified rhythm of the sculptor's existence. She overwhelmed him with her clumsy flattery (until now he had cared only for spontaneous praise), interrupted conversations with futile prattle and laughter (gaiety, she felt, should be the note), and indulged in familiarities which at their respective ages could only be regarded as comic: "I am your Muse," she would simper, running her diamond-laden fingers through the white hair on his handsome head; and on a copy of Hozier which she liked to show she had altered the date of her birth by ten years. She brought titled people to the Hôtel Biron with whom Rodin was not impressed. She reorganized his wardrobe and went with him to official functions. They appeared at the unveiling of the *Victor Hugo* in the Palais-Royal gardens: he, calm and majestic in fashionable clothes which did not suit him and a Prince of Wales top hat; she, chattering ceaselessly beneath a tray-shaped hat waving with ostrich plumes, painted, powdered, hair dyed, and slashed with red at the mouth—very like a vaudeville actress trying to break into society.

Strange things were happening at the Hôtel Biron; Rodin had bought a gramophone, and, after playing me some magnificent Hebrew chants and anthems by the Sistine Choir, he begged the Duchess to dance a *bourrée*. In a circus rider's hat and a black scarf which she manipulated with awkward gestures, "his muse" began to dance to an old Auvergne melody—Félicien Rops has amused himself by doing an engraving of this somewhat macabre performance. The effort she had to make almost banished the smile from her painted lips, and after going through some entirely impromptu rhythms which had no connection with a *bourrée* she flung herself down upon a couch where she remained for some time trying to conceal the fact that she was breathless. Rodin took out his note-book and jotted down:

"My amazing little friend dances with passionate ardour. She comes forward like Minerva of bygone days—a charming pose. She flings out her scarf, casts it forward, with her back in exquisite profile. She turns from side to side; then her scarf envelops her—an elbow forward with hand on hip—then it falls, motionless. Two hands raised now; the conquering smile—she is like a proud caryatid. Then her head sinks in meditation, the folds of her scarf are crossed. All her charms are in battle array."

His unbelievable sincerity saved this from being merely ridiculous. "Every day increases the grotesqueness and the absurdity of his old age," lamented Rilke. Not so those who loved him; for them his old age became every day more painfully imcomprehensible. What was happening in that ordered brain of his? What sort of day-dreaming had been evoked by this ludicrous woman? Was the son of humble working people dazzled by her title? Or had his passion for Michael Angelo and his unconscious desire to relive the great Florentine's life made him think that, in Claire de Ch——, he had found his Princess Colonna? An artist of humble birth is extraordinarily naïve and his power of self-delusion rather pathetic: valuable qualities, but, for Rodin, dangerous ones.

Fortunately, his genius survived this insane adventure; he did a bust of Mme de Ch——, her head turned sideways and her features convulsed by hysterical laughter: "it makes her look like a bacchante," he declared without realizing the exactness of the description. He was not aware of the cruelty of his realism and the bust did not please his sitter. He made another with somewhat stylized features and a fillet encircling the head; and to render it more valuable he had it cut from Parian marble.

Work always imposed limits to the affected foolishness of their life together. In that respect the Jupiter of Meudon was himself continually. He executed a bust of Clemenceau for the Argentine Republic which was anxious to offer a tribute to the statesman commemorating a series of lectures given in South America. The older Rodin grew, the more scrupulous he became. He had made a dozen heads of Clemenceau in clay, cut off at the neck; the studio was a nightmare of severed heads. He was practising sculpture as though it were etching. In order not to overwork his clay by too much remodelling, he took impressions, worked on these, going through the operation perhaps ten or a dozen times. To my mind none of these decapitations represented the powerful structure of Clemenceau's head, but there was a large bust in the corner of the room which took my breath away—authority, aggressive vitality, the head of a leader, of an already legendary being upon whose features lurked the melancholy lassitude, the subtle cynicism of an old Chinese philosopher. I voiced my enthusiasm. Again he had done something which made me think of Rembrandt.

"That one should be kept and the others discarded," interrupted Mme de Ch——.

"Just a moment," replied the sculptor, slightly annoyed, "Miss Cladel can judge for herself." And I imagined he had made her my mortal enemy.

Clemenceau refused to accept the bust. He was offended at being made to look like a Mongolian general. "But," said Rodin with some irony, "Clemenceau is Tamerlane; he is Genghis Khan too."

Several years before the world crisis, he had given us the Clemenceau of the War and no likeness of him will ever surpass it.

Mme de Ch—— adopted Rodin's manner to me and was more than amiable; she invited me to meet her husband—a man about town in whom there was evidence of deterioration due to heaven knows what misalliances but who nevertheless resembled in feature his ancestor, Louis XV's famous Minister; she came with Rodin to lunch with me and suggested that I should go to the United States and give a series of lectures on Rodin's work. The idea tempted me and the sculptor offered to put ten thousand francs at my disposal for expenses. Mme de Ch—— promised me letters to important society people in New York and began to introduce me to Americans then in Paris. In the summer of 1911, she arranged a reception at the Hôtel Biron. Among her guests were Mr. James Hyde, president of the Alliance Française in the United States, and Mrs. Lydig, an enchanting woman. They were both tall, slender, and graceful; Mrs. Lydig wore a tight-fitting gown of black satin and a little velvet beret on her small head, and she carried an ivory cane. I could not help thinking of *Le Serpent qui danse*. In the late sunlight we sat and talked on the wide terrace overlooking the gardens. After a half-hour of amiability, Rodin, who was doing Hanako's bust at the time, made his excuses and took the little Japanese actress off to his studio. He had been too preoccupied to dress for the reception and as he went slowly up the steps—a slightly bent figure in his long smock and soft hat, accompanied by the exotic little Hanako in her embroidered kimono—the gathered visitors maintained an admiring silence.

One Sunday in November—he always kept my American scheme in mind—he asked me to meet President Wilson's sister, Mrs. Howe, and her niece, Miss Cochrane. He had come in from Meudon for the occasion and was wearing his best frock coat with a large red rosette on its lapel. The ladies were a little late, so he threw a plaster-whitened robe over his shoulders, covered his carefully dressed hair with his beret, and set to work on a clay figure. His guests found him thus when they timidly entered the studio; they were slightly shocked by some of the figures, for the nude in sculpture was rarely seen in America.

Mme de Ch—— had been so sympathetic with my schemes that I was astonished to learn from one of the sub-editors of *Le Matin*, to whom M. de Jouvenel had turned over the matter of publishing the petition and who was unfamiliar with the situation at the Hôtel Biron, that "a lady named de Ch——" had written in to ask that publication be suspended or, at least, that my name should not be mentioned in connection with the petition. When Rodin was given notice to vacate the pavilion, I was horrified to hear her suggest to him, on the advice of a friend, the manager of an important newspaper, that he should move out temporarily and wait for the government's decision. I pointed out to Rodin the danger of such a proceeding, and on my telling Mme de Ch—— of my surprise at her letter to *Le Matin* she was full of friendly protestations and told me of her wish to arrange, through her influence, for me to be a regular and highly-paid contributor to that newspaper.

Until then I had believed in her great friendship for Rodin, perhaps tinged with snobbism and vanity, but on the whole disinterested and devoted. Among artists of those days and particularly in my own circle one could count on sincerity. Suspicion about people and their hidden desires was rarely indulged in; and this accounted for my credulity. But Mme de Ch—— asked certain indiscreet questions which put me on my guard. What exactly were the ties that bound Rodin to Rose Beuret? Had there not been a secret marriage? Why had it been kept secret? Had Auguste Beuret any legal claim upon his father's estate? All this information was essential to the concluding of an important arrangement between Rodin and an American museum. One day as I entered the room just outside his studio I found the Duchess alone, in front of a large open cupboard full of bottles. She finished drinking a glass of claret and told me that her life with Rodin was very exhausting and she needed to keep up her strength; her delicate hand, covered with rings and lined with blue veins, was shaking terribly. During our conversation Rodin's favourite pupil was mentioned, and "his Muse" informed me that he had completely forgotten all that; then she asked me, if I happened to hear her discussed, to say that Mme de Ch—— could absolutely guarantee that the sculptor was happy.

My desire to go to America weakened after this conversation. In any case I had an objection to the scheme, though perhaps it was a childish one. The question of money had never come up between us. When I had organized foreign exhibitions of his work, I had been satisfied with just my expenses and the usual lecturer's fee, both sums being paid me by the art circle or gallery. If I were to fail in America I would be deeply in debt to him and very much upset in consequence. Also, some New York friends had advised me not to come under the patronage of a person who was looked upon as an agent receiving commissions in the event of sales of Rodin's works; moreover, what would happen in my absence about the establishment of the museum? I gave up the American scheme and redoubled my efforts on behalf of the museum. Governments fell and I had to go through the preliminaries again with new ministers who viewed the proposal quite differently from their predecessors. Certain of these functionaries wished to establish a museum of sculpture in which the works of the great innovator would be lost among those of his bitterest opponents. M. Léonce Bénédite, curator of the Luxembourg, agitated for part of Rodin's work to be put in the former Saint-Sulpice Seminary. The *Institut* showed signs of perturbation. Malicious dwarfs seemed to be tangling the threads.

I concealed the bad news from Rodin and told him the good. He was not very helpful and frequently left Paris with his strange Egeria "to see cathedrals," often when his presence was most needed.

The transformation in his disposition grew more marked; he

216

lost his serenity and seemed unhappy. His affability and courtesy to women was unchanged, but with men he was arrogant and as capricious as Neptune. The casters, cutters, and founders who worked for him had to submit to harsh treatment; he expected his orders to be carried out before they were given. The poet Mario Meunier, his secretary, had need of all his affectionate veneration and the patience of a saint to endure the despot's unreasonable demands. The word "obedience" was continually on the sculptor's lips and he spoke sneeringly of Baudelaire's poem about the man who had a serpent in his breast, which, if he said: "I insist," would answer "No." When he was in a less severe mood his talk would take an ironical turn, with an occasional flash of Aristophanic humour. His good-tempered smile would give place to a faun-like grin that tinged his handsome features with meanness. His robust optimism and his acceptance of human limitations were altered: "I was wrong about human nature; people are imbeciles," he declared bitterly. Or: "What a tragedy the mere existence of a man can be! And how terrible it is to live out one's own without a thought for that of other men!" In June of 1914 he wrote to Emile Bergerat to thank him for a book:

My dear friend:
    Your book is as profound as life itself. It makes me love you more than ever, for you understand what a dreadful thing life is.
    With devotion, to Madame and to you, dear Bergerat,
                                                            A. Rodin

An evil spell seemed still to be hovering over the Hôtel Biron. Rodin was in the south of France with the Duchess. They visited Gabriel Hanotaux at Cabé-Roquebrune and went to Rome to see John Marshall who represented the Metropolitan Museum of New York in Italy, and to attend to another matter. In 1907 he had shown a reworked enlargement of *L'Homme qui Marche,* perhaps his subtlest and most powerful piece of sculpture. Despite Limet's skill in giving a metallic surface the appearance of antiquity, the sculptor had insisted upon his recommencing the patina three times. In 1911, a group of admirers bought this copy for the price of its casting and offered it to the French government, expressing their desire for it to be placed in the court of the Farnese Palace in Rome. Rodin was filled with joy at the prospect of seeing his work among the antiquities at the French Embassy. But the headless and armless figure offended M. Barrère and he declared it to be "nothing but a broken statue." "Are antiques never broken?" was Rodin's arrogant reply. He hoped then and there to convince the ambassador, but he did not succeed in doing so, and his friends nicknamed M. Barrère *l'homme qui ne marche pas.*

However, nothing could interfere with his delight at seeing Rome again after thirty years. The city dazzled him even more now than when he had first seen it. "Oh, Rome, how vividly alive you are, because of your beauty!" I was mortified on his return when I praised the charms of Paris in bright April sunlight to have him reply: "Paris is beautiful no doubt, but nothing to Rome."

Things had been going well for the proposed Rodin Museum when, in the spring of 1912, an incident occurred which seriously endangered its chances. There was no dancer of repute who did not want to dance for Rodin, the sculptor of movement; and he was grateful to them for the unusual opportunities for study which they afforded him. He knew and admired Loie Fuller and Isadora Duncan, had made studies of the latter, and was fascinated by the Javanese dancers at the *Exposition Universelle* of 1900; and in 1906, at the Pré Catelan Festival, he was greatly intrigued by King Sisowath's Cambodian ballerinas whom he followed to Marseilles in an attempt to learn the secret of their hieratism and the strange grace of their people.

In 1912 he saw the Ballets Russes, particularly *L'Après-Midi d'un Faune,* with Nijinsky's choreography and Debussy's music, and based on Mallarmé's poem. Parisians of that time remember the stormy scene when half the audience madly applauded the celebrated dancer's performance and the other hissed its disgust

218

with the realism of his choreography. The following day Gaston Calmette crucified Nijinsky in *Le Figaro*:

"We had an unseemly faun whose movements were brutishly erotic and whose gesturings were grossly indecent. . . . Well-deserved hisses greeted the too expressive pantomime of this mis-shapen animal-like body, hideous when it faced us and even more hideous in profile."

A select public, passionately interested in matters of art in those pre-war days, largely composed of artists and headed by Odilon Redon, proclaimed their admiration for Nijinsky in the press. Roger Marx begged Rodin to do likewise; he consented and Marx wrote an article to which no objection could be made except that stylistically it was pure Marx and not at all Rodin. This appeared in *Le Matin* over the latter's signature, and, the same day, Nijinsky went to the Hôtel Biron to thank Rodin who was childishly disappointed to find him an ill-formed little man in conventional clothes instead of the exquisite spirit whose flight towards the infinite had stirred his sculptor's heart.

Calmette's reply appeared at once:

"As for M. Rodin whom I admire profoundly as one of our most illustrious and skilful sculptors, I cannot accept his judgment in this matter of theatrical morals. . . . In replying to him I need only call attention to the fact that he has hung in the former chapel of the *Sacré Coeur* Convent School and in the empty rooms once occupied by nuns a series of lewd drawings and sketches exaggerating the brutishly lustful motions of the Faun who was deservedly hissed yesterday at the Châtelet. And, if I must speak my whole mind, the diseased pantomine of the dancer . . . offends me far less than the spectacle offered every day by M. Rodin in the former Convent School of the *Sacré Coeur* to his numberless swooning admirers or self-satisfied snobs.

"It is inconceivable that the State, that is, the taxpayers of France, should have spent five millions upon the purchase of the

Hôtel Biron for the sole purpose of housing, free of charge, the richest of our sculptors. That is the real scandal, and the Government must deal with it."

Thus the scheme for the museum was seriously delayed, if not permanently wrecked. I went to see Rodin at once. At the lofty entrance to the Hôtel Biron, I found a man leaning against the wall, bent with weariness and despair. It was Roger Marx and, greatly disturbed, I asked him if he were ill. He told me almost sobbing that a terrible thing had happened to him and that he did not feel at all well. He had just left Rodin who, alarmed by the attack upon him in *Le Figaro,* had written to *Le Matin* stating that he was not the author of the article signed with his name; whereupon the newspaper had demanded an explanation from Marx. He had gone at once to the Hôtel Biron to beseech Rodin not to discredit him, but had encountered a cold determination to leave things as they were. Marx, who had a weak heart, was on the point of collapse, and I begged him to go home at once. I had been present when Rodin had agreed to sign the article and I promised my confirmation if the need for it should arise. I also promised to speak respectfully but firmly to our terrible friend. How could he have fallen so completely under the domination of his disastrous adviser? Could such culpable weakness exist in such a great man?

Mme de Ch—— was with him and before I had said a dozen words she declared that the article could only make trouble for M. Rodin and that his action had been necessary. I was appalled by the sculptor's inflexible expression, but I made an earnest plea: his old friend Roger Marx; his unfailing supporter and the author of so many splendid tributes—but my effort was vain. Nothing could relax the unfeeling harshness of his determination, and I withdrew, doubly afflicted by Marx's despair and the great man's obstinate belittling of himself.

The disavowal, to which *Le Matin* gave no publicity, did no good. The war was on again, and there was a fresh crop of libellous

The Poet and Love (*Le Poète et l'Amour*). COURTESY OF THE MUSÉE RODIN

Head of Balzac. COURTESY OF THE METROPOLITAN MUSEUM OF ART

caricatures including one by Sem in *Excelsior,* with the odious caption: "The Sacred Goat," and one by Forain that filled half a page of *Le Figaro* showing a model undressing in the studio at the Hôtel Biron and captioned thus: "Master, where shall I put my togs?" "There, in the oratory." This was preposterous; Rodin never went near the chapel, which was a hundred and fifty feet away from the pavilion. Finally, certain headliners of the Ballets Russes being known for their peculiar tastes, it was one short step farther for Rodin, who had proclaimed his admiration for Nijinsky, to be accused of similar vices. The gossip-column editors took that step joyfully, and Galoché, his old caster, tells of seeing the tears falling down onto his employer's white beard as he groaned: "Now they're saying that I'm a pederast!" But devotion to art was his strongest preoccupation, when he was not depressed, and, being determined to make drawings of Nijinsky, the young dancer posed for him at Meudon.

Rodin was hotly defended by the newspapers that placed art above politics, such as *Gil Blas,* controlled by Pierre Mortier, and *Comoedia* by Pavlovsky, and they published my articles on the proposed museum. *Le Figaro, Le Gaulois,* and *La Liberté* dropped the affair till further orders.

He had a grudge against me for interfering on behalf of Marx for whose death he had very nearly been responsible. And this was not his first act of injustice; six years before, he had literally driven Rilke from Meudon, "driven out like a thieving servant," said the heart-broken poet in a letter of great dignity, since published. The cause of that trouble had been a trifle without the least significance. Later, Rodin forgot his anger and made it up with Rilke; but what bitter memories for those he had wounded! These incidents were not known of and could not be compared until long afterwards; otherwise they might have revealed a psychological disorder to some careful observer. But no one noticed it in time to prevent the unfortunate consequences.

Mme de Ch—— was polite to important friends like MM. Gabriel Hanotaux and Dujardin-Baumetz, but she misapprehended Rodin's true interests and sought to alienate those whom, in her ignorance, she thought would be of no use to him. One morning Mario Meunier asked me, for his employer, whether I would replace Charles Morice who was ill, and give a lecture at the Cercle Chateaubriand with Rodin in the chair. The lecture was to be a full statement of his ideas on Gothic architecture and would be called *Les Cathédrales de France*. Meunier brought me a large envelope full of notes taken by the sculptor during his cathedral pilgrimages.

The lecture was attended by a large audience. The Duchess was there, noisy and full of spirits. She overwhelmed me with congratulations, but I discovered later that she had done her best to dissuade Rodin from entrusting me with the task. My old friend's affection for me must have been steadfast indeed to have withstood the daily attacks made upon it. The Comtesse de Noailles, who had his admiration and deep affection, knew what this secret plotting could accomplish. She was ill and full of caprice, and he found it impossible to finish his bust of her. She liked it, nevertheless, and after the sculptor's death she asked me to come to talk to her about it: "No doubt after my death they'll put a bust of me somewhere," she said, "and I would like it to be that one." With this in mind she had previously asked Rodin for it, and he, usually so generous, had asked a large sum—one suspects at whose deplorable instigation—to repay him for the work he had done. Later he came to his senses and apologized to his friend, his "adored poet," who told me of the incident in her characteristic, half-melancholy, half-rebellious manner, putting all the blame on "the horrible Duchess."

Charles Morice had also to endure the sculptor's cruel injustice. He had been asked to revise the manuscript of *Les Cathédrales de France* and had written an introduction which was, to be sure, much too long and ponderous. Rodin was dissatisfied with Morice's revisions; he accordingly gave the proofs first to M. Hanotaux and then to M. Louis Gillet. Neither of these later revisions pleased him and he returned the proofs to Morice, but he postponed the book's publication indefinitely. The Duchess advised him to discard the fifty-page introduction. This infuriated Morice whom, though he had never admitted it to Rodin, she had already exasperated unbearably and sent off profoundly grieved at the way in which she was alienating the faithful band of his worshippers.

One cold rainy night near the Gare Montparnasse I met a tall thin figure hurrying through the downpour like one of the damned fleeing the wrath of Heaven. Charles Morice drew me towards a lamp-post and began to shout with the voice of a fanatic: I was to blame for it all; I had failed in my duty to Rodin; I had abandoned him to that ghoul who was stupefying and exploiting him. . . . When a woman was fortunate enough to win the affection of a great man, it was her duty to herself and to the world to protect him from adventurers—even against his own weaknesses. . . . I had shown myself unworthy of my good fortune and the evil bewitchment of Rodin would soon be irreparable. I protested weakly at first, then energetically. Had I not for the last fifteen years given him every proof of my devotion? Was it not true that, without fortune or influence, braving slander and ridicule, I had dedicated most of my time and strength to him? Would a man as dictatorial and peremptory as Rodin tolerate the least interference in his private life? The only thing possible was to continue my efforts for the establishment of the museum. Charles Morice left me not even half convinced that I could do nothing more.

It was true that poor Rodin was drifting towards the weakness and credulity of old age. He was confused and fatigued by endless receptions and useless visits. He had to listen to absurd stories: the Duchess declared that if the French Court were only in existence she would have her ancient rights and would be able to say "my cousin" to the King of England and the German Emperor; then, in another vein, she maintained that the soul of Maria, Rodin's beloved sister, was reincarnated in her. She would be taking him to fortune-tellers and hypnotists next. She worried him with tales of robbery, and after some supposed burglars had got into the gardens of the Hôtel Biron at night she made him ask the Prefect of Police for a special officer to guard the property. She also arranged that a watch-dog should be bought, to leap at the throat of anyone coming anywhere near the sculptor. Dora was a fine German shepherd bitch who understood no language but that of her own country. Knowing nothing of her ferocity, I put out my hand to pat her the first time I saw her. Mme de Ch—— turned pale, but Dora knew immediately that I was a dog-lover and seemed quite happy to be thus admired, and when she had forgotten the artificial maliciousness that her trainers had endeavoured to teach her she became gentle and affectionate.

Rodin's friends were angry with him for submitting to such servitude. The intemperate habits of the lady who continually exhaled the aroma of brandy and chartreuse were sneered at by the casters and other employees. They could have understood his passion if the object of it had been beautiful, but they failed to perceive the reason for the power exercised over him by this thin weasel-like woman, no longer young and much too foreign.

She got him to arrange a temporary separation from Mme Rose which she hoped would be a final break. This he had never before consented to do for anyone. On the pretext that his health required more comfort than was possible at Meudon—he actually had a touch of bronchitis—he settled in at the Hôtel Biron and only communicated with his wife through a trusted servant. Fresh upheavals and redoubled remorse on his part resulted. He could not help thinking about the ageing companion he had abandoned to poor health and great unhappiness at Meudon. When he travelled with "his Muse" he sent Rose instructions for her well-being:

My dear Rose,

I stopped off at Lyons to arrange a show of drawings.

I am anxious for you to do what I told you about putting a curtain at the second window and sleeping in my bed near the fire.

Auguste Rodin

Write me care of M. Hanotaux

Cabé-Roquebrune

Alpes-Maritimes

He was familiar with her carelessness in such matters and realized that she would try to hurt her tyrannical master by hurting herself. He wrote again more affectionately:

My dear Rose,

Are you taking good care of yourself? Have you done what I asked you to do? Have you put the Japanese curtain in front of the window, and is the wire fixed to the coachman's room at night? It is cold here this morning but yesterday at Lyons and on the way here it was warm.

Write me whether you are sleeping well. Don't get up early; and use the carriage whenever you like.

I was at Menton and now I'm at Cabé-Roquebrune with M. Hanotaux, where you are to write me.

Your devoted

Auguste Rodin

Even from Rome where there were so many things to distract him he thought from time to time of the desolation caused by his absence from Meudon:

My dear Rose,   27 January 1912

I'm at Rome and have had rain every day I've been in Italy. Write me your news and remember to be careful about staying out in the garden. Use the carriage; sleep longer in the mornings; it will do you good not to get up till about eight o'clock.

I send you my love and will write again in a few days to tell you if things turn out to my liking.

Your devoted

Auguste Rodin

Tell me whether you would like me to send some money. Write care of M. Marshall, 60 via Sistina, Rome Italy.

M. Fravaton, of the Ministry of Finance, informed me that M. Klotz was still being overwhelmed by requests concerning the museum project, and he advised me to tell Rodin that it would be to his own advantage to put an end to these importunities. This I did immediately, finding him less reasonable and less friendly to me. He was alone in his studio, care-worn and gloomy. He said the matter should be left to accomplish itself in several different ways, and that I seemed to want to "complicate everything." This hurt my feelings deeply, but my astonishment was greater. I told him I would leave it to him to continue the work which had occupied me for three years and was about to take my leave when he asked me whether I wanted to "say good-bye to Madame." I shook my head and the Satanic smile which I so disliked spread over his features. This was in June of 1912. I left Paris shortly, and did not see him again for three or four months.

IX. RETURN TO ROSE – ENGLAND – ROME

I KEPT on receiving official documents relating to the museum, and at the end of October I took them to Rodin. To my great surprise, he was alone; he looked rested and welcomed me warmly. In his long monastic robe he stood working at a little figurine, and he spoke with the discretion of someone trying to cast a veil over painful events, while his delicate fingers hovered about the clay.

He informed me that he had parted from Mme de Ch——, that he could no longer endure the disorganized life she had made him lead and that some very serious things had happened. Supported by two powerful newspaper men, and in the presence of a notary, she had got him to sign a contract or will conceding important rights to her and her husband relating to the reproduction of the works he was going to leave to the State. He had believed for a long time that her affection was disinterested, but finally discovered that he had fallen into a trap and would have to pay dearly for his self-delusion. There had been the usual presents: her bust, a large marble figure called *Le Sommeil,* and many water-colours; but he had also been obliged to supply her financial needs and those of her husband who was a gambler. Other more disquieting incidents, the nature of which he did not disclose, had convinced him that the only possible way out was separation. Then he had been very ill without being able to discover the name of the disease; a milk diet had been required to cure him.

All this was spoken uncomplainingly, moderately, and with all his former lucidity, with no trace of masculine vanity and a noble

227

acceptance of defeat. I would not have thought it possible to tell the story of a quarrel with such dignity.

I let him know how glad I was to find him free and able now to live his ordinary life and to work peacefully. "I ought never to have stopped living it," he said, as though unable to understand what insanity had been responsible for those six or seven years of slavery. "And there was my wife, poor little field-flower that I nearly crushed; and I had your friendship—these precious years of your youth. . . ." I protested and he continued, "Yes, my friend, it's all very well to spend two or three years defending an artist, but fifteen! . . ."

Every trace of my resentment vanished; his confession made everything clear: his fits of bad temper, the Duchess's deceptive kindness, her desire to get rid of me, that is, to send me and my museum project off to America so that she might be free to plunder as she pleased. The people round Rodin were delighted at her departure; her intimacy with the sculptor whom they deeply respected and her vulgar arrogance had offended them. They now eagerly awaited my visits to the rue de Varenne in order to horrify me with some outrageous tale of drawings taken from the studio, wrapped round her leg, or the filching of a portfolio of watercolours; the costly gift of a ruby sold and replaced by a garnet without Rodin's noticing it; and once the accusations were so frightful that I fled the studio, convinced that everyone in it had gone mad.

Immediately after the quarrel, Rodin returned to his old life. He sent a message to Rose at Meudon that he would be there in the evening after finishing his day's work. There was a simplicity and a nobility about this home-coming: she waited at the end of the avenue of chestnut trees for her ageing husband:

"*Bonsoir, Rose!*"

"*Bonsoir, mon amie,*" was her only reply as she took him by the arm and led him towards the house. Thus their life together began again, with its tranquil joys and its sudden storms.

Rose's faithfulness and self-denial could now be assessed at their true value, and one August evening in 1913, when alone on a visit to Gabriel Hanotaux, he wrote her these few lines:

24 August 1913

My dear Rose,
  This letter is just to tell you that my mind is full of the greatness of God's gift to me when He put you at my side.
  Keep this thought of mine in your generous heart.
  I return Tuesday.

Your

Auguste Rodin

La Pressoir,
Pargnan,
par Beaurieux, (Aisne) [1]

The Duchess did not accept her misfortune without protest. She overwhelmed Rodin with imploring messages, sent him such mementoes of their dead passion as the scarf with which she had danced the *bourée;* she also sent emissaries, one of whom was a relative, who pled her cause with emphasis on the financial as well as the sentimental aspect of the situation. And I thought I was dreaming when the Duke besought me to intercede with Rodin on behalf of his wife—the sculptor "had become so capricious." He explained that the Duchess was by nature fitted for the rôle of Egeria. Before devoting herself to Rodin, she had lavished her attentions upon an eminent prelate whom she had met in South America. "After all," I asked Rodin when I had told him of this incredible interview, "could M. de Ch—— be a decent man?" "A pimp is never a decent man," he replied serenely.

He was far from reassured as to the results of their intriguing, and was tormented by the thought of the contract they had got him to sign. I was unfamiliar with notarial practices, but I knew that one will could be nullified by another executed subsequently,

---

[1] The original of this letter belongs to M. Sacha Guitry who, when lecturing on "The Wives of Artists," called it "the most beautiful of all love letters."

while a donation was practically irrevocable. I told him this, but he could not remember the exact nature of the document he had signed. He asked me if I would get the advice of the Ministry of Finance and accompanied me to the foot of the stairs leading to M. Fravaton's office at the Louvre. M. Fravaton told me to urge the sculptor to write out again on stamped paper the details of his bequest to the State, and he promised to attend to the matter promptly. Rodin, happily in good health now, was almost seventy-three, and time was short. Early in January of 1913 I received the draft of a contract and a list of the members of the committee who were to deal, some with the financial part and others with the inventory of the contents of the Paris and Meudon studios. The list included MM. Fravaton, Maurice Reclus, from the Ministry of Fine Arts; Depeyster, Inspector of Finance; Doussot, Inspector of State Property; Collignon of the *Institut;* André Michel, Curator of the Louvre; Dayot, Inspector-General of the *Beaux-Arts,* and Léonce Bénédite, Curator of the Luxembourg.

I carried these documents enthusiastically to Rodin, who told me he would have to examine carefuly and that this would take him some time. Again he seemed inexplicably withdrawn and anxious.

Actually, his last adventure had left him disorganized and easily worried. Several months before this I had told him of an article: *L'Enseignement d'art de Rodin,* which Marius and Ary Leblond of *La Vie* had asked me to write. Upon my reading him the proofs of it, he became unaccountably agitated. The article was quite an ordinary one, its only fault being its lack of novelty. I had mentioned some of the sculptors whom Rodin had many times referred to as representatives of the new School: Desbois, Bourdelle, Maillol, Despiau, Schneeg, Dejean, and Halou. He reproached me sharply with having got him into terrible difficulties and declared that the article must absolutely not be allowed to appear. In spite of my confusion I thought he seemed afraid of making enemies of the sculptors whose names were not mentioned. I promised to communicate at once with my friends, the Leblond brothers. In the studio at the time was Br——, a journalist, greatly annoyed and embarrassed by what had taken place; he was up to his ears in the famous *Notes* which the sculptor allowed too many scribblers to make use of. As I was preparing to go, Rodin declared in the same harsh tones that he was ready to indemnify the editors of *La Vie* if they would agree not to publish the article. I was upset by this unnecessary and absurd treatment of my friends and took my departure, disgusted and unhappy. Life seemed very difficult and I badly needed the support of Rodin's friendship and enthusiasm. Now this support was failing me. He was changeable, forgetful, and unjust—exactly like other men. I was so depressed when I reached the Gare des Invalides that I stood there weeping miserably. Then I heard heavy hurried footsteps behind me and a hand was slipped under my arm:

"Now you're cross with me," said Rodin, his voice gentle again.

"I'm not cross, but why must you be so harsh with me when all I want is your happiness?"

"I know—I know . . ." he replied, pressing my arm, "your affection for your friends is amazing, but don't be cross with me because I'm old and hard-pressed. . . . And that fool Br—— had to be there!"

I laughed at his reference to the innocent man who had been present during the scene and Rodin's expression showed his gratitude for my returning good spirits. He kissed my hand affectionately and went off to catch his train to Meudon.

The next day brought a fresh reversion; the following letter arrived by messenger:

We must send a summons or something to stop that article. The injury to me would be horrible. Come as soon as possible and do what you can. The magazine will have to be satisfied with an indemnity.

Yours,

Rodin

I hurried off to find Marius Leblond who, out of deference for Rodin, offered to accompany me to his studio. It was too late to suppress the article; the November 23rd issue of *La Vie* had just come out and Leblond brought along a copy for the man to whom he wished once more to pay tribute. Rodin grasped the magazine and looked at the forbidden page, but he said nothing. At that moment Mme Martin, his secretary, returned from the police station where she had been sent to have the publication of the magazine stopped. She laughingly told us of the amusement her request had caused, and the teapot tempest subsided even more quickly than it had arisen. Rodin never mentioned the insignificant article again.

Mme Martin, whom I met then for the first time, had taken an active part in the quarrel between Rodin and Mme de Ch——, and his old friend Edmond Bigand-Kaire, formerly a captain in the merchant marine, had been similarly involved. He had the force of a man accustomed to battling with the elements. Intelligent, cultivated, a lover of the arts, this native of the Franche-Conté lived at Marseilles in the winter and in the summer at Saint-Mitre du Martigue. He was interested in the study of Provençal and longed to have Rodin know Frédéric Mistral. During his travels he had exercised his good taste by purchasing many precious objects for Rodin, among which were a Persian manuscript, an Egyptian cat in bronze, and a bird beautifully carved in wood. These the sculptor would take from his cases and show to his guests with the ceremony of a priest at the altar. The Captain would frequently send him Virgilian gifts of wine from his vineyards, figs and olives from his garden, and bundles of lavender cut on the hill-sides of Provence.

My dear Friend,

Thanks for your always devoted friendship which declares itself in my difficult moments. Thank dear Durand for me. Perhaps I can come to visit you, but I don't know. I can't keep promises and don't dare to make them.

My work is so exacting. Thanks, friend, for what you tell me about the vintages—but I impose on you; you shouldn't be so generous.

Your friend,

Rodin

Having been informed, by persons unknown to me, of the manoeuvres of "the black gang," as he called them, the Captain courageously interfered. He came to Paris in the middle of summer and exhibited positive proofs—no one knew where he obtained them—of the plot against "the Sultan of Meudon," and he declared flatly: "As long as I live and with all my strength, whether you like it or not, I will fight any of your enemies, French or foreign, who attempt to carry out their sinister schemes." Whereupon followed a lengthy argument and Rodin, who was extremely sensitive about his private life, took his brotherly advice in good part, acknowledging it with touching frankness:

My dear Friend,

I have received your sympathetic letter and I send you my best wishes too.

I've done what you told me and I'm working hard, but I don't take very good care of myself. I need exercise. You don't tell me enough about yourself. I believe you get happiness from being a true friend—which is unusual; the ancients praised this conception of life and wrote essays about it.

I don't see what can happen to me, but I'm being as careful as a man walking in a forest after dark.

Au revoir, my dear Bigand,

Your grateful friend,

Rodin

Knowing that the winter was difficult for Rodin and his wife on their windy hill-side at Meudon, M. Bigand-Kaire tried to lure them to Hyères, where Stevenson had attempted for several successive years to re-establish his health. But Rodin declined his offer:

233

77, rue de Varenne,
20 January 1913

My dear Friend,

Your active kindness to me makes me very happy. The break is absolute and I don't know whether there are or will be any complications. I'm going today to see your friend, the former Prefect of Versailles.

I like the idea of coming to Hyères, especially because my wife cannot stand the Paris climate, nor can I.

I've been waiting for two months for the authorization from Rome to put the new pedestal under *L'Homme qui Marche*. I've seen M. Bérard and M. Poincaré and expect to hear any day now. I couldn't think of leaving Paris. The Hôtel Biron affair has to pass the budget committee, in order to have the financial end of it absolutely certain, and I must get all the support I can. The proposition is such an ideal one for me that I cannot afford to neglect anything. The Ministry of Finance has sent me a contract and I am examining it now.

So you see things are moving. The President, the new one, is favourably disposed.

I am touched by your kindness and I hope your legs are better in that good climate, but you must keep away from the marshes. Be careful about that.

I hope to have a visit from you here in the spring.

Your friend,
A. Rodin

Please thank your friend Dr. Melchior.

A month later he thought everything was settled and did not realize how much had still to be done or how long it would take to obtain the final vote.

77 rue de Varenne
25 February 1913

Monsieur Fravaton,
Ministry of Finance,

I hear that the question of the museum has been settled satisfactorily and I am very happy about it. Many thanks for the great assistance you have given me.

Will you please tell the Minister of my appreciation. I hope soon to have the honour of expressing this to him myself.

My sincere regards,
Auguste Rodin

In the meantime, the functionaries of *Les Musées Nationaux* prepared the inventories. In May I encountered M. Léonce Bénédite at Meudon. He spoke of Rodin with honeyed deference, but underneath could be discerned the anxiety of a man who feared the lion's claw. He was hated by Rodin's disciples because of his denunciation of their idol's sculpture (caused by lack of understanding, said Desbois, rather than hostility). The wind now blew from another quarter and M. Bénédite's opinions had changed accordingly, but he was afraid Rodin would remember his criticisms.

The sculptor had as little confidence in the State authorities as he had in individuals when his emotions were not involved, and he asked me to take duplicate inventories. M. Bénédite was very much occupied elsewhere and he begged me to make up a list of the drawings and engravings. I found that some of them were not "fixed," particularly the fine vigorous academy figures which had been done in Rodin's young days at the *Petite Ecole* and preserved in tissue-paper coverings. I suggested that the fixing might be done by my young artist friend, Mme Villedieu-Pautrier, who had often been to his Paris studio. To this the sculptor agreed at once and she went with me to Meudon. When our visit was over he took us to the station, stopping on the way to cut a bunch of his finest gladioli which he placed silently in Marie Villedieu's lap.

M. Bénédite wrote me an extremely civil letter thanking me for the lists I had sent him and telling me confidentially that M. Léon Berard, who had been made Under Secretary at the Fine Arts Ministry, seemed apprehensive about getting the approval of the Chambers. I had found this eminent statesman, as well as his young predecessor, M. Jacquier, to be in favour of the project, but other personages now in power were hostile, especially M. Guist'hau, the Minister of Education, upon whom his friend Briand had been requested to exert his influence.

The making of the inventories pleased Rodin and his spirits improved. He occasionally asked me to go with him to the antique dealers on the left bank where he bought Empire console-tables and benches to complete the furnishings for the museum; and often on Sundays he and his wife would lunch with me before going to vespers at Notre-Dame. He loved to listen to the plain chant which evoked memories of his religious youth and spoke to him across the centuries of his ancient progenitors, the cathedral sculptors. He was interested in the book about him which The Century Company of New York had, at the suggestion of my translator Mrs. J. K. Star, commissioned me to write. But storms continued to rumble both in Paris and at Meudon. Mme Martin, who was deciphering with great difficulty and typing the "notes" which filled twenty note-books, covered endless scraps of paper and even cuffs, had been bluntly thanked for her labours: "I'm going to leave literature alone; it interferes with my sculpture. Go back to your own writing; I'll help you. If I need you I'll let you know."

As a matter of fact, she had a vivid and caustic style, and he had promised to write a preface for her forthcoming book of short stories. When the volume was ready for the printer, he asked me to write the preface, and when I told him that a few lines from him would be of far greater value to the author he flew into a rage.

Mme Martin was a curious person; she was of humble birth, voluble and sharp-tongued—a little dark woman whose eyes glowed in a rather Japanese-like face which was ugly in such an interesting way that Rodin should have modelled it. Without fully appreciating the sculptor's greatness, she had a strong emotion for him, in which affection, ridicule, admiration, and sarcasm were compounded; and for those who schemed to exploit him a savage hatred—she called herself his watch-dog. She would patiently endure his capriciousness, then leave him for a time, but she could not long resist the magnetism of his genius. She handled him perfectly with her caressing Southern impudence, and fed him pills of bitter truth coated with sugared flattery. In this manner she had been able to open his eyes to the intrigues of Mme de Ch——.

Though she had succeeded, with the help of Captain Bigand, in dethroning the Duchess, no one had been able to cure Rodin of his weakness for women, of his need of their presence: "I did not realize that, though they aroused my scorn at twenty, they would delight me at seventy," he wrote. "I scorned them because I was frightened of them." And again: "My old age is adorned with roses; I am surrounded by ministering women and there could be nothing more delightful."

Georgette D——, a pretty young creature, who had been his model for three years and was well aware of this weakness, resolved to profit by it. She began by throwing a doubt upon the honesty of the servants at the Hôtel Biron. They were quickly discharged and her mother, a sly woman obviously ready for any mischief, was employed. The stage was now set for one of the most sinister of his experiences. Upon information supplied by Georgette certain works on sale in Paris and London were seized and declared false by the sculptor. Both mother and daughter were in league with several of the dealers, and they persuaded Rodin to employ dishonest agents. Confused by this plotting and scheming, he sent his caster, Paul Cruet, to England to make inquiries there. The whole affair was extremely obscure. Although certain pieces were clearly imitations, Rodin was forced in the presence of the police commissioner who was astounded at such mistakes to authenticate those which had been seized in Paris. Obliged thus to withdraw his charges, he had to pay heavy indemnities. In short, he again became gloomy, exhausted, and was, as he admitted to his friend Bigand, "in despair at the confusion in the rue de Varenne." The Captain besought him again, for the sake of his dignity, his self-respect as an artist, even his security, never again to take up with any scheme suggested by this new "black gang."

This miserable affair, which got into the papers at the most crucial moment in the campaign for the museum, was the more distressing in that it seemed to justify those who had always alleged that Rodin was insane.

Following his private conception of distributive justice, he rid himself of honest servants and kept the rascals. The devoted Paul Cruet was discharged, but recalled several months later. Then the tenant of the Hôtel Biron, feeling that the atmosphere should be cleared, resorted to flight; he went south with the woman who had never betrayed him, his "kind Rose," and he dismissed Georgette and her mother by telegram. They were replaced by an honest couple, relatives of Rose, but they continued nevertheless to extract money and gifts from the man they had bewitched.

Fortunately nothing could interfere with his art. He did much less sculpture now, but he drew and painted constantly; thousands of drawings and water-colours accumulated, and, as though his means of reproduction were inadequate, he devoted hours to setting down his thoughts and impressions. The rebellious school-boy, the former artist-artisan, paying little heed to grammar and spelling, had now become, thanks to his acute observation and his poetic gifts, the subtle notator. The man usually called illiterate by his enemies used images which caused the secret envy of more than one writer. With the determination of one who feels that the gift of knowledge may elude him, he kept on studying. He read and re-read Homer, Aeschylus, Virgil and Ovid. He meditated upon Plato; Tacitus seemed to him a genius at portraiture, almost a colleague; Ronsard, and Longus in Amyot's translation delighted him; he had a passion for Rousseau's *Confessions,* not to mention the Romantic poets, or Balzac, or Flaubert, and he was filled with curiosity about certain philosophers, such as Spinoza and Schopenhauer. Since he did not read the books of his contemporaries, who bore him a grudge for it, the legend of his indifference to things of the mind became established. Two or three years before the war he asked me to make him a list of "good books" for reading at night during the long vigils caused by an arterial disease. Classical music intoxicated him, but on going to Bayreuth with the desire to enter the Wagnerian forest he was profoundly disappointed; *Parsifal* seemed to him nothing more than bad church music. Nor did he understand Debussy who came to Meudon and played him some of his own favourite passages. He furnished his mind untiringly from the best sources. Is it therefore surprising that he produced extraordinary things, luminous ellipses?

Georgette often posed at full length on a couch and he would sit leaning forward, exploring the face encircled by blond hair with a gaze so penetrating that the young woman occasionally lowered her eyes. Then he wrote, handed me his *notes* to copy, and I would piece together the exquisitely sensual fragments:

"This head lying on a pillow is a bas-relief. The features are perfectly placed, the eye-brows straight, the nose, a region of beautiful parallels, expresses unmarred regularity. . . . The eyes of a child beneath a woman's eye-lids. . . . The serenity of the eyes, their tranquil lines, her own calm ecstasy. . . .

"Sometimes the eyes seem to be the abode of spirits.

"The lovely head rests at the edge of the couch.

"An animal-like gentleness . . . a fainting heart when the tyrant Passion has vanished. Like a vampire he drains away the slender remnants of tranquillity, the delicate modellings of serenity. . . .

The hair falls about the cheeks . . . the golden pyramid of the hair.

"The hair is a veil tinted like autumn leaves; the ears are transparent and almost hidden by it, loosened and escaping its bonds. . . .

"This lovely fringe amply outlining the face—a corn-field with sheaves of gold. . . .

"The moist red mouth is delightful, serpent-like in its delicate curves; the rounded eye-lids are closed, crossed by a seam of lashes. . . .

"There is a tender harmony between the eyes and the mouth. . . .'

He leaned closer to the recumbent figure, and, fearing lest the sound of his voice might disturb its loveliness, he whispered: "Hold your mouth as though you were playing the flute. Again! Again!" Then he wrote:

"The mouth, the luxurious protruding lips, sensuously eloquent. . . .

"Here the perfumed breath comes and goes like bees darting in and out of the hive. . . ."

How happy he was during these hours of deep serenity, when he could enjoy the untroubled play of his faculties! A supreme ecstasy, for it had no end:

"What a joy is my ceaseless study of the human flower!

"How fortunate that in my profession I am able to love and also to speak of my love!"

At Meudon, Mme Rodin had engaged a pretty young cook; the sculptor was very attentive to her, and, since his reputation was not of the best in these matters, the virtuous young woman, who had a jealous husband and was greatly attached to her mistress, became somewhat uneasy. "You have the profile of the Bour-

Balzac (*Balzac*). COURTESY OF THE MUSEE RODIN

Falguière the Sculptor (*Falguière*). COURTESY OF THE MUSEE RODIN

bons," he told her, "and a lovely neck like Mme de Montespan's. I would like to do a bust of you." She had never heard of these illustrious people and was astounded at his request, but she consented and had no reason to regret doing so. Rodin treated her with the respect he accorded great ladies who paid him large sums to execute their busts. This one of Mme Grégy was very beautiful —one of his last works—and he generously rewarded his sitter for her patience.

Early in 1914 René Viviani took M. Guist'hau's place as Minister of Education. Léon Bourgeois arranged for me to see him and his first words showed him to be completely unaware of what had been accomplished. In the peevish manner he often adopted, he told me that he had other matters to occupy him that were more urgent than the wishes of M. Rodin. Did he have a presentiment of the terrible events that were soon to take place? Then, in a more reasonable mood, he promised to look into the matter and advised me to see the new Under Secretary at the Fine Arts Ministry, M. Albert Dalimier. Marcel Sembat of the Fine Arts Commission in the Chamber declared that he would bring the question up in the Chamber himself.

I saw little of Rodin then, for he was ill and scarcely ever left Meudon; and my own health was far from good. When he came again to Paris I told him what I had been doing; he was coldly disinterested and said that his health and that of his wife required a long stay in the south; he was on the point of leaving. Besides, why should I waste my time in efforts that never accomplished anything? They were quite useless.

"Useless?" I exclaimed, deeply hurt. "You are mistaken, as you will soon realize."

"I only judge by results," he answered coldly.

The Duchess had failed in her efforts to get rid of me, but his model and her house-keeper mother had been clever enough to warp his judgment. Moreover, after a long career of beating off attacks, he had acquired a touch of persecution mania, was always unconsciously on the defensive and suspicious, even of a friend of twenty years' standing.

Three days later, the Under Secretary announced the deposition of a bill at the offices of the Chamber regarding the establishment of a Rodin museum. M. Fravaton asked me to arrange at once for a conference with the sculptor and I was obliged to tell him that Rodin had left Paris for two or three months.

I had a letter from Marseilles in which he withdrew the authorization he had granted me for the taking of the photographs to illustrate my book: *Auguste Rodin, L'Homme et son Art,* but he rashly—though with great reluctance, it is true—allowed his *Aphrodite* to be used on the stage of the Renaissance Theatre in a play based on Pierre Louÿs's famous novel. As he had feared, several journalists criticized him severely, and *Le Figaro* expressed its regret that "the nation's pride" should have turned himself, as it were, into a theatrical property-man.

M. Bigand-Kaire had undertaken to find Rodin a furnished apartment at Hyères, but on arriving at Marseilles with his wife and a servant in the midst of a terrific storm, the sculptor gave up the idea and could not even see his friend who was laid up with rheumatism at Saint-Mitre du Martigue. He sent him a letter the handwriting of which betrayed his gloom and fatigue:

24 February, 1914

My dear Bigand,

Exasperated at not seeing you. Both of us ailing and we [sentence not finished]

I catch a fresh cold every morning with this infernal wind. I'm going straight to Menton. I am completely exhausted—my wife too, and she sends you her best regards. The weather has worn us out.

Your friend Dr. Melchior Robert is a charming man like yourself; he is lunching with us at Basso's and we shall drink to your health, dear friend, and also to our meeting at Maillane.

We are gradually getting rid of small discomforts.

Things appear to be moving in Paris; Marcel Sembat has become interested in me and has taken up the affair. But all the same it's a big responsibility for me.

How is Moreno? [2] It's terrible to think of her.

Your devoted friend,

Auguste Rodin

From Menton he occasionally visited Gabriel Hanotaux at Cabé-Roquebrune; once he dined there with Léon Bourgeois to whom he complained of neurasthenia. On his way back to Paris at the end of March, he stopped at Marseilles and finally saw Captain Bigand-Kaire who was grief-stricken at the recent death of Frédéric Mistral. He had hoped to take Rodin to see him at Maillane. The Captain was greatly troubled at finding his old friend "very much changed physically, as well as mentally."

I had started a correspondence with this sincere and loyal man, and, having told him of my vexation at Rodin's incredible changeableness, I asked him if he could explain it. He was far more perceiving than I, and he unhesitatingly put the responsibility for it upon "all those filthy Parisian vandals, French and foreign, who are using his great name for their own advancement, or, which is worse, exploiting him shamefully in his old age. And these swindlers have an easy time of it, because of his excessive friendliness and confidence at a first meeting, however casual; whereas, of those who sincerely admire him for himself and his prodigious accomplishments, he sometimes harbours inexplicable suspicions which can only come from some deep-seated disorder. I have occasionally been greatly troubled by his astoundingly paradoxical behaviour, despite a feeling that one should make an effort to take the great man as he is. Those who are privileged to be his friends

[2] A young dancer at the *Opéra Comique* who was one of Rodin's favourite models.

cannot help knowing that his sulkiness is neither malicious nor of long duration."

His stay in the south only partially re-established his health, and he and Mme Rose spent April and May with the Viviers at Châtelet-en-Brie. He wrote me from there that the *Pygmalion et Galathée* group which he had promised me long before was finished and that, on account of the great weight of the marble, I would have to arrange for a special stand.

This was the first important gift I had ever received from Rodin. The little marble group he once promised me for my mantelpiece had turned out to be much too large; this had greatly embarrassed him—he was so kind in those days—and he had asked me if I would object to his selling it in America. Thus the charming group went to the Metropolitan Museum of New York. A smaller one had been cut in marble and it was this group that he now offered me. But the floor of my apartment in the old house where Eugène Delacroix had died was found inadequate for its support, and, having been ordered to the country by my doctor, I was for the moment unable to accept the gift.

During the spring, Rodin's health improved and he went to London to be present at the opening of an exhibition of some of his works at the Duke of Westminster's palatial residence, Grosvenor House; the reception he there received cheered him greatly.

At the beginning of July, 1914, he was in such a torment over a fresh delay in the settlement of his gift to the State that I went again to the rue de Valois. Edmond Guiraud and M. Népoty of the Fine Arts Ministry introduced me to M. Dalimier, who arranged for a meeting in the rue de Varenne. The Under Secretary was anxious to act quickly, because a new project was being discussed for the transformation of the Hôtel Biron and its gardens into a sort of hostel for the numberless hordes of children for whom the city of Paris was responsible. This meeting took place on July 25—how far the government's thoughts must have been in that golden summer of 1914 from the quickly approaching disaster! M. Dalimier declared that he would like to make himself personally responsible for the establishment of the Rodin Museum. On the first of August, M. Léonce Bénédite took the Minister of Commerce, M. Etienne Clémentel, to Meudon.

On August thirtieth I met Rodin at the Fine Arts Ministry where the *Société Fraternelle de Secours aux Artistes* for which I was working had been established. His face was pale and his usual half-smile was absent.

"I'm leaving Paris with my wife. Do you think I can get a safe-conduct from the Minister?" he asked in a stricken voice.

"I doubt if M. Dalimier has to do with such things. May I ask where you intend to go?"

"To Marseilles," he answered with a shrug of his shoulders, indicating that his destination was more likely to be settled by fate than by his own preference.

"But not in this terrible heat! It would be too much for you, and for Mme Rodin."

I quickly forgot his recent unjust treatment of me and was filled with compassion for his feebleness and his helplessness: "I am taking my mother to England where one of my sisters has lived for fifteen years; would you like to travel with us? You have many friends in London."

His face brightened: "I think it would be a good idea." Then deciding rapidly: "We'll go with you to England."

"Then you must return to Meudon at once and get ready. I will attend to the tickets; also the safe-conducts if you like. We must be ready the day after tomorrow, September first."

Rodin and his wife met us at the Gare Saint-Lazare; a servant was carrying their luggage. People of every nationality crowded the station. There were no porters and each group trundled its own luggage on a barrow. I installed my three old people at the lunch counter with instructions not to move, and Rodin, for once, saw the value of obedience; I realized that if necessary he would wait there all night. Mme Rose looked very frail beneath a large hat of black lace, but she was revelling in the one pleasure that counted for anything: that of being near her husband.

Two hours later, the formalities were over and we boarded the train. The crowd poured into the compartments, paying no attention to class, and I feared we might have to stand all the way. But we managed to find seats and the train glided out of Paris towards the setting sun, and Dieppe.

Rodin kept his patriarchal dignity throughout this hurried exodus. Leaning against his massive shoulder, Mme Rose seemed to regard as matters of course the events which he spoke of with the serene melancholy of a prophet. For many years he had told me that Europe would return to a state of barbarism, that Europe knew nothing of discipline, duty, or justice, cared only for material pleasures and was hopelessly ignorant of the highest refinement of civilization: scrupulous honesty in work and a love of art. In his unpretentious language, but with a certain dignity, this son of the people who had joined the aristocracy of the mind, said: "France cries out against Germany for destroying with fire, without noticing that she herself smells of smoke."

When I spoke of the safety of the contents of his studios in Paris and at Meudon, he said: "I have left everything in charge of my caster and a watchman." Then he added gravely and with admirable resignation: "They contain the results of a great deal of work. And my antiques! If the Germans take them it won't matter, for they will still exist; but if they destroy them . . . ! Can our masterpieces in the Louvre be protected?"

We admired him less when he voiced his doubts as to a victory for France and the valour of our generals. A mystical faith, with no foundation save the memory of the calamities from which our country had splendidly emerged, enabled us to believe in her eventual triumph, and it was painful to have this faith undermined.

There were endless delays for the passage of military trains, but at dawn we arrived at Dieppe. The English boat looked many times too small for the multitude it was to carry across the Channel, and I shuddered with apprehension on realizing that I was responsible for three people over seventy. However, we were soon aboard and I began to wonder how we were to be comfortable for the five-hour crossing when, above the sea of heads, an arm signalled to us; its owner, a little Japanese man, made his way through the crowd and bowed low before Rodin. He made way for a doll-like figure no taller than a little girl of ten, clad in the costume of her race with a heavy ebony head-dress. It was Hanako, accompanied by her secretary, on her way to London to join her company. The little secretary soon found chairs for us and, after an exchange of friendly greetings, the young actress withdrew with true Japanese discretion.

London seemed far removed from blood-stained France and Belgium, and its people appeared outwardly to be living their customary existence. My mother and I had arranged to join my two sisters at Cheltenham in Gloucestershire, but I offered to take Rodin wherever he wished to go. He seemed lost and could speak no English.

"I would like to go to Cheltenham with you," he said; "I will have to see too many people if I stay here. I can't remember these English names and that will make everyone think me rude."

I told him I did not know whether the modest lodgings in Cheltenham which my sisters had taken for us would suit them, but he insisted.

Cheltenham was a charming little town and our friends were made comfortable by Mrs. Gandy who gave them her best bedroom and a small sitting-room. The other lodgers were politely discreet and there was no publicity beyond a simple announcement in the papers of the great sculptor's presence. Rodin appreciated this respect shown him by the English. He was, however, the object of profound interest for the little group of Mrs. Gandy's lodgers at Sussex House.

Outwardly our life was calm, but we were tormented by anxiety. The French newspapers had been cut down to less than half their size and contained the minimum of strictly censored reports. In England the ten- or twelve-page editions overflowed with news. And such news! The irresistible German advance, the continual driving back of our forces, and the maps which made everything terribly explicit. The heavy black line that drew nearer and nearer to Paris transfixed us with horror each morning.

The tragedy at Reims affected Rodin profoundly; he had refused to believe it until the publication of a photograph in the *Daily Mail*. Finally he regained his placidity, but Mme Rose was nervous and excitable; she was never able to forget her grudges against the sculptor for his past treatment of her, and he was continually trying to pacify her. New dresses and furs were of little avail.

"I won't wear them," she grumbled to me one day as the three of us were leaving one of London's smartest dress-shops. "It's the same at Meudon; he has the hair-dresser every morning, and he makes me have my hair done too, because he thinks it looks untidy. It doesn't suit me at all and I always pull my hair down over my eyes as soon as the man goes."

Her outpourings were not confined to me, and I was in a continual state of anxiety lest she might disclose the fact that she was not Rodin's legal wife. But Mrs. Gandy and her lodgers spoke little French and the secret was kept.

In spite of the inactive life imposed upon Rodin at Cheltenham, he did not accompany us back to Paris at the end of September. He and Mme Rose stayed with Mrs. Gandy until the cold weather came and then fled to Italy. I had no news of him that winter beyond one or two short notes and reports from returning friends. Mme Martin told me that she had seen them on their way through to Rome where Rodin would probably be doing a bust of the Pope. He had merely told her that my sisters and I had been very helpful in England.

Albert Besnard, who was then director of the Villa Medici,

said in his interesting book of reminiscences, *Sous le ciel de Rome* (published seven or eight years later): "Rodin would like to take an old palace here for several months, and would use one of its rooms to work in. . . . It will be delightful to have him among us. . . . His talk about art and nature is amazingly beautiful." Why did Besnard write so cruelly, later in the book, of the friend who always generously praised his painting. Was it because he envied the master-sculptor his prodigious reputation?

"He wanted to see people—a little Benvenuto Cellini—and we took him to M. de Billy. He came here firmly resolved to amuse himself, and I believe that in his heart he felt Rome was too much taken up with the war and not enough with him. He had aged and wore his hair *en brosse* again, having given up the curled fore-lock advised by the Duchess. This must have been the in-fluence of his wife who went everywhere with him. He was very silent and seemed greatly withdrawn from the world whose sup-port, nevertheless, he sought continually. . . . Once when driv-ing along the Appian Way, he said: 'All this is what made Poussin.' He never tired of admiring Bernini's busts and he was obviously attracted by the skilful posing. He hovered about them as though trying to discover their secret.

". . . He seemed bewildered in a city where people had some-thing to think of besides his arrival. He fled from Paris to escape the rigours of the war, and upon Italy's joining in he would flee Rome. This man needed repose, but not yet that of the tomb. In order to console himself he went occasionally to look at the two bronze legs which he had high-handedly placed in the centre of the forecourt of the Farnese Palace, and when he came to the Academy he spent two hours among the casts, lovingly stroking the admirable legs and the powerful torsos of the Greek stat-ues. . . ."

Though it was the custom to admire legs and torsos modelled by the old masters, modern ones had not yet achieved this privilege, and Rodin knew it only too well. He said, however: "Beauty is like God; a fragment of beauty is beauty complete." The "two bronze legs," otherwise known as *L'Homme qui Marche,* had been since 1912 awaiting their permanent fate. The Ambassador remained firm in spite of the intervention of influential officials, and the museum at Lyons was finally privileged to receive this work which would not have been repudiated by the best Greek or Roman sculptors. About that time, at Cyrene, archaeologists discovered a marble Venus consisting of a torso and two legs; and despite the anguish of the war, the art world flew to see this apparition and to offer its amorous tributes.

A group of Francophiles at the Vatican were anxious to arrange for Albert Besnard to paint the Pope's portrait and for Rodin to execute his bust. "A large canvas in the style of Rigaud was required," the great painter said. "The Pope, being a little man, wanted something grand, even sumptuous. He desired to reestablish the papal taste in art and would therefore favour an elaborate setting." The Sovereign Pontiff would certainly insist upon a decorative bust in the manner of Coysevox or Bernini.

Benedict XV granted Besnard only four sittings with which the latter managed to satisfy himself, and despite all his diplomacy, the head of the *Ecole de Rome* failed to engage his illustrious sitter in any conversation whatsoever, either concerning the sumptuousness of the Vatican, religious painting, portraiture, or the fame of Rodin.

The execution of the bust was postponed and Rodin was obliged to return to Rome several months later, this time without his wife. A modelling stand, clay and tools had been sent from Paris, and a studio was discovered to the sculptor's liking; it was a large room, once a pastry-shop, in a wing of the ancient Colonna Palace. He started work on a nude, but the tragic events of the war got on his nerves and he accomplished little. His visitors had the impression that he worked a great deal and then destroyed what he had done. He was weary and profoundly distressed by the war, but obviously anxious to do the Pope's bust, both because of his personality and, as he naïvely said, because he wanted to talk about the war with him. He was astounded, as was half Christendom, that Benedict XV had not protested against the invasion of Belgium. "No one in Rome," he was told, "knows what the Holy Father really thinks. He is believed to be on France's side because he was at one time Papal Nuncio in Paris and has always been in sympathy with her; but that is all." Someone should have pointed out to Rodin that, at a time when the Pope's smallest gesture was a revelation, the fact of two well-known French artists being commissioned to do portraits of him was of undeniable significance.

John Marshall accompanied Rodin to the Vatican when the first sitting took place. After the second, the sculptor was asked if the bust was progressing well: "Yes," he replied, adding in an undertone, "we talked about the war and I told the Pope the truth about it." No doubt this sort of conversation proved distasteful to His Holiness, and, whether for this reason or because of a genuine lack of time to spare, he showed signs of fatigue during the third sitting and, at the next, he announced that he would not be able to sit again. Rodin was furious at having his work interrupted and attempted briefly to explain his method of procedure, but the Pontiff cut him short: "Finish, finish, Monsieur Rodin!" He could not understand the long scrutiny of his profile, and when Rodin walked round his august person he persisted stubbornly in turning his full face towards him. He would not allow the sculptor to look down upon him from above: Rodin above; the Pope below, at his feet; that could never be permitted. . . . Upon looking closely at the lump of clay upon which the careful fingers of the creator of the *Balzac* were at work, he voiced his bitter disappointment: "What! Is that it?" Then, being as naïve in matters of art as Rodin in diplomacy, he added: "Why don't you copy Count Lipai's bust of me? It would go more quickly then."

Rodin had followed his usual method, first working on the head alone—the head separate from the neck—turning it this way and that in his skilful hands and undoubtedly regretting his inability to do likewise with his sitter's head. The Pope, merely confused by Rodin's vague explanations, was obviously horrified at the idea of being preserved for posterity as an anatomical fragment and not as the imposing figure he had dreamed of. He did not realize that Rodin would have endowed the completed bust with his august expression and given it the desired sumptuous setting.

Albert Besnard saw the mortified sculptor himself removing his unfinished work from the pontifical apartments. With the help of a footman he carried the modelling stand with the shrouded bust upon it. Besnard had introduced Rodin to Boni de Castellane who had come to Rome in order to arrange for the annulment of his American marriage; his amiability and cleverness at once appealed to Rodin who took him to see the Venus of Cyrene, and, being uneasy at the thought of returning to Paris alone, decided to make the journey with him. The day preceding their departure a large parcel containing the Pope's head in clay was delivered to the Marquis de Castellane with a note from Rodin begging him to undertake its transport to Paris. He did so with the utmost care, even going with Rodin to his studio. This was in April of 1915.

X. ILLNESS –
CONSPIRACIES

O NE day in June of 1915 I met Rodin in front of the Palais-Royal accompanied by someone I did not know. He seemed embarrassed and ill at ease, omitted the customary polite inquiries—even for my relatives at the front—and spoke of something he had done about his museum. He said he would see me one day about the marble group for my apartment and the articles for *The Century Magazine*. He had been conferring with MM. Clémentel and Métin who had added their support to that of the Under Secretary, M. Dalimier. The latter had asked me for certain information regarding the contents of the Paris and Meudon studios and had said that he would entrust me with the task of making the catalogue of the museum.

Friendship as well as love has its tragedies. Rodin had said twenty times at least: "We'll arrange the museum together." Friends whose help I had often called upon and who knew of my long years of effort and the sculptor's ignorance of administrative affairs, felt that a modest collaboration would be not only a recompense for me but an added service to him. They were also fully aware of Rodin's recent changing moods and advised me to ask for a secretaryship at once. Léon Bourgeois was very anxious for this to go through, and, though on the point of undergoing a serious operation on his eyes, he telephoned to the Ministry of Fine Arts—a touching gesture which did not, however, ensure a cordial reception for the young man who was sent to discover Rodin's desires regarding me. This well-intentioned effort was not of my suggesting. I did my best to forestall it, for I was only too familiar with Rodin's dislike of young men—due perhaps to his own youthful errors, such as his failure to appreciate Barye and Carpeaux. Léon Bourgeois, himself a master of eloquence, believed, as did Gambetta, in the power of the spoken word, but Rodin was as impervious to its spell as Bismarck.

In July I saw him again in the gardens of the Hôtel Biron. He appeared to be in better health, but he looked anxious and depressed. He immediately broached the subject of his bitter disappointment regarding the museum and said he was being kept in such a state of uncertainty that he was considering a division of his works between several European museums, keeping the larger share for Belgium. I replied that this would be a grievous loss to France, that administrative delays in war time were to be expected, and I made the humble suggestion that if he had not discouraged me and showed his unwillingness to grant me a small official title of secretary—or whatever he wished—I would then have had the authority required for the uninterrupted pursuance of my efforts.

In icy tones he replied that he wished to arrange his museum himself and needed help from no one; that I had interested myself in it for personal reasons entirely.

A blow in the face could not have shocked me more profoundly. I was so hurt and disgusted that I cannot remember just what I managed to say. I did remind him of the many years during which I had never betrayed his confidence in me and of his own frequent references to my disinterestedness. He admitted financial obligations to me and said he was ready to reimburse me for certain expenses and also to give me the marble group he had promised me. Didn't he understand that what he was saying only made matters worse? I replied that he owed me no money whatever and that, though I would have been happy to accept the group when it was offered in friendship and affection, I could no longer do so, since it would now merely remind me of his abominable injustice.

Then I took my departure, assuring him I would never come back.

It was unbelievable that the close friendship which had filled my youth with such perfect happiness could end in this way. Its loss was an affliction more grievous than any save the loss of life itself. Life? In these days of insanity, with nations devouring one another, life seemed to me an orgy of crime and wickedness.

When M. Bigand-Kaire learned what had happened he suggested writing to Rodin, but I persuaded him not to. My mother, however, even more hurt than I, sent him a letter which vehemently expressed her stupefaction and her anger. After this, though the deep wound I had received did not heal, the war and those who were being sacrificed to it filled my mind completely.

A few months later, I was told by some friends in high authority at the Ministry of Fine Arts that MM. Clémentel and Métin, in speaking of my quarrel with Rodin and of his desire to keep me out of the museum affair, had made some extremely discourteous remarks about me. My friends added that, having seen me working for Rodin, they were astounded by his ingratitude and thought very badly of him for it.

I was anxious to clear myself and wanted to have the facts established, so, despite a feeling that it was rather contemptible of me to bother a statesman in war time with a question of personal dignity, I begged M. Etienne Clémentel—now Minister of Commerce and Industry—to see me. He granted my request at the end of November, 1915.

M. Clémentel received me with some coldness. I protested vehemently against Rodin's allegations and showed him a copy of my mother's letter. He listened to my statements and read the letter carefully; then in a more amiable manner he asked me to remember that old people often had peculiar ideas, that Rodin wanted no one to help him with his museum—neither me, nor Gustave Coquiot, nor Armand Dayot who had asked for the privilege, nor even Mario Meunier whom he greatly liked. He said he was sure that the sculptor had been set against me by someone and that time would straighten out this difficulty. It was *my duty* to accept his gift—the group was of *very great value,* he insisted—and he advised me to forgive a great man who was old, tired, and in bad health.

I thanked M. Clémentel and begged leave to disagree with him as to what my duty was. I did not wish to see Rodin again or accept his gift.

One evening in December I was not a little surprised to receive a visit from Mme Martin. Rodin, she informed me, was at Meudon with a heavy cold and could not go to his studio at the Hôtel Biron since the heating system, guaranteed him in the proposed contract, had not been installed. Would I be willing to go to the Ministry of Fine Arts and ask that the matter be attended to? I was astounded by this message and pressed Mme Martin to tell me whether her coming to see me had actually been suggested by Rodin or was merely her own idea. I told her I saw no reason to spend my energies again in behalf of the man who had caused me so much pain and had said such slanderous things about me to his new friends. Mme Martin replied that it was wrong of me to attach such importance to an old man's humours; he had several times expressed regret for the quarrel, and had even said: "I don't know how it happens—I quarrel with all my friends." He was very much changed, became tired the moment he tried to work, and had no inclination for the things which had once delighted him. I must go to Meudon to see him and finish the book I had begun two years ago. This would be a welcome distraction for him in his affliction and his cruel loneliness.

For the sake of our former friendship and of my unchanged admiration, I promised to do what I could about the heating system, but I refused to go to Meudon.

The heating system could not be installed before the bequest was formally accepted and then the Chambers would have to vote credit. This stage in the proceedings was still a long way off, though the following letter to M. Dalimier proves that Rodin did not realize it:

To the Minister of Fine Arts: [1]

Our friend Clémentel tells me that the Minister of Finance is ready for my signature. I am ill and cannot come to Paris for about ten days. It would save time if you could send me a draft of the deed of bequest. Then I could examine it, and by the time I am able to go to the offices of the Ministry you will have my comments on it; thus the signing will not be delayed.

I must tell you that the lack of heat at the Hôtel Biron has caused my illness, and the furnace will have to be put in at the earliest possible moment. I want to move in as soon as I am well enough, but I can do nothing there unless I have heat in all the rooms. Moreover, if the furnace is not installed before the winter, I will be obliged to remove my drawings; they would be ruined in the cold damp rooms.

My kindest regards,

Auguste Rodin

My reception at the Ministry in the rue de Valois was one of friendly amusement. I was told that the illustrious tenant's long absences and interminable objections were largely responsible for the delay.

I continued to receive letters and visits from Mme Martin: the sculptor's health was worse; he had periods of complete physical prostration; he was not being properly cared for. . . . I told her that since this was the state of affairs I would go to see him, but that I would not set foot in his house without an invitation from him in his own handwriting. I was getting urgent letters and cablegrams from The Century Company in America and a dummy of the proposed book had also been sent, showing binding, paper, and typography. It resembled the finished book, except that only twenty pages had been printed—the rest were blank; the publishers anxiously awaited my complete manuscript. I felt that the appearance of a book of this kind in the United States in war time would be splendid propaganda for France. Mme Martin insisted upon

---

[1] Albert Dalimier: *Quatre Ans, rue de Valois* (*Beaux-Arts*, September 15, 1933.)

my letting her take the dummy to show to Rodin, and I heard from her that he was both pleased and surprised. She also said he had given her to understand that there had been intrigues to prevent the completion of my work on it. Who had poisoned his mind this time? Mme Martin assured me, however, that Rodin was now ready to give me his entire co-operation, and I soon received a few words in his own hand, fixing a time for me to come to Meudon.

Our meeting took place one morning in February, and I found his appearance not so alarming as I had feared. He spoke cautiously and his manner was constrained. I talked to him only of my book. He said very little and his few words came slowly; there was the same despair and disillusionment in his tired voice as in his face. He lamented the destruction in the war of our public buildings and monuments, and he talked in disjointed phrases about the beauty of Rome:

"The ruins of Rome are magnificent, but the city is being destroyed day by day. . . . Those who did not see it in the nineteenth century do not know Rome. . . . Unless something is done there will be nothing left of its grandeur. People do not see how beautiful the Appian Way is, and it will soon disappear. . . . We are in a period of decadence; this is shown by the war; we live in a barbarous age. . . . We are told that Reims is to be rebuilt, but it will be destroyed utterly. Ignorance triumphs and restorers destroy the sculpture. If there is not a reaction soon, France will have no history. . . . Europe is finished; it will soon be like Asia. . . . There are students in Rome but it is not their work that makes Rome. The Italians were surprised at my saying this and they discussed it when I left. As soon as its truth is realized, something will happen. . . . Rome is Bernini—he was a fine man, a great sculptor—as great as Michael Angelo, but not as subtle. He made Rome what it is and no one knows it. . . . The Church is ignorant; so is the Pope—he's only a little parish priest."

What ingenuousness! Words of one monarch about another! Napoleon talked like this of Pius VII.

He showed me the famous bust of Benedict XV, or rather, a plaster cast of the head lying on a slab. The features were austere, a little hard and full of nervous strength; the curiously oblique nose was like that of a toucan. What a pity it could not have been finished!

Together we took the train for Paris. He had recovered a certain ease of manner, but the look of depression was still upon his face. He told me to come again to see him if I needed his help, and he put his notes at my disposal.

I did not realize then that I had had my last conversation with the real Rodin, with the man of impeccable artistic conscience, with the man whose lucid mind had, for more than thirty years, guided the troubled spirits who came in contact with him.

On March 29, 1916, at the end of a winter which had added its rigours to the anguish of the war, I received a melancholy letter from Mme Martin; Rodin had caught a heavy cold and had also had a bad fall on the steps leading up to the door of his house. He was seriously ill and no competent doctor was available. Some strange foreigners had arrived by motor and were looking after him; they were Red Cross nurses to judge by their uniforms. Mme Martin besought me urgently to come to Meudon and she warned me that "anarchy prevailed." Mme Rodin, herself ill and nervously exhausted, was unable to get on with her son and daughter-in-law whom the sculptor had summoned to the Villa des Brillants at the beginning of the war. The poor woman, exasperated by the presence of so many suspicious characters, was jealous of everyone, and there had been a succession of violent scenes. "How terrible it is that the end of his life should have to be so dreary," the devoted secretary continued; "so lonely and without the affectionate care that he needs! Try to get him to listen to your advice when you come."

259

My distress was as great as hers, but what could I do? Go to Meudon and struggle uselessly with those ignorant people, with fresh distrust of me implanted in Rodin, with those mysterious nurses who had taken over the care of the great man, following God knew what sort of treatment? . . . I wrote to M. Bigand-Kaire, feeling that he alone could influence his old friend and clear up the situation for him. He telegraphed from Marseilles: "Terribly disappointed ankylosis of the knee cannot walk otherwise would come at once beg Rodin for me to follow your advice absolutely both medical care and artistic interests. . . ."

A message from Rodin's son to Mme Martin informed us that the patient's condition had improved and that he had gone with his wife to recuperate at Châtelet-en-Brie. Mme Vivier was there alone, her husband having been mobilized despite his age.

On going one day to Meudon to inquire for Rodin, I had seen a man of about fifty in workman's clothes, digging in a corner of the garden. He did not look up until I called to him; then he came forward and spoke to me very politely. I had never seen him before, but I recognized him at once. Auguste Beuret's hair was turning grey; he had Rodin's sloping forehead and prominent nose, but his eyes were like his mother's.

At the outbreak of the war he was living at Saint-Ouen in the rue Latérale—a quarter inhabited by hucksters and pedlars—in a collapsible hut, with the widow of a rag-picker. She was older than Auguste and he was deeply attached to her. In August of 1914, his cousin Edmond Beuret had gone there to find him and tell him that Rodin wanted him to take up his abode at Meudon immediately. The next day the sculptor became impatient and sent Mme Martin with instructions to bring him back with her, alone. Auguste flatly refused to desert his beloved Nini, and the two of them were accordingly installed in the little house near the villa which belonged to Rose.

Despite the assertions of his slanderers, Rodin had never completely abandoned his son. He had wearied of the boy's continual disappearances—Auguste was a true Bohemian—and though he soon gave up trying to discipline him and was annoyed by his presence, he nevertheless gave him money and copper plates to engrave for him. Auguste did not want to go in for an art which required mental effort, but preferred to try all trades, even the lowliest and the most laborious; he was incurably changeable and intemperate, but not lazy. He always did a little engraving, but he became by turns mover, dealer in old clothes, and foundry labourer, and he had been employed in this last capacity at a weekly salary of 45 francs when war was declared; he worked until his death in 1934 which came after that of his wife. When he was in desperate straits he went secretly to Meudon and his mother would give him food, Rodin's old clothes, and a little money.

On a snowy winter's evening, during one of these desperate periods in his life, he had collapsed, either from hunger or too much drink, in front of a hovel in Saint-Ouen occupied by a rag-picker and his wife. He was revived and questioned: "Who are you?" "Auguste Beuret, but Rodin is my father." "Who's Rodin?" "The sculptor—the famous one." He stayed with his rescuers, and, at the death of the husband, took his place with the wife. Eugénie Doré, otherwise Nini, was a curious specimen of the slum population; she was short and dumpy, intelligent, even crafty; as polite to "the gentry" as she was loud-mouthed to her own kind; sloppily clothed, untidy hair, red face, breasts inadequately confined beneath a short jacket, protruding stomach covered by a blue apron —even so, Auguste Beuret loved her truly and she lavished a similar emotion upon him.

The ageing sculptor was very much alone at the Villa des Brillants; his servants had been mobilized and he needed a dependable and honest person near him—Auguste had inherited a share of his parents' integrity. So he put up with them both. What material for a novelist with a weakness for antithesis! The great Rodin harbouring these two creatures from the lower depths of the Paris slums! Unbelievable scenes were recounted to me by Mme Martin. She had made friends with them both and her southern loquaciousness amused them hugely. They took everything that fell from her lips as gospel truth and she seemed able to make them see life through rosy glasses. "You're an artist," she told Auguste, which was true; "you're doing your little Mürger, living *la vie de Bohême*. You two are just like Rudolpho and Mimi." Then the three of them drank to the delights of life and love.

At the end of May, she wrote me that she could not make out what sort of schemes were being hatched at Meudon. New influences were at work upon Rodin and he was being robbed again; I would do well, she told me, to ask for my *Pygmalion et Galathée* group before it fell into strange hands.

On April 1, 1916, the provisional contract was signed at Meudon, and M. Clémentel urged M. Paul Painlevé to hasten the State's acceptance of the bequest and begged Maître de Monzie to approve the deed so that it might be presented to the proper committee in the Chamber at the earliest possible moment.

In June I saw Rodin again at the Hôtel Biron. He was very feeble and his features had the despairing look of a wounded animal. With a shawl about his shoulders he walked slowly along one of the garden paths, supported by two persons whom I did not know. One was a sculptress, Mme G——, who called herself his pupil; the other, her daughter, was a girl of twenty-one. Rodin had met them in Florence the year before.

At Meudon, several days later, I saw him again, this time with his wife and Loïe Fuller; he was in a much better state and after an hour's chat the three of them accompanied me to the station.

Mme Martin, ever watchful, informed me that a good many pieces of sculpture had, despite their weight, been removed from the Paris and Meudon studios, how or by whom she could not discover; my group would surely disappear before long. She suspected several people—possibly the Duchess de Ch—— behind the scenes. I asked Rodin if I could have my group and he replied that it had been ready for some time. In spite of his feeble condition he came twice to Paris to supervise the moving and was greatly annoyed with the firm he had chosen to do the work, because, owing to war-time difficulties, it had disappointed him on the first occasion.

On July 8, in the presence of Mme G——, her daughter, and Loïe Fuller, he ordered the young Japanese whom he employed for certain delicate jobs to engrave his signature upon the marble base: *Aug. Rodin*. The three women, who seemed to be on terms of great intimacy, were most amicable and asked me to come to see them. Mme Rodin stood behind her husband, apart from the talkative group, her eyes flashing with disapproval of the foreigners.

I went to see the G—s in their apartment in the Montparnasse quarter; one of the rooms was large and rather tastefully furnished, and here the sculptress worked. Lying about on the couches like dolls were some small bronze figures that showed real talent despite a vulgar realism. The daughter missed being pretty; there was nothing remarkable about her looks and her true character was not easy to read. While she and I were talking, her mother, a stoutish woman with a fierce look in her eyes, came to the door to have a surreptitious glance at me before joining us, and I had a most unpleasant impression of her appearance. Later, when her daughter was out of the room for a few moments, she told me that Rodin would frequently escape from "his poor crazy wife" and take refuge in her pleasant studio where he could work in peace; that Loïe Fuller was an angel of goodness with a heart of gold, and so clever, and that she, Mme G——, loved her "like a sister." But there was such great insistence upon Mme Rose's disastrous influence and the necessity for separating her from her husband, and such a clear implication that I was to help them persuade the sculptor to go without her to their villa at Clermont-Ferrand where an excellent doctor would care for him, that I began to be suspicious. Rodin had already seen the doctor in question, during a visit to the G—s at Clermont-Ferrand, and he had artfully declared that the sculptor would certainly live to be eighty-five or more, and that he could easily recover his health if given immediate treatment. On the other hand, his wife, in her all-embracing ignorance, was submitting him to a disastrous régime, and if left to her tender mercies he would soon be dead.

On July 24, Mme Martin paid me an unexpected visit. In frightened tones she told me that Rodin was very bad again, he was completely irresponsible. Also, she had discovered what the people at Meudon were plotting; they had even tried to get her to help them. She had heard it all from Auguste Beuret's wife, to whom poor Rose had unburdened herself: Mme G—— had got Rodin to make a will in her favour; Loïe Fuller had bribed the servants, and the cook, whom she had herself employed, was under her orders; Rose, crazed and hysterical, now visited her wrath upon her daughter-in-law and her son whose ears she permitted herself to box as though he were not fifty but an urchin of ten.

I was horrified at this picture, but I could not help giving Mme Martin a long look; had she perhaps become affected by her fantastic surroundings? Rodin had once maliciously admitted to me that his secretary's imagination was like that of a successful writer of trashy novels. She evidently thought I suspected her story, and she besought me with pathetic seriousness to interfere and save the unfortunate man and his works.

The very least I could do was to establish the facts. I set out for Meudon in the blazing heat and, upon arriving at the Villa des Brillants, was shown directly up to Rodin's bed-room. It was five o'clock and he had just been helped into bed; Mme Rose was with him and he had already fallen into a deep sleep. His head had slipped down from the pillows and one massive shoulder was raised above it—a torso of Hercules fallen from its pedestal. I helped Mme Rose to lift him up and settle him among the pillows. He woke, smiled like a child, and seemed glad to receive these small attentions. On the wall opposite his bed a great Gothic Christ rose up to the ceiling; it was a fine piece of sculpture and he loved it. When it was cold a fire was kept alight, not for the patient's comfort but for the preservation of this masterpiece. The huge cross seemed to protect him in his feebleness. . . . He asked me to come again soon to talk about the museum and gave me a fatherly kiss.

I was very anxious to speak to Mme Rose alone and we went down to the drawing-room. She did not appear to be greatly weighed down by the misfortune; her semi-awareness prevented her from perceiving its infinite pathos. Could it be that this amazing brain was affected—this noble mind destroyed? Couldn't his health be restored if he were cared for intelligently? We sat in a corner of the large room. Mme Rose looked more emaciated than ever; her features were drawn and there was a feverish look in her eyes. She was almost sobbing with emotion now, and I took her hands in mine:

"Tell me what is happening here."

"Oh, Mademoiselle Judith," she burst out, "I'm not the only one now!"

"What do you mean?"

"No, I'm not the only one now. Those other women are trying to take him from me, but I won't let him go. I'm going to stay with him till the end!"

"What women do you mean and what is it they want to do?"

"It's Mme G——, she came here with Loïe Fuller and a man. She made Monsieur Rodin sign a paper."

"When was this?"

"I don't remember exactly. Two or three days after he got ill."

"Were you there?"

"Yes, but Mme G—— took the man into Monsieur Rodin's room and told me to go downstairs."

"Who was he? A lawyer? Had you ever seen him before?"

"I think I saw him once . . . then they made me sign a paper and told me that Monsieur Rodin wanted me to do it."

"Did you sign it?"

"Yes. Monsieur Rodin wanted me to do it."

"But you know he's not clear in his mind. What did the paper say?"

"I couldn't read it. They told me that Monsieur Rodin was dividing everything between Mme G—— and me. When I signed the paper, she pinned it inside her dress. Oh, Mademoiselle Judith, I can't stand these women any more; they've made me suffer too much. They want to take us both to their house at Clermont and get a doctor that I don't know. I would never get rid of them. They're after his money," she cried with savagely glowing eyes, "and they can take it, but they won't ever get rid of me!" She shook her mop of white hair angrily. "I'm his wife—I've looked after him like a child for fifty-two years! It won't do them any good to say I'm crazy and ought to be shut up. I won't leave him. . . . Just fancy, they've been all through the house, studios and all, opening his letters; they act just as if they owned everything. And they've taken away some of the statues. . . ."

I tried to quiet her by promising to speak to Rodin's real friends: M. Peytel and M. Clémentel whom she knew, and I urged her to keep everyone out of the Villa des Brillants except Mme Martin and these two gentlemen.

"But, Mademoiselle, Loïe Fuller is a good friend."

"By the way, what did she do while the paper was being signed?"

"She went back to Paris to get something for Monsieur Rodin."

"And what happened when she returned?"

"She was angry with Mme G—— and they had a quarrel. Before that, they were such good friends. And in two days everything was changed. . . . Loïe is very fond of us; she wants to rent La Goulette so she can be with us more. She couldn't have it because Monsieur Rodin has it full of casts and frames."

"Be careful, dear Mme Rodin, even with Loïe, and, above all, don't talk about any of this till we can make some arrangement." I felt that she paid little attention to what I said and was engrossed in her daily worries.

"Things always go against me," she confessed. "I'm really never happy. Monsieur Rodin has tormented me with his women, and now it's my children. They're not good to me; they don't love me. They're never satisfied. They get a house and coal and two hundred francs a months, but they won't do anything for me, and I can't tip them like servants . . . they're always drinking; she's just like him that way."

I tried to hide my fears and urged her to be patient, to have a mother's indulgence. Then, realizing that she was worn out and, having heard her complain of all she had to do for her invalid, I told her she ought to have someone to help her, a nurse.

"Oh, no!" she exclaimed quickly. "I want no one—no one. It is my duty to look after him, and I'll do it until the end."

What a novel! Oh, Balzac, Balzac! Balzac's *Rodin,* one of my friends said; and Dostoievsky's and Gorky's too.

I returned to Paris in a state of intense alarm. The situation was precarious. What could be done for these two old people alone in the country with the incompetent Auguste, one lost in the fog of semi-consciousness and the other almost unbelievably simple-minded—both of them the pathetic victims of ignoble intrigue and covetousness? How could Rodin be protected? No one with him had any legal status; Mme Rose was not his wife in the eyes of the law, and his son did not even bear his name; his friends were either in some other part of France or completely absorbed by war jobs; the bequest was still unratified by a government too busy with the country's defence to prevent the plundering of its poten-tial art treasures.

Had I been a man, the situation would have presented no diffi-culties, but a single woman is an object of suspicion in this con-ventional France of ours, even when she is sincere and disin-terested. Her motives are obscure compared with those of an ad-venturess and people are alarmed lest she make inordinate de-mands; in short, the unknown is always to be feared.

It was however imperative to act at once. I went to the Ministry of Commerce and asked M. Clémentel's secretary to arrange for me to see the Minister as soon as possible. I wrote a long letter to M. Bigand-Kaire asking him to give me a letter of introduction to

M. Joanny Peytel, president of the administrative council of the Crédit Algerien, Rodin's banker and friend. I begged M. Edmond Guiraud to urge his colleague, M. Clémentel, to see me at the earliest possible moment, and from him I discovered that the matter of the bequest had been held up by the finance committee of the Chamber. I apologized to Mme Martin, thanked her for having warned me of the trouble, and urged silence, caution, and a discreet inspection of all those who appeared at Meudon: "We shall soon discover the details of the plot," I told her. "Mme G—— and Loïe Fuller are at swords' points now and each will provide us with a full account of the other's behaviour."

I did not realize then how soon this supposition would be confirmed. Mme G—— called at my apartment and, not finding me there, sent me a *petit bleu* in which she said that she was glad to find that I had gone out to Meudon and would be interested to know what I thought. She then announced her intention to call again the next day. Her hasty and carelessly written note did not betray an easy conscience.

Despite a violent thunderstorm she and her daughter arrived punctually at the hour mentioned. They were both dressed with great care, and I was rather surprised by the youthful elegance of the mother's appearance. The daughter was attractive, though somewhat lush, reminding me of a Dutch peasant girl.

Mme G—— began immediately to denounce Loïe Fuller. Had this woman, whom I had thought was at least intelligent, forgotten her enthusiastic praise of the exquisite creature she had wanted two weeks ago for her "twin sister"? Now such close contact was out of the question; a sheet of paper lay between them—a will—and today the beloved friend was merely an American dancer, perhaps German, concerning whom Mme G—— had heard the most discouraging reports: an alien who, with the Duchesse de Ch—— as accomplice, was pillaging Rodin's studios and re-selling his works in America at huge profits. "She wants you to sell her your group," said Mme G——, "so that she can dispose of it there for at least twice what she pays you." Poor Rose came in for her share of hatred: owing to her stupidity and her half-demented state, she was preventing Rodin from going to Clermont for treatment, and getting rid of some suspicious people at Meudon, particularly a Russian nurse, Mme X——, and her niece or adopted daughter, who stepped into Rodin's motor "as they would into their own slippers," used sixty gallons of his petrol a day, and pestered him continually with their unintelligible chatter. One day, after a violent quarrel in the sick man's room, Mme G—— had ejected this woman who said she was a sculptress and had insisted upon ensconcing herself at his bedside to do a bust of him. Mme G—— had thrown the bust out of the window and the woman down the stairs.

"And Rodin?" I asked. "What did he do while the brawl was going on?"

"Nothing. He was looking at a pianoforte method, muttering: "It's nothing but words, words."

O Shakespeare!

". . . He's not responsible. He sold some little bronzes, and when I asked how much, he told me 150 francs. There was a large bronze head of one of *Les Bourgeois de Calais* at the Hôtel Biron, but it's gone. Loïe Fuller took it to the foundry. . . . Poor Rodin! No one thinks of him. Loïe trundles him about in the motor, wearing him out with her tiresome chatter, and Mme Rodin quarrels with her all the time. People should be kept away from the Villa; I would be willing to attend to that, but Mme Rodin won't hear of it. What's to be done? I've got no rights [except those, I thought, set forth in the precious sheet of paper]; he's not my father, or my brother, or my uncle—what can I do?"

Then, finally, the purpose of the visit was disclosed: my help was requested in getting Rodin to Clermont, and I was also to see that the works spirited away by Loïe Fuller were seized at the customs. It was an astounding conversation, or rather, monologue, for I had fortunately scarcely been required to utter a word. I was wrong about Mme G——; she was not the high-class adventuress I had taken her for. She was too flat in her denials, lacking in finesse, and she blundered continually. She declared Rodin to be irresponsible. Of what value, then, was the document which she had obtained from him and to which she naturally made no reference? And why had she rushed into the lion's mouth like this? It was well known that my energies were concentrated upon the establishment of the Rodin Museum. Possibly she thought I used this cloak to conceal personal designs like hers, like those of all the gluttons who were enticed by such magnificent prey. . . . I was sincerely sorry to discover Loïe Fuller involved in these piracies—Loïe Fuller, the enchantress whose divine dancing had charmed the public of two hemispheres and had been the delight of all artists! The fact remained, however, that she too was dangerous, because her lack of physical attraction and her flattering attentions to Mme Rose had easily won the latter's confidence. I could not help feeling an increased apprehension for the unprotected and fragile occupants of the Villa des Brillants.

I heard nothing from M. Clémentel and wrote him another pressing letter. Finally I received an appointment, but not until August 1 and it was then only the 27th of July. I had been to see M. Peytel in his offices in the Place Vendôme; full of middle-class caution and a desire, common to old gentlemen, to avoid troublesome matters, the banker merely replied that Rodin needed rest. No hope therefore from that quarter!

On leaving the Ministry of Fine Arts, after discovering that M. Dalimier was out of town, I met Loïe Fuller who had also wanted to see him. She was excessively amiable, and made me sit with her in her taxi for a moment; then she made a little speech to the effect that I was an excellent writer, but that "the intellectual must be reinforced by the material" and therefore I would have to be made curator of the Rodin Museum. In the meantime, considering my well known devotion to my family, I should be thinking of my heirs. She would be glad to arrange with her friends from America to buy the marble group that Rodin had given me. Would it not be a splendid and profitable thing for me to sell this work of the great sculptor to the San Francisco Museum?

XI. READJUSTMENT –
SUPREME CONFESSION

I HAD an interview with M. Clémentel at last. Believing perhaps that I had come upon a personal errand, he was cautious at first; but when he had heard the facts he thanked me warmly for having come to him, telling me how all this intriguing annoyed and troubled him. He would go to Meudon that evening to see what might be done, and I told him I was going to get Mme Rodin's permission immediately to interview her husband's doctor at Bellevue. I proposed to ask Dr. Godefroy whether or not, in his opinion, Rodin was responsible for his acts and, if he were not, whether, as attending physician, he would be willing to certify his patient's enfeebled mental state in writing. M. Clémentel was in favour of this measure and asked me to let him know the result immediately. Then, taking off the telephone receiver, he asked for the Ministry of Fine Arts. He was an intimate friend of M. Dalimier and told him in no uncertain terms that the plundering of the Paris and Meudon studios and the disappearance of works of art destined for the State would seriously injure the reputation of his administration. The Minister's complete shift to my way of thinking was very satisfying and I felt that I had at last found someone who could put everything in order.

Dr. Godefroy was careful and straightforward, very much the country doctor, and, as befitted his calling, very cautious. He stated quite frankly, however, that Rodin had had an attack of congestion of the brain on the 10th of July and that he was definitely not in full possession of his faculties. He also stated that he was prepared to certify his patient's condition in writing. He suggested that Mme Rodin should obtain similar certificates from several specialists. On being told briefly of recent developments at Meudon, he seemed greatly amused by the prospect of the "walloping" in store for the lawyer who had witnessed the will. Who was he? Would we ever find out?

Dr. Godefroy's statement had affected me deeply. So it was on July 10 that, after another fall on the stairs, he had been carried to his bed, perhaps never to regain the full use of his mind; and only two days before, with a determined haste which was very like a presentiment, he had come to Paris for the second time to supervise the moving of the *Pygmalion et Galathée* to my apartment.

On going to Meudon, I found him unchanged. "Four years ago," Mme Rose told me, "he had an attack like this one. He was having his lunch and his fork dropped on the floor. He leaned over to pick it up and after that his arm hung stiff at his side; he couldn't move it. He got slowly better and he told me not to speak to anyone about his attack. Since then, in case he has another, I've been keeping some leeches ready to use," and in the room next the dining-room she showed me a jar containing the sinister black objects, half hidden behind a small plaster cast of *Les Faunesses*.

Four years ago! The very summer when we were all so shocked at the change in him! The summer when he had broken with the Duchess and had referred mysteriously to some "serious things" which had occurred. What a price to pay for his illusions, for this belated indulgence of his amorous desires!

He was in his bed-room sitting in a chair which had been moved close to the open window on account of the oppressive heat. It was the first time I had seen the indomitable worker avail himself of the comfort of the one upholstered chair in the house. Mme Rose came and went, preoccupied by her domestic duties. Rodin was gazing out the window at the familiar landscape. His face had grown thin and his eyes, usually screwed up because of his nearsightedness, were now wide open and clear as a child's. I talked

273

to him quietly; his conversation was limited, but fairly consecutive. We re-arranged his pillows for him, and his compliance with the smallest request was touching. He had been such a demon of determination! By another of fate's perversities he had been deprived of his essential virtue, of that iron will which he had relentlessly exercised for more than sixty years; this prodigious gift had suddenly been taken from him as if to punish him for abusing it, and also to terminate a great career with a great misfortune.

"People have tried to make trouble between us," I said to him. "They wanted to keep me away from you. None of it was your fault and fortunately it is all over now." The furtive blush that coloured his features showed me that his sensibility was unimpaired, despite the corroding attacks made upon it. He laughed and took my hand in his, tapping it with the ends of his fingers.

"What have you done this morning?" he asked.

"I've been working."

"That's for me, I know," he said, with a vaguely unhappy look in his eyes. "I can't work any more."

"It's because you've worked too much. You've always told me that periods of rest are necessary in life as well as in art."

"Well, perhaps."

"You're comfortable here with your statue of Christ to protect you."

"Ah, He was a man who worked."

I was so moved that I could not answer. He looked out with dream-like gaze across the valley of the Seine, its colours bleached by the blazing summer sunlight. The rumbling of the frequent military trains seemed to tire him.

"What place is that out there?" he asked suddenly.

"It's Meudon," I answered, greatly upset, for it was the first time I had noticed his mind wandering.

"You talk like my wife. It's Meudon to me, but not to other people. Is that train moving north the one that goes to that great city—what is it? Saint-Georges? Something like Saint-Georges."

At that moment M. Clémentel arrived, with Rudier from the

274

foundry. In the bright voice one uses in speaking to children, he told Rodin that he must ask the Ministry of Fine Arts to have his various studios guarded. We brought up a little table and with the obedience of a school-boy he wrote out correctly the few lines dictated by the Minister. M. Clémentel put the letter in his pocket and said he would give it himself to M. Painlevé the next morning. Then we made a rapid inspection of the studio and the other rooms, and the Minister offered to take me back to Paris in his motor. I availed myself of this opportunity to ask him a question: would it not be wise and also no more than her due that Mme Rose should be made Rodin's wife in the eyes of the law? If they were officially united it would then be possible to have Mme Rodin take the necessary measures to protect the sculptor and his works.

"You are right; we must get them married," declared the Minister. "Talk it over with Rodin and I will speak to Peytel."

He was infuriated by the disappearance of certain pieces of sculpture, one of which had not yet been listed; for these Rodin had been persuaded to accept ridiculously low prices. The proposed bequest would not come up for discussion in the Chamber until the end of August, and not in the Senate until September or October. In the meantime the State's inheritance must be protected. M. Clémentel advised me to consult Maître de Monzie the following day as to how a provisional organization could be established. "I'll see that you are appointed director or curator of the museum," he said amiably.

I thanked him and said: "No one can be curator of the museum during Rodin's lifetime; there is a clause in the contract naming him as curator. Any insignificant post that will permit me to watch over the sculpture that I know so thoroughly will be quite sufficient."

"Well, we'll make you general secretary now and curator later on," decided M. Clémentel. Then he mentioned the bust that Rodin had done of him before his illness; though not quite finished, it was a very fine one and he wanted to have it cast as soon

275

as possible. He asked me whether I knew of a sculptor, perhaps my brother, who could undertake its completion and casting.

"My brother is at the front, and anyhow he, a young sculptor, would not dream of touching a work by Rodin. One of his expert assistants, Jules Desbois for instance, might do it." M. Clémentel begged me to speak to Desbois about this.

Maître de Monzie, courteous to the daughter of a writer whom he admired and who had come from his own province in the south, considered it necessary to select some neutral individual, lawyer or magistrate, of whom Rodin would not be suspicious. Such an administrator could act with my help in the matter of transferring the contents of all the other studios to the Hôtel Biron. Maître de Monzie suggested M. Monnier, a magistrate whose reputation was unblemished. Then he blurted out, watching how I would take it, that Rodin had been afraid that I wanted to participate in the organization of the museum so that my brother might have the chance to retouch his works. This story was so absurd that I could only laugh. So that was the invention of the plotters who wished to get rid of me and be free to accomplish their villainy. Rodin must have been already in a bad way to believe a tale at which he would have been the first to laugh several years ago. My brother had encountered the arrogance with which the sculptor usually greeted young men, and had never returned to his studio. I was sorry that Maître de Monzie had not heard M. Clémentel's conversation of the day before.

I was called immediately to the Ministry of Fine Arts and found several of those high functionaries still greatly upset by the telephoned warning from M. Clémentel. The Under Secretary arrived in frock coat, high hat, and varnished boots; he was on his way to lunch at the Elysée. The heat was frightful and M. Dalimier seemed to be in a rather bad humour: "Are you coming, Mademoiselle? We're going to the Hôtel Biron." In the motor, he asked me about the little Japanese man, then the sole guardian of the

Death of Alcestis (*La Mort d'Alceste*). COURTESY OF THE MUSEE RODIN

Miss Eve Fairfax. COURTESY OF THE MUSEE RODIN

contents of the studio in the rue de Varenne. On the 14th of July, a lively discussion had taken place between M. Dalimier and the Jap who spoke little French and laughed continually. There had been a charitable affair in the Hôtel Biron gardens, presided over by Mme Viviani and M. Dalimier. The Jap had refused to let them enter the studio.

"Monsieur Rodin not here, nobody come in."

"But I control this property," the Minister answered crossly, unused to such treatment. "I'll throw you into the street."

"I throw you into street," the little yellow man had replied.

He was the only person Rodin now trusted, and he had been employed by him for years on account of his ability to do delicate jobs. He was married to a French woman and had never, the concierge told us, carried off the tiniest parcel.

As we approached the pavilion he appeared, wreathed in smiles. M. Dalimier walked up to him and, bending over so that their two faces were on the same level, he spoke severely in simplified French:

"Police come here at once if anyone enter, you understand? No one enter, or police will come. Understand? He shook his finger and rolled his black eyes—a real Grand Guignol scene.

"Me very glad," said the Jap with his rattling laugh, "house of Monsieur Rodin well guarded."

He took us through the rooms and told us that Mme G—— had just removed a marble figure of a young girl about three feet high; Loïe Fuller had taken an *Homme au Nez Cassé* and two plaster casts of hands, on producing Rodin's informal receipt: "Loïe gave 3,000 francs."

"Why did you let these things go without authorization?" shouted the Minister.

"But those ladies always with Monsieur Rodin, always, always. . . ."

M. Dalimier decided to do the inventories over again in order to discover how great the losses were, and then to put the Hôtel Biron under the guardianship of the *Musées Nationaux* with in-

277

structions to let nothing go, even if a receipt from the sculptor were presented.

The heat blazed and heels sank into the Paris pavements as I set forth with M. Dalimier the following day for Meudon. The Minister had regained his serenity and this time was wearing white trousers and a straw hat. The luncheon the previous day at the Elysée was in honour of the King of Montenegro and he told me it had been an extraordinary affair. When the monarch, in his sky-blue pleated skirt, offered his arm to Mme Poincaré to escort her to the dining-room, it was only with the greatest difficulty that the assembled guests remembered the King's misfortunes and controlled their immoderate laughter. "I've still got my watch," said Aristide Briand later, as he left the table. It required an occasion of greater solemnity to silence Parisian flippancy.

We sat round an iron table in the garden at Meudon, and Rodin listened with great satisfaction to M. Dalimier's statement that the Paris and Meudon studios were to be carefully guarded. "That was necessary," said the sculptor quietly. "Someone had to issue an order." Mme Rose, pleased by this news, generously offered to present her large marble bust to the museum. She had considered giving it to the San Francisco Museum—it is hardly necessary to say at whose suggestion—but now preferred to have it remain in Paris: "Remember, Auguste, it's not signed," she warned him. But the Minister reassured him with a smile: "It doesn't matter; we'll know it is yours just the same."

It was pleasant to sit in that cool garden after the suffocating heat of Paris, with these two old people who were perhaps happier now that the enfeebling of one mind had brought it down to the childish level of the other.

Mme Rose told me in an undertone that Mme G—— had only just left. Fearing the displeasure of the man whom, even in his present state, she still regarded as the dreaded master, she had not dared to send her enemy packing.

On the way back to Paris I told the Minister of my idea, which pleased him, that the Villa des Brillants should be kept exactly as

278

it was now, so that it might become, as had the houses of so many famous men, a hallowed spot for pilgrimages. He then asked me how dangerous people were to be kept from calling at the villa and I mentioned Mme Martin, whose devotion and knowledge of the situation would be invaluable; I also ventured the opinion that some such small employment would repay her for the undoubted service she had rendered the State by her persistent sounding of the alarm. M. Dalimier decided to interview her the next day and he instructed me in his official capacity to verify the inventories.

I was beginning to believe that the museum would be saved.

Two days later I went again to Meudon with MM. Clémentel, Dalimier, Valentino, and Bénédite who was as supercilious now as he had been affable the previous year. He knew nothing of the recent disturbance, but was told about it on the way. "What a novel!" one of them exclaimed. "What a film, you mean!" said another. Dr. Godefroy had been asked to come to Meudon also, and he again advised consultation. "Do you know any specialists who are in town at this time of the year?" asked M. Clémentel. M. Dalimier mentioned Dr. Paul, skilled in medical jurisprudence, and Professor Dupré, head physician of the *Dépôt*. I suggested Dr. Stéphen-Chauvet who, I had been told, was a clever diagnostician.

"All right," said M. Clémentel, "let's have him; let's have two, or ten, if you like. We've got to protect ourselves against these brigands."

". . . and we've got to get back the stolen works," added M. Dalimier.

Several days later, the Minister informed me that M. Léonce Bénédite was to have charge of organizing the museum. I was very much surprised at this, for the curator had favoured a different arrangement by which the Luxembourg would get Rodin's works. M. Clémentel explained quickly: "He will fall in with all Rodin's wishes and he will be glad to work with you. He told me he would. His present scheme is to move the Luxembourg to the Hôtel Biron and to build a new museum and a restaurant around the pavilion. The plans are to be sent in to the Ministry of Fine Arts presently."

I did not realize then the rapidity with which ministerial projects could bloom and fade away. This one filled me with apprehension:

"May I be allowed to say that we are getting far away from Rodin's ideas. He is determined to be isolated. After his death he wishes his work to represent the artistic principle for which he laboured ceaselessly; he wants the Hôtel Biron to be not so much a museum as a school for young sculptors. Would it not lose its true significance if surrounded by huge galleries and restaurants?"

"It is certainly a matter for discussion."

"May I tell you of another of his wishes? He is anxious for the appointment of an advisory council to include his best friends, Claude Monet, Besnard, Mirbeau, M. Fenaille, and particularly the sculptors who were his assistants, Desbois, Bourdelle, Despiau, and Halou."

"Bénédite will be only too pleased to go into that with you."

It was imperative for the specialists to see Rodin at the earliest possible moment. In their ignorance and plebeian prejudice, his present entourage was giving him meat and red wine. How would he receive the doctors? In general he had no patience with those "ignorant men who denounce a Frenchman's two essential foods: bread and wine," but he now submitted with smiling benevolence to a long examination by Drs. Godefroy and Stéphen-Chauvet, and he kept repeating: "But I'm not ill, I'm not ill."

Treatment was prescribed and the two doctors prepared a certificate in duplicate, which, alas, established the great sculptor's complete irresponsibility, due to cerebral hemorrhage. They then went to the Mairie to sign the duplicate certificates; Dr. Chauvet, a cautious Norman, arranged with Dr. Godefroy for both documents to be sent by registered post and simultaneously. They would find out just when the documents would be required by the Fine Arts administration.

They were both to have visited Rodin again with Professor Dupré, three days later, but were mysteriously instructed not to come at the last moment; Professor Dupré was not told of this and he arrived alone. He was a very shrewd man, extremely civil, considerate of his patient, and he treated Mme Rose like a great lady. He could only confirm the diagnosis of his two colleagues, and added that, apart from the circulatory trouble, "the master was quite all right, perfectly comfortable, serene, and smiling like a god." There was no hope for the recovery of his mental faculties. Mme Rose listened without understanding, and answered the doctor's questions with nods and shakes of her head.

In order to be nearer my daily occupation, and to escape the fiery heat of Paris, my mother and I moved to a house in Meudon, not far from the Villa des Brillants. M. Clémentel had asked me to keep him informed as to how things were going. I saw him from time to time, and he told me that the question of the will in favour of Mme G—— made Rodin's situation very disquieting, that, if he should die before the voting of the Chambers, the establishment of the museum would be seriously endangered and Rose Beuret might find herself without a sou. I told him that, if Rodin were in possession of his mind, he would be greatly troubled, for his intentions had been unchanged for the last ten years: "All my works to the State and the rest to my wife." I asked M. Clémentel whether it would not be possible to discover the name of the man who had helped Mme G—— in her illegal attempt to gain an inheritance. He shrugged his shoulders. "To avoid all danger we should have Rodin make another will embodying his original desires. I'll give you the text of it."

This seemed to me a rather doubtful proceeding, but M. Clémentel replied to my scruples: "Since no advantage can come to you or to me, and since we are merely seeking to legalize Rodin's original intentions, no one will find our action blameworthy."

I pointed out that his other relatives ought not to be left out. M. Clémentel agreed, and after reflecting for a moment he handed me a blank sheet of paper and dictated the following formula: "I *hereby revoke and declare null and void all wills of mine except that will in favour of Rose Beuret, dated ——, and in addition to the provisions therein contained, I give and bequeath to the said Rose Beuret, in recognition of our fifty years together, the remainder of my fortune. At her death this remainder shall become the property of my natural heirs.* Then leave blanks for place, date, and signature. M. Peytel agrees that they should be married as soon as possible. Mme Rodin deserves it, poor woman."

Mme Vivier, the Rodins' great friend, was staying at the villa, and I was pleased to have her there when I performed the task with which I had been entrusted. I waited for a favourable moment.

One afternoon Rodin was sitting in the little dining-room, vaguely reading a newspaper; he seemed a little stronger and I took Mme Rose aside, explained M. Clémentel's proposal, and asked her to keep the cook, whom we more or less suspected, in the basement. Then, inviting Mme Vivier to sit with us, I asked Rodin whether he would confirm his first intentions in favour of his wife. He nodded and I put before him a sheet of stamped paper, pen, and ink. He immediately began to write clearly and rapidly, even anticipating my dictation; he seemed to know the terms by heart. Actually, he had often written them out, for we soon discovered ten or twelve wills and drafts of wills embodying the identical provisions. When he came to the clause regarding his natural heirs, he said: "This is how I want it," omitted the clause and signed his name at once. Was it the word "death" that troubled him, or had the clause not lain for a sufficient length of time in his subconscious? I glanced at Mme Vivier and said: "Don't you want to write down the rest?"

"That is the way I want it," he repeated, and, taking up his newspaper, he went back unconcernedly to his reading. I then called Mme Rose, showed her the will which M. Clémentel had asked me to take at once to M. Peytel, and besought her to prevent her husband from putting anything more on paper, no matter who might suggest it. She thanked me for my kindness and kissed me, her satisfaction being due more to the knowledge that the women who had tried to supplant her were now put in their places than to the establishment of her financial security.

I asked Rodin whether he did not think it would be fitting for him to marry Mme Rose whom he had for so long introduced to everyone as his wife. He blushed slightly and took my hand:

"You always have such good ideas."

"We will attend to it all for you. The marriage can take place here in your garden, in the presence of a few of your intimate friends."

"Yes, it must be like that," he said quietly.

For some time Mme Martin had occupied a little room in one of the annexes. She had been instructed to help me with the inventories and to keep an eye on all visitors. We had assumed the task of taking care of Rodin's correspondence; his memory had so failed that he could supply us with no help whatever. M. Clémentel had told me to have the marriage banns published and to draw up a proposal for the organization of the museum for him to give to M. Simyan of the Ministry of Fine Arts who was working on the budget for the Chamber of Deputies.

First of all we had to identify and classify the keys. There were two hundred of them, perhaps more, and the right one could rarely be found, for Rodin had omitted to mark the carefully attached labels; each one had to be tried in each drawer. This required hours and we finally gave up and called in the locksmith.

A huge chest disgorged a mass of papers, among which we discovered some cheques to Rodin's order, uncashed and several months old. In a large envelope were four wills, three of which arrogantly revoked the provisions formerly made in favour of the Duchess; it also contained three drafts of wills in favour of Rose, and another in which he stipulated that, if the State did not accept his bequest, it was to be divided among several European and American museums. Finally there were some letters he had written, the contents of which tore at my heart. They bore witness to

283

the confusion of this lonely man who did not know in whom to confide just before his tragic descent into the valley of shadows. They contained words of gratitude to friends who had enriched his life. Some of them were merely beginnings; others were in their envelopes, ready for posting: to the Duke of Westminster who had had an exhibition of thirty of his works at Grosvenor House in 1914, to Lady Sackville, to an unknown friend, to the Comtesse de Noailles, to the brother of M. Dujardin-Baumetz who "courageously fought for the cause of art," to Emile Verhaeren, to Gabriel Hanotaux, and to others whose names were not set down.

To His Grace the Duke of Westminster:

The situation is too grave for me to thank you as I should. You have granted me your esteem which is as great a reward as I have ever received.

Allow me, in the midst of this terrible war which magnifies and enhances you, to sign myself

your humble and devoted servant,

Auguste Rodin

2nd October, 1914

To Lady Sackville from whom he was expecting a visit, he wrote: "We will talk about your daughter whose great beauty is, I judge, no less than her goodness." To M. Hanotaux: "I've got influenza now which means that I am very tired. . . . I have lacked proportion—I've not been so expert in life as in sculpture —or rather, like an astronomer, I kept looking at the sky as I fell lower into the well. In short, I am only complaining of myself." To an unknown friend: "My dear, your sweet letter has arrived. So you are in Holland! Will you be coming to England in the spring? —England which has given you strength and restored you. It is like a benediction and keeps you young. Are you still as beautiful as ever? I think so, without having seen you." He had a vague presentiment of his approaching collapse and sought instinctively for support among his intimates—fortunate beings still in possession of their powers; he stretched out weary hands to them to save

e Bather (*Devant la Mer*). COURTESY OF THE METROPOLITAN MUSEUM OF ART

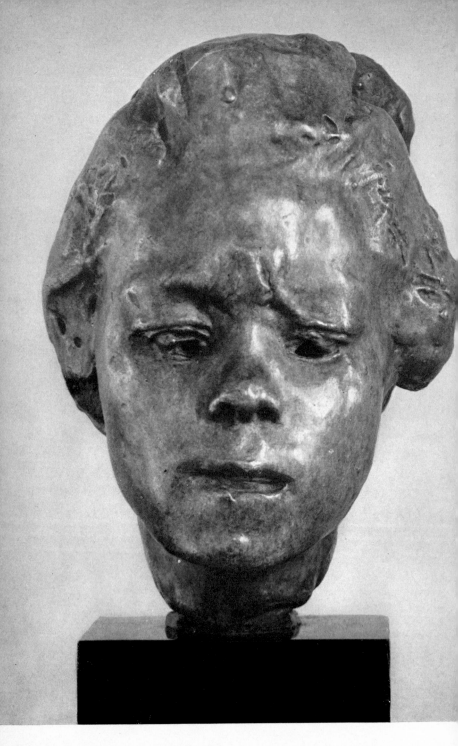

Hanako, the Japanese Dancer (*Hanako*). COURTESY OF THE MUSEE RODIN

him from the unknown abyss at his feet. To Anna de Noailles: "You say the simplest things in the world—no one has ever said them but you. You discover treasures for us, treasures which, like radium, have been for centuries within our reach, and I am grateful to you. You cut into the marble and your fine, intense personality begins to appear; you enrich us all and you are very consoling to me. Others take away; you give. You are like a flower; I lean closer now; I read a verse and the rose is more fragrant; its perfume speaks in your own words. I read you like that and draw near to Heaven."

His appeal to Verhaeren is the more urgent for being merely a fragment; it is like the cry of an exhausted sea bird straining to reach the deck of a swiftly passing ship:

"You are a great poet whose strength nourishes me and whom I love because you say things that are true.

"Like a farmer's plough your mind throws the earth to right and left; then you sow the true seed; I express myself badly, but you understand me. . . . I am greatly troubled. Tares grow up where I sow. . . ."

There were a few more fleeting reflections, most of them scarcely legible, except for the following confession:

"We live a life of our own invention and, when it is ended and has proved difficult, we learn what was wrong by remembering the religious instruction which we laughed at in our youth. These precepts, like a gathering of wise friends, speak to me now as I lie in my bed. Nothing in my whole life can compare with the gentle peace of this remembering. Men of old show me how my life should have been lived, point out my mistakes, my stupid vanities, my mad ambitions. Their wisdom makes plain the foolish errors I have committed. Great men are severely thinking for me now. Punishment must clear out the mind and prepare it for the beauty contained in good books. How comforting to realize one's faults even though it is too late to remedy them."

How pathetic this return to the humility of his young belief, this groping for the solution of the great mystery towards which his life was leading him, half in dream and half in reality. Finally, upon a thin sheet of paper, a few wavering lines in a hand that trembled with the beating of his sad heart:

"I have wanted to give my country the Hôtel Biron for four years, and my desire cannot be realized. I am coming round to my other idea: Belgium will have my works. She saved France and is therefore our country now, and her King and Queen are the two noblest people of our day.

"But perhaps it would be better for France if I kept my works here."

Thus, in his final lucid moments, he was obsessed by the idea of his museum, and it was the duty of his true admirers to accomplish its establishment.

One day I was immersed in thoughts of this man who had so often thwarted his own progress, when the cynical words of Mme Martin intruded upon my musing: "Well, here are the trouble-makers in full action. They've made up their minds to go down to posterity with the visual consent of their victim." She held out a ghastly series of photographs showing Rodin sitting in a chair in his dressing gown, with head drooping, eyes glazed, and mouth distorted—the face of a paralytic in the midst of an attack. Beside him were his nurses, the stout Russian woman and her niece. One of his hands was held by his wife who sat huddled in a low chair; the other lay in that of the Russian, who stood behind him and saw to it that the hand rested upon the clay head she had done of the dying sculptor. The sinister scene had been set for the purpose of authenticating the bust which had eventually been thrown from the window by Mme G——.

The G—s had also provided themselves with photographs; one showed a cozy scene in their studio: Rodin modelling the daughter's bust, the sitter and her mother in evening dress, and a little bust of the sculptor done by the latter in full view. Another showed

Rodin, swathed in wraps, holding one of the daughter's pretty hands, while Mme Rose sat apart, gloomily contemplating her position as wife of a famous man.

The guarding of Rodin's studios did not completely discourage the intriguers. Mme G——, exasperated at being refused admittance to the Hôtel Biron, complained bitterly of measures that she had advised me to take against Loïe Fuller. She came to Meudon and declared that, since the State seemed unable to establish the Rodin Museum, she would herself undertake "to put the revered master's works where they belonged." Later, realizing that she was beaten, she told M. Bénédite of her intention to spend several months in Florence.

Loïe Fuller's position was strengthened by the old couple's pleasure in her company and she became more insistent. One evening late in August, about ten o'clock, Mme Martin, who had been instructed to inform me of anything unusual, hurried courageously along the roads, unlit because of the "gothas," to tell me that the American dancer had taken M. and Mme Rodin off in a taxi at two o'clock, and had not yet brought them back. She deplored the carelessness of Rodin's friends who were unable to get rid of intruders, the crazy atmosphere that permeated the villa, Auguste's uselessness, and the incapacity of Mme Rose who was just as irresponsible as Rodin himself. It was serious. Why had Loïe spirited them away like that? Where should she look for them on such a dark night? "That wretch," I said, "is capable of having taken them somewhere in order to dictate a new will to Rodin. Go back to the villa and if they have not returned send Auguste here and we'll go to the police."

I heard the next day that they had returned sometime after ten, having dined at Villebon. If stamped paper had been used again, all our efforts were vain, also my instructions to the incorrigible Rose.

On getting up in the morning I habitually glanced at the opposite hillside where the villa stood almost hidden by its surrounding trees; I could see the façade of the Château d'Issy wreathed in morning mists and I always wondered, as my eyes rested upon this little temple exhaling incense, placed there by Rodin to recall the beauty of Greece, what fresh madness might be taking place within the walls of the villa. Had not Auguste's wife Nini, a shrewd observer of the melodrama, suggested the probability of a secret marriage between Rodin and Mme G——? Such a move might easily have occurred to that crafty tactician, and her hatred of Mme Rose—a fragile but insurmountable obstacle—would thus be explained. In that case our scheme to get Rodin married with several ministers as witnesses—the banns were already being published at the Mairie—would make him a bigamist. This prospect was appalling, but so ludicrous that I could not help laughing.

XII. DONATIONS TO THE STATE – RODIN'S LAST WORK

M. BENEDITE'S amiability increased. He admitted that he had been suspicious of me at first, as of all the women in Rodin's entourage (he might, I thought, have taken the trouble to inquire about me); he told me that the police were looking up the records of Rodin's friends (so I had the police to thank for his changed attitude!); and he added that he was delighted to have me work with him. Then, no doubt with the idea of showing his confidence in me, he told me an incredible story about M. Clémentel.

M. Bénédite was not a sympathetic person in matters of art, and his subordinates complained of his unpredictable moods and his despotism; however, I managed to respond fittingly to his friendly advances and promised to second him faithfully and earnestly in the task which had been allotted to us. His appearance was rather pleasing: medium height, good figure, and, though nearly sixty, youthful alertness in his movements. His hair was crisp and curly, his beard pointed, and his full face resembled that of a Valois of the Renaissance, but his weak profile and the line of his jaw were rather commonplace. He called one day at the villa when I was lunching there, and seemed nervous and timid, even frightened, standing at the dining-room door, as though he feared another of Rodin's outbursts. But alas, the lion was now as gentle as a lamb and on that occasion completely absorbed in his feeble dreaming. In order to put M. Bénédite at his ease, I said to Mme Rose that she could henceforth count upon him as a sincere and devoted friend. Later, he informed me that, to facilitate my dealings with undesirables at Meudon, he would have me made an unsalaried member of the staff of the Luxembourg, with special duties at the Rodin Museum; he also told me that he would ask for the appointment of a small advisory council composed of MM. Clémentel, Peytel, and ourselves. He further stated that, since Rodin would have to bear the expense of moving his works from Meudon to Paris, it would be necessary for him to sell several of the properties that belonged to him. The proposed marriage was in his opinion dangerous. Who could tell what result it might have? Auguste Beuret's position would be legalized, an heir would thus be created, and Mme Rodin would be far less amenable to the State's wishes if given the status of wife in the eyes of the law. All this troubled me greatly, and I spoke of our promise to Rose. "Yes, but later," replied M. Bénédite. "We cannot allow sentimental considerations to interfere."

The classifying of the drawings—it actually took six weeks—was the most urgent of my duties, so I began at once. There were hundreds of them: cartoons, crayon sketches, drawings in black-lead pencil, and water-colours—all were given their number.

Towards the end of his career, Rodin had done far less sculpture than drawing. Several adaptations, a few busts of women, the unfinished model for *Le Monument au Travail*, groups and subjects such as *Bénédictions, Crépuscule, La Terre et la Lune, Psyché, Mirage, L'Homme et sa Pensée, La Main de Dieu* seemed a scanty harvest in comparison with that of his earlier years. But he was all the while producing works, the richness and abundance of which are still not realized by the general public. "No one drew like Rodin," the painter Ernest Laurent maintained, despite his association with officialdom, "no one—not even Michael Angelo." Art critics have erred through carelessness and have temporarily harmed these astonishing productions of Rodin's maturity which will soon be fought for by collectors. The critics claim that they see in them nothing but rough sketches to which the artist could have attached no importance. Nothing could be farther from the truth. They must have merely glanced at the drawings; otherwise they could not have helped perceiving, beneath the freedom of the line and the fulness of the modelling, the sum of all his knowledge and experience, as effective as the power which brings a flower or a fruit to maturity. "The mind draws, but the heart models," said Rodin. Quickly, as though afraid that the images would escape him, he contrived to capture living forms by means of a few essential lines and colours. It was a synthetic method of transcription; the impression passed with the speed of electricity from his brain to his fingers without, as it were, a break in the contact. There was an uninterrupted current that flowed between him and external objects. Tirelessly he made his drawings; they were compact with life—not steps towards some accomplishment, but ends in themselves; not sketches, but completed drawings. In an undated letter to Bourdelle, written about 1903, Rodin said: "My drawings are the direct results of my sculpture."

He came to value his drawings more than any of his other work and, when asked to exhibit them, he often sent carefully made copies because he feared the originals might be lost or carelessly handled. He never presented them even to understanding and appreciative friends without a twinge of regret.

Slowly these marvellous sheets passed under my eyes—by hundreds, by thousands. When evening came I would go up to say good-bye to the man who had produced them. He sat in his chair, often so detached from the world about him that he did not recognize me. The weather had turned cooler and a wood fire burned in the grate. Mme Rose sat near him and he held her hands in his to keep them warm. Once I spoke of his drawings and told him it required much strength of character not to take some of them away with me.

"I believe you," he said, "especially when one can appreciate them."

"How wonderful they will look in the Hôtel Biron!"

"Yes—the lighting is excellent. I will go there this winter when my wife is better." Embers sometimes glowed for a moment in the dying fire of his mind.

Mme Rose took me downstairs. "He thinks he is still in Belgium," she said. "Now and then he doesn't know me. He says, 'Where is my wife?' and I answer, 'Here I am. Aren't I your wife?' 'Yes, but my wife in Paris—has she any money?'"

I was careful not to enlighten Mme Rose. His wife in Paris! He must have meant his former pupil whom he had never forgotten and to whom (Mme Martin assured me of this) he had until recently been paying a small allowance.

M. Bénédite and I had a delicate task to perform. Rodin's actual state had to be concealed from all save his intimate friends. His enemies would have leapt at this opportunity for doing him further injury. We let it be known simply that he was seriously ill and could not leave Meudon. We were obliged to answer all his letters, merely asking him to sign them, and to get rid of visitors without hurting their feelings. Our conferences took place at the Ministry of Commerce and Rodin's lawyer, Maître Ph——, whom I had not seen before, attended the first one. I had been thinking so much about the will extracted by Mme G—— and her daughter that the presence of a member of the profession filled me with suspicion. I asked the Minister privately whether he had confidence in Maître Ph——: "Oh, he's one of the best known in Paris," was the smiling reply.

There was some discussion about Rodin's leaving the Villa des Brillants and its surrounding buildings to the State. The question was a complicated one, because the sculptor had made Mme Rose a joint owner of the land upon which the studios had been erected. She would therefore be obliged to sell her share back to him. I was asked to hunt for the title deeds which no one else had been able to find. I imagined they were in the mysterious room of which Rodin himself kept the key; it was forbidden to Mme Rose and she called it Blue Beard's Chamber. I was unwilling to enter it without a witness and I asked that either the Minister or M. Peytel might accompany me.

One afternoon I climbed the stairs to this secret room with Rodin, Mme Rose, M. Clémentel, M. Bénédite, and Mme Martin. It was almost too small to contain the six of us at once with all its piled boxes and bundles. These were labelled: *Manuscripts, Notes, Bills, Letters;* there were nine containing letters from his feminine admirers.

Pointing to some bundles of papers marked *Opinions on Art,* the Minister exclaimed: "There's some work for you. All those notes will have to be put in order." M. Bénédite opened an envelope and drew out a paper headed: *Draft of Bequest.*

"Look at this," he cried indignantly, "about Mademoiselle Cladel! Who could have written it? '(1) M. Rodin will offer a marble group to Mlle Cladel and she will sign a paper in which she will undertake not to enter or attempt to enter the Hôtel Biron at any time. (2) The Minister of Fine Arts will appoint the personnel to be suggested, or at least approved by M. Rodin. . . .'"

"But it's Mme G—'s handwriting," exclaimed Mme Martin. "Wait, here are some letters from her daughter. They're idyllic as befits her age."

"Keep these documents carefully," advised M. Bénédite. "One day we'll ask these ladies to explain themselves and they will be useful."

We had found the title deeds and I took them to Maître Ph—— at his chambers in the Boulevard Bonne-Nouvelle. The out-of-date atmosphere, the Louis-Philippe mahogany benches, and the tiers of green cardboard boxes pleasantly recalled similar offices described by Balzac. Maître Ph—— was approaching sixty; he was of medium height, thickset, smooth-shaven, and was less distinguished than the chambers in which he drew up his documents. We exchanged a few remarks about the plotters at Meudon, and he told me Loïe Fuller was a dangerous woman who had tried to get Rodin to sign documents to which he, his lawyer, had been absolutely opposed.

"And what did Rodin say?"

"He said, 'You are right,' and turned his head on his pillow."

"This was after his illness?"

"Of course."

After leaving Maître Ph——, a vague but persistent uneasiness, rather like the beginning of a headache, began to oppress me.

On the 13th of September, 1916, at the Villa des Brillants, Rodin's second bequest to the State was executed. In the huge drawing-room which had been carefully put in order were gathered MM. Clémentel, Dalimier, Bénédite, Valentino, and Paul Painlevé. Mme Rose and Mme Martin were also present. The documents to be signed dealt with the second of the three bequests and included "all works of art, without exception, contained in M. Rodin's different studios, whether his own work or of other origin; all his writings, manuscripts or printed works, published or not, with full rights in them." This meant that, in addition to the sculptor's bequest of the preceding April, he now presented to his country twelve marble figures and groups, twenty bronzes, a hundred terra-cottas, and more than three thousand drawings and sketches. The whole was undervalued at 347,000 gold francs. The deed for the Villa des Brillants and La Goulette, representing a sum of approximately 190,000 francs, had not yet been drawn up. This third bequest was executed on October 25, 1916, with a clause attached in which the State appointed M. Léonce Bénédite as Rodin's representative "for the administration and the management of its artistic heritage."

The divestment was complete, but it seemed legitimate since the dispositions were made for the sole purpose of preserving the works of one of France's greatest geniuses.

Maître Cottin for the Ministry of Fine Arts and Maître Ph—— for Rodin solemnly read the documents. The Minister accepted provisionally for the State and two distinguished names were affixed to the contract: Auguste Rodin and Paul Painlevé. The others present were privileged to affix theirs, and when Rose Beuret leaned laboriously over the table I looked at M. Clémentel, for there was a clause in the contract in which Rodin declared that he was a bachelor and had no heir with any claim upon his property. Not legally, perhaps; but in equity? . . . When my turn came I took a pen and dipped it in the inkstand.

"I beg your pardon," interrupted Maître Ph——, handing me the fountain pen the others had used. "All the signatures must be written in the same ink."

This done, he held out to me, as temporary secretary, a paper he had taken from his portfolio; then, suddenly withdrawing it, he tore it into small pieces and gave them to me.

"Burn this," he said.

"What is it?" I asked M. Clémentel, who sat next to me.

"The Mme G—— will."

"Oh! I would have liked to see that."

"Piece it together."

I gave the handful of pieces to Mme Martin: "Paste them together on a sheet of paper and keep it carefully." Then, with rapidly increasing curiosity, I questioned my neighbour again: "How did Maître Ph—— get hold of that will?" The Minister must have been secretly amused at my artlessness.

Rodin had made an effort to follow the reading of the contract. He was calm and, as usual when a number of people were present, silent; his natural dignity and politeness were in evidence. It was suggested that he give drawings to those concerned in the museum project; whereupon his face lit up and he stretched a generous hand towards the piles leaning against the wall. Comparisons and lively discussions ensued; the choosing was prolonged and finally MM. Clémentel and Dalimier each took two water-colours; M. Bénédite one. M. Painlevé was somewhat withdrawn and had to be questioned as to his preference. He accepted the gift offered with the utmost courtesy, took his leave of Mme Rodin as though she were a woman of the world, and told Rodin that many flattering things would certainly be said of him during the forthcoming discussions in the Chamber and the Senate. "Flattering things have already been said here," replied the sculptor. Then, as we took our departure in order not to tire him further, he turned to Mme Martin and to me: "I want you both to have drawings too."

The following day, Mme Martin brought me the will which she had pieced together: *I appoint Marie-Rose Beuret and Julie G—— (née B——) as my joint residuary legatees, with accretion to the survivor. I revoke all previous wills. Auguste Rodin, Meudon, 12 July, 1916.* The handwriting was wavering, misformed, with lines that sloped towards the bottom of the sheet; it was like that of a dying man and showed clearly that there had been criminal coercion.

Two days later I showed this tragic document to M. Bénédite whom my mother had asked to lunch with us. I told him I was going to burn it.

"No, you mustn't do that," he said, gazing at the paper greedily. "We will be bringing suit against Mme G—— for unlawfully withholding some of Rodin's works, and this weapon must be kept."

"Yes, but Maître Ph—— told me to burn it."

"He was wrong. The document is in pieces and therefore not valid, but it is nevertheless an incontestable proof."

"Take it then; it belongs among your papers."

M. Bénédite put it quickly in his portfolio.

On September 14 I received a telegram from the Ministry of Fine Arts informing me that the Chamber of Deputies had just passed the bill dealing with the Rodin Museum by a vote of 379 to 56. The day's session was curiously animated. Vigorously attacked by several members of the right and three or four spokesmen for the *Institut*, M. Simyan's excellent statement was brilliantly defended by M. Léon Bérard, and by M. Anatole de Monzie whose short speech, with its decisiveness and its somewhat insolent references to his opponents, was responsible for many votes. M. Dalimier closed the discussion.[1]

I took this news at once to Rodin who listened to it with smiling optimism. Towards noon, Loïe Fuller, just back from England, arrived for lunch at the villa. I told her of the vote in the Chamber, adding that Rodin's works were at last, irrevocably, the property of the State. She turned pale, almost choked, and was unable to speak for some moments. Then, suddenly, she got up, saying she was obliged to keep an important appointment in Paris and would come back later. She did not return that day.

Actually, the acceptance of the bequest was not as definite as I had given her to understand. The Senate's more doubtful vote had still to be obtained. Two days later M. Clémentel encountered Loïe Fuller at the villa. She had recovered her equilibrium and was trying to dazzle the sculptor with an extraordinary scheme to establish a museum in San Francisco to be endowed by two American millionaires. Before going to England the impetuous dancer had taken from the studio a *Tête de Saint Jean-Baptiste* in marble worth at least 25,000 francs. She began by making flattering speeches to M. Clémentel, but this merely irritated him and he asked coldly where the head was. She replied serenely that the sculptor wisher to offer it to the Queen of the Belgians, and that she herself, through the kind offices of some highly placed friends, was attending to the presentation.

"You have no power to make such a gift," said M. Clémentel. "M. Rodin's works are the property of the State. The head must be brought back at once. I was about to lodge a complaint with the State's attorney."

"Oh, you wouldn't let that happen to your friend Loïe!" she turned to Rodin with a forced laugh.

[1] *Journal Officiel:* September 15, 1916.

"Why not?" said the sculptor, with the logic of one in his mental condition.

The *Tête de Saint Jean* was restored to Meudon and Loïe Fuller tried to obtain a cast of it. She had actually announced the sculptor's intention in high places, for, some years later, the Belgian Court asked for the head and the French Government complied with its request.

This ministerial reprimand had little effect, and the dancer went constantly to Meudon; but Mme Martin had strict orders to increase her watchfulness and to see that paper, pen and ink were kept out of reach. One evening we left the villa together and she asked if she might take me home; she stopped her taxi on the way, and for almost two hours I was obliged to listen to her ungovernable chatter. This was fatiguing after my day's work at the villa, but she had several amusing things to say about her meeting with Rodin and Mme Rose in Italy the previous year: Rodin, lumbering as placidly as an elephant through old churches, emitting opinions after interminable contemplation, with Mme Rose at his side, gaping with exhaustion and boredom.

Discretion was not one of her qualities, so I listened, hoping for confidences. Apparently there had been any number of wills made in favour of Mme G—— and herself. She was aware of Mme G—'s dislike of her and told me that the sculptress was terribly jealous of her and furious because she, Loïe, had discovered her scheme to marry Rodin after Mme Rose's death which she expected would occur soon. In July, on finding that Rodin was in a bad way, she had said to her then intimate friend: "He wants to see a lawyer," whereupon both she and Loïe had gone to Paris to get one: "He was very polite to Mme G——, but rude and disagreeable to me," declared the latter bitterly.

At the word "lawyer" my curiosity flamed up and, though afraid of putting her on guard, I could not help hazarding the question:

"Who was the lawyer?"

"I can't recall his name."

"Where did you find him?"

"Somewhere in the Boulevard . . . the Boulevard Bonne-Nouvelle."

"Could it have been Maître Ph——?"

"Yes, that's who it was."

This information was so astounding that I decided to keep it entirely to myself.

From the torrent of words that poured over me I was able to gather that there had been three successive wills: one leaving half his fortune to Mme G——, a quarter to Rose Beuret, and a quarter to Loïe Fuller; in a second will he left only an eighth part to Loïe; a third reinstated Rose as his sole beneficiary. "And there is still another," she added.

"Yes," I said, taking a long chance, "the one you got Rodin to sign at Villebon."

"How did you know that?"

"We know everything; the police are in charge at Meudon. Won't you let me persuade you, an artist whom we all appreciate and are grateful to for so many beautiful performances, not to involve yourself in this unpleasant situation? Let the State manage Rodin's affairs. You say you have some papers he has signed. Give them to M. Bénédite. Go to see him; he is a very charming man."

The Curator awaited these papers impatiently; according to Loïe Fuller they granted her the rights in several of Rodin's works. Finally after endless evasions, she went to the Luxembourg empty-handed, saying she had just dropped in on her way to her manager's office. I happened to be with M. Bénédite at the time and we were obliged to listen for two hours to the incredible flow of her conversation—an extraordinary mingling of her commercial instinct and her vanity—the extravagance of which was something very like lunacy; she had a frenzied desire for possessions. M. Bénédite was suffering from a severe headache and had been making frantic signals to me for some time. I finally succeeded in getting her away, and, in the taxi, she tried to persuade me to have an impression taken of Rodin's hand which she could have cut in marble for each one of the twenty-three millionaires who were going to contribute to the establishment of the museum in San Francisco. I would have one, of course; also Mme Rodin and Mme Martin.

At last M. Bénédite, at the end of his patience, threatened her with legal proceedings and she then brought him several papers signed by Rodin in his pathetic invalid's handwriting. The most shocking thing of all was a promise to sell her a bronze casting of the *Balzac* for the absurd sum of 3,200 francs—the *Balzac* which, when in full possession of his mind, he had persistently refused to sell at any price!

M. Bénédite wrote to me:

"If she comes to Meudon again, will you and Mme Martin see that she is not left alone for a second. . . . We will never be able to get the sculptor's affairs in order or guarantee him the peace he deserves for the remaining years of his life unless we can get rid of these women. This last schemer is, in spite of everything, more dangerous than her predecessor; her audacity is appalling and her present behaviour is merely assumed for the purpose of hiding what she has done and intends to do."

Granted, but this work of surveillance was definitely beyond the compass of an artistic assignment. It was for the police and not for me to guard the door of the Villa des Brillants and protect the old people from this influence. Her attentions were unremitting; she took Rodin and Mme Rose out to lunch continually and the sculptor's régime was dangerously interrupted. She employed a nurse for him at her own expense and after dark she would have long consultations with her hireling in the road that ran past the villa. . . . No, my job was to classify drawings and attend to correspondence.

Rodin was pleased at the establishment of order and took a lively interest in our activities; he and Mme Rose would often sit with us in the drawing-room. Once when he got up to go, he had a flash of memory:

"I promised to give you each a drawing."

"How marvellous! But hadn't you better wait until M. Bénédite is here?"

"No," he insisted, "things that are not done at once often don't get done at all."

"I want one too," said Mme Rose pathetically.

She could have taken as many of them as she liked, but could not endure being excluded when her lord and master was conferring favours. She was given a water-colour, as were Mme Martin and I, and when Rodin signed and dedicated mine—the body of an adolescent, as straight and slim as a young tree or a jet of water—his writing was so firm and well formed that I had a gleam of hope for an improvement in his condition.

Jules Desbois came to Meudon that day. He had gone with me to see M. Clémentel, and to the Minister's astonishment—he had supposed that the task of finishing one of Rodin's busts would have enchanted Desbois—the scrupulous and frank-spoken sculptor had replied:

"You are not suggesting an easy task, Sir. If the bust turns out well, it will be Rodin's, of course; but if it is a failure, people will say it is my bust or that I have spoiled it. I must see it first."

At Meudon, Mme Rose took the damp cloths from the clay that she had been carefully attending to. It was a distressing consultation; Rodin stood there with clouded mind and the gift of creation gone forever. He looked silently and with apparent unconcern at his last work which, happily, was as fine as its predecessors, then at Desbois and the Minister.

"It is very beautiful," said Desbois, "and it must not be touched. The back of the head is not quite finished, but that is of no importance. Nothing remains now but to give it to a good caster."

He agreed to supervise the casting himself.

XIII. THE BATTLE
FOR THE MUSEUM –
MEUDON IN DISORDER

DESPITE the favourable report of the Fine Arts committee in the Senate, the museum proposal encountered a strong opposition. The academic party, having recruited several members from the right, hoped to prevent the vote of the Chamber from being ratified. A protest was drawn up and handed to the committee, signed by a dozen or more members of the *Institut*. An opponent of the project, M. Jules Delahaye, came to Meudon with the obvious intention to hunt for indecencies and report them to his fellow senators. He was refused admittance on the ground that the studios were being rearranged and could not be visited. He spoke politely and his sarcasm thus became the more apparent; we did not reply to his questions about "this famous secret museum."

It now delighted Rodin's enemies to speak of the "secret museum," despite the fact that the studios at Meudon did not contain a single figure or group that could be regarded as offensive to any educated person; and of the almost four thousand drawings and water-colours which had passed through my hands, perhaps, at the most, thirty water-colours, twenty pencil drawings, and as many sketches might, if stripped of their artistic quality, have been considered as gynecological plates. Like a scholar searching relentlessly for the solution of the mystery of creation, Rodin had set himself to represent the springs of life in woman. Or were these few drawings the evidences of a sex obsession due to the deprivations of old age? It is difficult to settle this point.

In the whole course of our long friendship, I had never heard him utter an indecent word, and it infuriated him to hear this sort of thing in the streets. Someone knowing him less well than I might regard this as hypocrisy, but it was no more than his simple approach to nature and her ways.

The manifesto of the *Institut* had to be answered, and Rodin's friends undertook to do it. The heads of the different sections of the *Société Nationale des Beaux-Arts:* Alfred Roll, Bartholomé, and Jean Beraud congratulated him publicly upon his "splendid gift to France." Albert Besnard, director of the French Academy in Rome; Frantz Jourdain, president of the *Salon d'Automne;* Rosenthal, president of the *Association de L'Art Français;* the *Société des Peintres et Graveurs;* the *Société des Peintres Orientalistes,* and other groups expressed similar appreciation. M. Bénédite and I organized a petition for which M. Bigand-Kaire obtained the signatures of the mayors of Marseilles, Nice, Cannes, and Toulon; this led us to ask for the support of other large cities. Lyons was the first to comply—by letter from Edouard Herriot who was a personal friend of Rodin's—and Toulouse, Bordeaux, and Rouen followed suit. Many well-known persons signed the petition, including Colonel Deport who was responsible for the famous '75 gun; his name was like artillery fire directed against those who were slow in giving their support.

Several of Rodin's friends and fellow-artists, among whom were Roll and Bartholomé, asked if they might see him, but it was impossible to grant their wish and no little diplomacy was required to prevent people from discovering the mental affliction which had fallen upon the most powerful genius of the beginning of the century.

Though the man had to be concealed, it was important for his works to be shown. M. Dalimier brought several delegations to

Meudon; with the group from the Senate came M. Murat, an intimate friend of Clemenceau's and a man of great sensitiveness. There were tears in his eyes as he stood in the lofty studio filled with gleaming statues. "This is infinitely moving," he said. "Everything should be kept just as it is now."

In spite of these favourable signs, M. Bénédite was anxious. He took up the cause of art with M. Dubost, President of the Senate, whose objections, obviously moral, had to be met: Rodin was unmarried, yet he had encumbered his estate with a reserve in favour of Mlle Marie-Rose Beuret (the name suggested someone in her twenties to those unfamiliar with the sculptor's private life); the sculptor would enjoy a great privilege as occupant of the Hôtel Biron which should really be made into a residence for visiting sovereigns. To this objection Léonce Bénédite replied: "There is a precedent, Sir—the Louvre!"

The debate in the Senate took place on the 9th of November. It was prolonged and, if anything, more animated than that in the Chamber. M. Lintilhac hotly defended his report; he had the support of M. Théodore Steeg and M. Dalimier, and his spirited discourse triumphed over the speakers for the opposition: MM. de Lamarzelle and Gaudin de Villaine. Whereupon the Senate passed the museum proposal, by a vote of 212 to 27. Owing to certain formalities, the final decision of the two legislative bodies was not definite until December 15, 1916.

"At last, we can breathe easily," said M. Bénédite when he heard the news. "We can begin work now."

There was plenty to be accomplished. Rodin's works were a world in themselves, in fact several worlds: models, drawings, and moulds. The complete inventory to include the contents of several buildings round Meudon would require months to complete.

But it was imperative, first of all, to see that Rodin and Mme Rose had certain comforts which up to now they had lacked. Winter had come and the heating system was both out-of-date

uchesse de Choiseul (*Duchesse de Choiseul*). Courtesy of the Musee Rodin

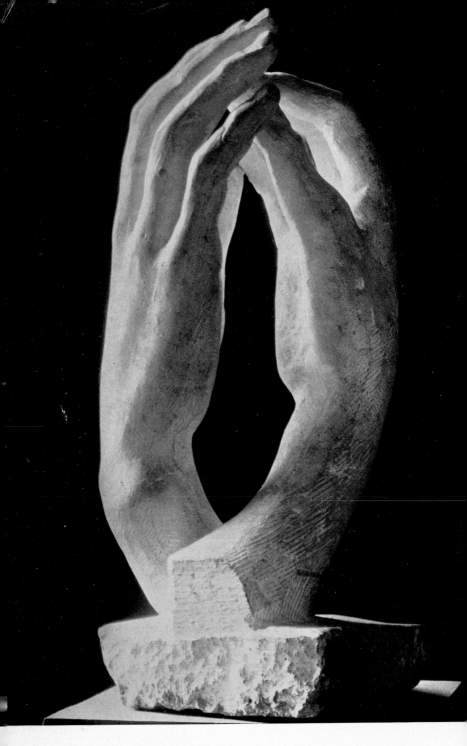

The Cathedral (*La Cathédrale*). COURTESY OF THE MUSEE RODIN

and badly managed by ignorant servants. Its premonitory rumblings had already terrified them. The ill-fitting doors and windows let in freezing draughts; defective drains filled the house with poisonous odours; the dogs had undermined the fences and wild rabbits had ruined the garden. The little house occupied by Auguste Beuret and Nini was just habitable in summer, but now the water which ran down the slope had found its way into the ground floor, and the floor above was so damp and cold that the poor souls had to have a huge dog sleeping on their bed to keep them warm.

Mme Rose suffered during the first weeks of winter. She lost weight and coughed a great deal, showing the poor state of her health; the last remnants of her strength were being used up in caring for her master. They were both horribly bored and for their amusement a competent chauffeur was engaged to drive the car Rodin had bought just before the war. M. Clémentel had persuaded Mme Rose to get a nurse to help her, recommending a woman of unusual serenity who had nursed his mother through her last illness.

Another urgent matter was the straightening out of Rodin's financial affairs. Some believed him to be very wealthy, for it was known that, since 1900, he had been selling from 150,000 to 200,000 francs' worth of sculpture a year; others feared that he might not be able to afford sufficient comforts for his old age. His capital was scattered about in different banks. But what banks? He could not remember. Mme Rose knew less than anyone about his affairs; she had her own small personal fortune which she had built up out of savings and occasional sums placed to her account by Rodin. She also kept in her room a sum of money in gold, and it delighted her to count and recount her treasure. Often, when one passed her door, the soft clink of gold louis and ten-franc pieces could be heard.

It was decided to collect Rodin's scattered resources and place them in the *Crédit Algérien*. He had a strong-box at the *Crédit Lyonnais* and I was asked to find the key to it at Meudon and to bring Rodin and Mme Rose to the bank with M. Peytel's lawyer.

The key was finally found in a little silver purse in one of the sculptor's pockets, but he had forgotten the combination of the supplementary lock, and an expert from the Maison Fichet had to be called in. The contents of the strong-box—60,000 francs in securities and about 20,000 in cash—were taken and put with the 250,000 finally gathered together at the *Crédit Algérien*. This total seemed small, considering the sculptor's long years of work, but he had invested a great deal in antique sculpture.

Mme Rose's condition improved slightly, and, now that she had followed her companion's example and given to the State all the works that belonged to her, there seemed to be no objection to proceeding with the marriage. The "family council" felt that the time had come, except, inexplicably, M. Bénédite. Mme Rose had never asked that her position be made legal; in fact she had recently said to me that if it were not M. Rodin's wish it should not be forced upon him. I reminded her of how gladly he had received the proposal, and when I looked at her ravaged features I was more than ever anxious for it to be carried out. After our visit to the *Crédit Algérien*, I suggested to Rodin that he should buy a wedding ring. We went into a neighbouring jeweller's shop and the sculptor ran his fingers through a tray of little gold bands with childish delight. Then he held one out to Mme Rose who joyfully slipped it on her emaciated ring-finger. But the man who had just bequeathed millions to France did not have a sou in his pocket and I was obliged to lend him twenty-five francs for his modest purchase.

When the inventory of the drawings was finished, M. Bénédite instructed me to supervise their moving to the Hôtel Biron. I had counted and marked three thousand four hundred at Meudon and there must have been almost as many more in Paris. I tied up the last bundle regretfully, for I had been in close communion for many long weeks with the supreme achievement of a great artist and such an opportunity would never occur again. I was fully aware of the great value he set upon his drawings and watched over their transfer with the utmost care. On arriving at the villa to attend to the packing of the second van-load, I found that the movers, coming earlier than the time fixed upon, had, with the help of the villa servants, hurriedly brought up the lot from La Goulette, confusing all the series. Who had given this order? I received evasive replies. Therefore I applied immediately to M. Bénédite for permission to supervise the unloading at the Hôtel Biron. He gave me an appointment, but when the day came there was no sign of him and the guard informed me that the Curator had neglected to leave the keys of the cupboards in which the drawings had been placed. I asked for another appointment and M. Bénédite said: "It's too cold at the Hôtel Biron to do the revising now." I tried to hide my exasperation, and resolved not to let the matter drop.

At Meudon, after the second van had disappeared, I was given a finely engraved card, bordered with black. Two ladies had asked to see the sculptor and were waiting at the gate of the court. The card bore the name: *Countess Grosvenor* and I went at once to speak to them, for Rodin had frequently mentioned the widow of George Wyndham, the handsomest of all English statesmen, and of her affectionate appreciation of the noble bust he had done of the man she adored. Lady Grosvenor had a friend with her and these two distinguished persons, whose costumes recalled the days of Queen Victoria, had asked, as though it were the greatest favour, to be admitted into the presence of Rodin. Before taking them into the little dining-room I begged them to forgive me for suggesting that, since he was so very easily fatigued, their visit should be a short one. The two old people were as usual sitting close to one another. Rodin got up at once and took off his beret without recognizing—or so it seemed to me—the visitors he was welcoming. They bowed and greeted Mme Rose; then, after a few moments' chat, they kissed the great man's hand with the ease and grace of the well-born and took their leave. Rodin did not appear in the least startled and smiled serenely. Lady Grosvenor and her friend did not suspect that the venerated artist's mind was veiled in shadow.

To my great regret, the unity of our "family council" was broken. M. Clémentel was nervous and impulsive and commenced to get on M. Bénédite's nerves. He insisted upon the employment of a caster of his own choosing for the museum. I was presently informed by the Curator that, in order to effect a proper surveillance, I would have to live at the Hôtel Biron in a room with north exposure. This, owing to my indifferent state of health and the necessity for me to be with my mother, was extremely annoying, but M. Bénédite persisted, telling me that he expected to find me installed there in January.

Things were in a state of revolution at Meudon. The cook refused to provide for the chauffeur; Mme Martin was in a rage with the nurse recommended by M. Clémentel and I sympathized with her when I saw the woman; the caster began to work under the direction of the Minister without consulting the Curator who loathed having his province invaded; the large drawing-room, which had been so tidy for the reception of government officials, now resembled a gipsy encampment; the sculptor himself was being given the wrong treatment and Mme Martin threatened to smuggle beefsteaks and wine into his room to prevent his dying of hunger.

Dr. Chauvet was asked to report to M. Clémentel upon Rodin's condition, but his advice was not heeded. The Minister blamed me for all the absurd mismanagement at Meudon; he then told me that M. Bénédite should have known better than to suggest my living at the Hôtel Biron. The thing was impossible. Where was my self-respect?

I understood nothing of this and protested, but he did not listen to me and began to expound his own ideas as to what the sculptor's régime ought to be.

Fortunately I was not required to live at the Hôtel Biron, and my activities were confined to the catalogue, which work could be done at home; but, in a few days, this was changed and I was given letters to write to Senators and Deputies; my duties were supposed to include an anquiry into the doings of Loïe Fuller, just returned from England and again a frequent visitor at Meudon. This last, I determined to neglect, since it was outside my province.

Mme Martin, who had just married a pleasant young electrician named Tirel, informed me that the nurse was disrespectful, even brutal, to Rodin; that Loïe Fuller, thanks to copious tipping, was on the best of terms with the woman, and that, despite the repeated orders of MM. Clémentel and Peytel, Mme Rose had threatened to have anyone thrown out of the villa who attempted to keep the dancer away.

On the last day of December, Dr. Chauvet stopped to get me on his way to the villa for his monthly visit. We had an altercation with the taxi driver who refused to wait there for us until he was given twenty francs. We did not pay this and he went off to fetch the police. The nurse was present during this scene.

The dining-room table was covered with toys brought by Loïe Fuller; Rodin and Mme Rose, the dancer, a young soldier, and the new Mme Martin-Tirel were gathered round it, and the sight of Rodin listlessly playing with a mechanical rabbit was painful. The nurse was very obsequious and attentive to Loïe who soon made the excuse of having to wash her hands and went into the adjacent bed-room for a confidential chat with the woman. Dr. Chauvet took me out into the passage and told me of his astonishment at finding Rodin in such a vacant state of mind. He asked to see the medicines he had prescribed and, on discovering that they had not been administered, he reprimanded the nurse severely.

In the meantime, our taxi driver had returned with a plainclothes officer. The former's demands were now more reasonable, but I told Mme Tirel and the nurse that we might need them as witnesses; I asked the latter to give me her name and address. She blushed furiously and told me that she would never tell me and would not dream of having anything to do with the police. Later, Mme Tirel informed us that this "perfect servant" had refused to sign a receipt for her wages until she realized that the money would not be given her otherwise. Mme Tirel then showed us her business card which we could not imagine how she had come by:

MME VEUVE T——

Medical and Surgical Nurse

Cupping

"She might have added 'Procuress and Abortionist,'" said Mme Tirel. "She looks the part."

I refrained from enlightening M. Clémentel as to the "admirable woman" of whom he had spoken so sentimentally, but he learned of her dishonesty elsewhere and she was discharged. A Russian woman, who seemed to me excellent, was engaged to replace her.

During the last year of his life, Rodin was destined to be surrounded by ignorant and useless people, and these accounts of their wretched intrigues may seem superfluous, but I feel them to be essential to a full understanding of the state of affairs at Meudon.

XIV. RODIN'S MARRIAGE – DEATH OF MME RODIN

RODIN'S marriage was at last fixed for the end of January. It was high time, for each day that passed took its toll of Mme Rose's vitality. I had frequently encountered Miss O'Connor at Meudon. She was a great friend of the Rodins, of good family, and secretary to the Comtesse Greffulhe. It had taken us some time to get to know one another because of the unfortunate atmosphere of mutual distrust surrounding Rodin, but a common desire to make the ceremony as agreeable as possible for the old couple finally brought us together.

MM. Clémentel and Peytel were to be Rodin's witnesses, and Mme Rose had asked Miss O'Connor and me to be hers. The contract was signed on January 22, 1917, and the wedding fixed for the 29th. When I informed M. Bénédite of Mme Rose's choice he told me that Miss O'Connor, being a foreigner, could not be a witness. "Anyhow, Mme Rodin has had enough of these women who flutter round her husband; she certainly doesn't want one of them for a witness." He himself and M. Weiler, from whom Rodin had bought his motor, would be Mme Rose's witnesses. I wondered whether I should ever discover the reason for the inclusion of this complete outsider.

I had performed my duties satisfactorily and M. Bénédite had shown his appreciation, but my friends kept advising me to be careful. "He has a mania for domination," one of his assistants confided to me. "He must control everything himself and complains continually of those who work with him, never allowing them to act upon their own initiative. He is as changeable as the moon. In short, though perhaps he doesn't mean to be, he is a dangerous man."

Recently his attitude towards me had altered somewhat. I felt that he was a little resentful of the affection shown me by Rodin and Mme Rose. The latter often asked me to lunch with them, and, though I rarely accepted her invitations, M. Bénédite seemed to grudge me this little intimacy. Though hurt by his high-handed substitution of the motor dealer—why on earth had he chosen that man?—I tried not to show it and merely asked Mme Rose why she had changed her mind. "Monsieur Bénédite said it was necessary," she replied.

It was impossible for them to go to the Mairie, and in order that the formalities might take place at the Villa des Brillants a marriage *in extremis* was necessary. The matter had been hanging fire for six months, but no arrangements were made and the time was short. Four days before the 29th, M. Bénédite sent word that he was ill and that I would have to attend to everything: find the two birth certificates, approach the proper authorities for permission to have the ceremony at the Villa, and see that the large drawing-room was put in order for it. Mme Rose asked me if I would invite several of her relatives from the Haute-Marne, "her niece," Mlle Coltat, and Rodin's first cousins, Emile and Henri Cheffer. The authorizations required were almost impossible to obtain in war time, and, worst of all, there was a serious shortage of coal at the villa. The man power of France had other duties and very little could be brought from the mines to Paris. The staff of the villa had no conception of saving anything and little thought for the comfort of the old people. I had been begging the sculptor's friends in the Government to send supplies ever since the beginning of the cold weather, assuring them that one night without heat would be the death of the two invalids, despite the fact that they had been moved to the ground floor where it was easier to keep warm.

Could the wedding take place on the 29th? Nothing was ready

on the 27th and the 28th was a Sunday. At the villa, Miss O'Connor and I found Mme Rose feverish and coughing continually; the Russian nurse had kept her in bed. Rodin smiled at us good-humouredly from his chair near Mme Rose's bed: "I never felt better and tomorrow I'm going to be married." Miss O'Connor laid her muff on the coverlet and he put his hands inside it to warm them. Whereupon Mme Rose, mistaking the source of his pleasure in so doing, snatched the muff and threw it across the room—jealousy would torture her till the very end. A box of old lace was fetched to appease her; it contained a gauze scarf, and Rodin, whose taste had survived the shipwreck of his mentality, spoke of the manner in which scarves, if subtly used, could enhance the charms of the feminine body.

"Do you remember the scarf?" asked Mme Tirel, glancing mischievously at the sculptor; "the scarf and the *bourée?*"

I squeezed her arm and whispered: "Why talk to him about that?"

"The *bourée?*" he questioned vaguely, and I realized that the past was indeed buried.

Mme Rose, who was too feeble to undertake any of the details, asked us to bring from Paris the necessary articles for a buffet lunch. We promised to do this for her without knowing how it was to be managed. In order to get the authorization for the house wedding, a certificate from Dr. Godefroy was required, stating that Rodin and Mme Rose were unable to go to the Mairie. We obtained this and also, miraculously, the promise of ten bags of coal from a merchant in Bas-Meudon for the morning of the 29th. Then we proceeded to the Luxembourg to confer with M. Bénédite; from there to a caterer's shop where we discovered that we ourselves would be obliged to arrange for the transport of the food to Meudon.

On Sunday the 28th the weather was dry and clear. We found our two old friends in much better spirits than we were; they knew nothing of our difficulties or how much remained to be done. Mme Rose was up and about; she had been trying on her wedding

313

hat joyfully, and when asked what she was going to reply to the Mayor when he asked her whether she would take M. Rodin for her husband, she said: "I will answer, 'Yes, your Honour; with all my heart.'" And her quavering voice was so eager that we refrained from telling her how legally superfluous the second phrase was.

During the afternoon two terrific explosions shook the windows of the villa. Rodin and his companion fled hand in hand towards the door, and servants came rushing up from the basement. Mme Rose turned pale and sank into a chair. Her heart was none too good and the possibility of her death before the ceremony so ardently desired flashed through my mind. Grotesque events usually occurred in the lives of great men, but why did this Jupiterian manifestation have to accompany one of Rodin's last acts?

Scarcely had we recovered from the fright caused by the explosions—we found out later that a munition factory at Puteaux had blown up—when another detonation shook the villa and cries broke out afresh. The heating system had finally burst, and streams of dark brown water flowed through the house. No heat could now be hoped for from that source, and Mme Tirel suggested bringing up two stoves from the casters' quarters. When the water had been sponged up, her husband, Auguste, and the guard got them into place with the utmost difficulty and lit them. But the drawing-room flues had been sealed up and smoke poured into the room, covering the freshly polished furniture with soot. We were soon as black as chimney-sweeps, but the flues were opened and at last all was in order again.

At nine o'clock on Monday morning, January the 29th, Miss O'Connor and I arrived at the villa with some rugs for the drawing-room lent by M. Bénédite, cakes and glasses from the caterers' shop, a butler, some flowers, and a wedding ring for Mme Rose to give Rodin. The coal had arrived and the little stoves were sending forth sufficient heat. Marie-Rose Beuret looked frail but distinguished in her wedding costume, and Auguste Beuret was radiant—convinced, according to Mme Tirel, that he would be legitimized during the ceremony—and Nini had been lent a muff and a lace scarf which gave her an unexpectedly respectable appearance. In his frock coat and large velvet beret, Rodin contemplated the order and elegance of his drawing-room with amazement. The furniture shone in the winter sunlight. "Don't the pictures look well in this light," he said, "especially the Falguière. It's a superb painting."

Guests and witnesses arrived, and the latter took their places round the table behind which the Mayor's assistant was preparing for the formalities. "What a setting!" murmured M. Dalimier who sat next to me. "I'll have you made directress of the Odéon." I moved close to Rodin, fearing one of his fits of absent-mindedness. When the Mayor came to the usual question he was absorbed in contemplation of a Van Gogh, so I leaned towards him and whispered the necessary "Yes, your Honour," which he repeated at once in a perfectly natural voice. Then Mme Rose laid a hand upon her breast and, in a feeble voice, made her touching reply: "Yes, your Honour; with all my heart."

Several photographs were taken by Choumoff and his assistant, and after brief congratulations and a few toasts the guests departed. Mme Rodin and her husband both seemed to be in a good mood; Miss O'Connor and I were asked to stay, and the four of us sat at a table near one of the stoves and lunched on the remains of the wedding buffet. "How delightful it is," we said to them, "to be able to celebrate your golden wedding on the day of your marriage! Fifty years together; it's marvellous!"

Other members of the group were less happy. Auguste was cruelly disappointed at not being legitimized, and Mme Tirel had gone off with him and his weeping Nini to try to bring back their gaiety with the help of several bottles of wine.

When we had finished lunch, Choumoff suggested more photographs, and Mme Rose asked that one might be taken of the group round the table. This touched me very much and Miss O'Connor was delighted at the prospect of being able to send a souvenir of this sort to her sister, Lady G——, in England. We then asked Choumoff to take Rodin and his wife alone, which he did with splendid result.

During the first part of February the shortage of coal was worse than ever. I could find none anywhere to replenish the supply at the villa and was without a scrap myself. Warmth was necessary for Rodin and Mme Rose and they were kept in bed most of the time. Who would have believed that the Minister of Commerce was one of Rodin's friends? This question was always in the foreground and it seemed to be particularly exasperating to M. Bénédite, already sorely tried with the Rodin relatives—not with the Cheffers who had gracefully accepted the situation, but with the Coltat sisters:

"They are being very silly," he complained. "They're going to make trouble and have already threatened legal action. They declare they have been robbed by the State, and are furious about the marriage, because they noticed you forcing Rodin to say 'yes' to the Mayor's question. And that fool Clémentel laid himself out to be polite to them; he even received them at the Ministry that evening. His lack of judgment is appalling."

Miss O'Connor lost no time in calling at Choumoff's studio to see the photographs, and was greatly disappointed not to be shown the one of the group. She was told that M. Bénédite had suppressed it; the sculptor's appearance of fatigue and dejection was such as to make this action necessary. Otherwise, said Choumoff, the photograph had been excellent and he had suggested, when showing the plate and print to M. Bénédite, that another head of Rodin could easily be substituted. But the Curator had objected violently; he had taken the plate and print from Choumoff in order to destroy them. Certain members of the family, he said, were accusing Rodin's friends of having forced the marriage upon him, and it was therefore important that this proof of his mental deficiency should not exist.

When I asked my employer to let me see the condemned photograph, he seemed rather confused for a moment; then he replied, in the crisp tones he always employed when he believed his authority to be even slightly doubted, that the plate had been broken and the print burned, because there had been an expression of "appalling bestiality" on Rodin's face. Poor Rodin! What evil demon, during the two or three seconds of that pose with his wife and his two friends, could have imprinted an expression upon his face which I had never seen there in my whole twenty years' association with him?

Despite the warnings I had received, I could not account for M. Bénédite's new attitude. He had allowed photographs to appear which showed Rodin in a grievous state of collapse and mental vacancy, and he now suppressed one which obviously displeased him because it included me. I suppose he was unable to believe any woman could be disinterested.

Choumoff's assistant, astonished at the inexplicable suppression, had secretly made a print from the condemned plate. Several years later, this precious document was sent to me and I found that my suspicions were correct: Rodin's expression was one of perfect naturalness and serenity.

On the 14th of February I received two letters which sent me hurrying to Meudon. One, from the nurse, Mme Markovitch, informed me that Mme Rose was very bad; the other, from M. Bénédite, brought me the more precise information that her bronchitis had turned into pneumonia and that there was no hope for her recovery.

A bitterly cold wind swept the Meudon hillside. The front door of the villa was partly open when I arrived, and I heard voices as I entered the drawing-room. Nini and the laundress were standing by a large brass bed covered with a sheet and seemingly empty.

"Do you know what's happened?" asked Nini.

"No—what?"

"She is here."

The sheet, beneath which the emaciated body had been almost imperceptible, was turned back and I gazed upon the wax-like features and closed, sunken eyes of Mme Rodin. Upon a table at the bedside were a burning candle and a goblet containing some sprigs of box; a glacial cold pervaded the room.

"When did she die?"

"Today at noon."

M. Bénédite and Mlle Coltat were going through the contents of the writing-desk in the little dining-room, and Rodin sat in the bed-room with sadness and resignation written upon his face. He was holding his wife's hand-bag from which Mme Tirel took some money to pay the laundress. A large envelope bearing Mme Rodin's name was then removed from his coat pocket. He made no objection to any of this and his dignified indifference seemed to signify: "Nature gave me the power of perception and admiration, and I have repaid her in work and love. I have given all that lay in my power to give. Nothing else matters to me now."

M. Bénédite and Mlle Coltat emptied the contents of the envelope upon the bed and counted two thousand francs in notes. They had already opened the little boxes and bags in which Mme Rodin had kept her savings, and these had been counted in the presence of Auguste Beuret, her heir. They amounted to about twenty thousand francs in gold and silver. The remainder of her fortune, one hundred and sixty thousand francs, was in the *Crédit Algérien.*

I had never before been present at a discussion of this sort in the presence of death and was surprised at the amateurishness of the procedure. Nini had removed the rings from Mme Rose's fingers immediately after her death, but Auguste had angrily ordered her to put them back.

During the last three days of her life, Mme Rose had been in a peaceful state of mind, full of gentleness and gratitude to everyone. That morning she had kissed her husband, thanking him for the great happiness he had given her and telling him that her only regret was that she had to go first and leave him by himself.

318

. . . There was true nobility in the concentrated love of this simple woman. Those familiar with her sufferings were profoundly relieved to know of these moments of serenity at the end of her life.

At M. Bénédite's request, I returned the next day to attend to getting some black clothes for Auguste. The cold was much less severe and there was a spring-like softness in the air; birds flew in and out of the hedges and bushes, chattering gaily; two huge aeroplanes crossed the clear blue sky.

Rodin had slept well, but when I saw him in bright daylight he looked much thinner; the bony structure of his face and head seemed more easily perceptible and his eyelids were red. Before he was dressed, M. Clémentel arrived, bearing a huge bouquet of flowers. His effusive greeting was rather confusing to Rodin, always so moderate in such demonstrations, but he admired the bouquet, saying that flowers were always beautiful anywhere, and laid them upon the bed. He then lifted the sheet and bent over the drawn face, examining it closely. "She is beautiful," he said, "just like a piece of sculpture."

The Minister spoke to him about the tomb to be erected in the garden of the villa, in which Mme Rodin's body would eventually be placed. Then he explained at much too great length that when the time came the sculptor himself would rest beside her, beneath a stone slab upon which was to be placed *Le Penseur*. Rodin was not afraid of death and he replied serenely: "Yes, and I shall be there for years—millions of years." When the Minister had left the room, he asked me to go after him and beg him to present his compliments to Mme Clémentel, and I took this opportunity to ask him to lose no time in having the heating system repaired and to do what he could towards having some coal delivered. The feebler of the two old people had died from lack of heat and it was imperative to prevent a repetition of the tragedy.

On the 16th of February we saw Mme Rodin for the last time;

319

and Rodin, realizing that the final separation was drawing near, went more often to gaze upon his wife's body. He would leave his chair silently, open the door, and make his way quickly and resolutely into the drawing-room, and would have struck anyone who dared to oppose him. At the bedside he took off his beret: "She is like an antique statue." Then he laid his hands tenderly upon the marble-like feet to warm them. That evening he insisted on being present when she was placed in her coffin.

A mortuary chapel was improvised in the garage, in order to protect Rodin from too many visitors. It was hung with black and filled with flowers; the body remained there for three days. The funeral took place on the 19th of February at eleven o'clock, and was attended by the same friends and relatives who had been with Rodin on the morning of his wedding three weeks before. Since no one had thought of summoning a priest to the bedside of the dying woman, the Church refused to officiate and the coffin was taken, without the usual services, to its temporary resting place. Rodin drove to the cemetery with his son.

The nurse gave me some alarming accounts of the behaviour of the occupants of the villa during the days preceding the funeral; she said that the dreadful scenes of drinking, shouting, fighting, and weeping frightened her and were clearly dangerous to the sculptor's health. I spoke of this to Léonce Bénédite the next day, but he had nothing to suggest. Surely it was possible, I thought, to find servants and caretakers who could be trusted. But no one with authority felt as I did. The "family council" no longer met and M. Peytel seemed unable to suggest anything but economy. With only fifteen thousand francs income, Rodin had only just enough to live on. He spoke as though a man already seventy-seven had to be assured of enough money to last for many years.

The moving of Rodin's sculpture to Paris was undertaken just as carelessly as that of his drawings, and with no regard for the aged artist's feelings; with a little tact, he could have been spared the sight of the disorganized studio. His adored *Christ* had been brought down from the bed-room and was leaning precariously against the staircase leading to the gallery. No order had been given to disturb this cherished statue and when Rodin saw it he was greatly upset. With face deathly pale and eyes full of distress he lifted the statue with his own hands, and, muttering to himself, started to take it back. Whereupon I asked two of the movers to carry it immediately to his room.

Two days later I found him wandering about the devastated studio with tears rolling down his pale cheeks. I discovered that an order had been given to set up *La Porte de l'Enfer* with several of the figures in a different arrangement from the one settled on by the sculptor. I could scarcely contain my anger and disgust. What a scandalous way to treat a man who had just given everything he possessed to his country! This blundering insolence was not difficult to trace; the man responsible for it had become despotic, undertaking far more than he knew how to accomplish. M. Bénédite's schemes for the Hôtel Biron and the garden at Meudon were appalling, and the preoccupation of M. Clémentel with other pressing business gave him full control. No administrative council for the museum was appointed, "because," said the Curator, "a council would complicate everything. It is much better to organize the museum first."

Despite the daily visits of Mlle Coltat and Mme Charles Cheffer, Rodin was cruelly bored. I sometimes tried to get him to discuss matters of art, and he expressed himself in disjointed phrases, but for the most part clearly. Pens and pencils had to be locked up to avoid any further papers being signed, and I suggested that he be given clay and tools; he might have been able to amuse himself by modelling something. But it was not thought advisable for him to have this distraction.

One afternoon Paul Cruet, instructed by M. Bénédite, took a

cast of Rodin's hand. It was cleverly done, but, unfortunately, no amount of care in the execution could produce anything but a lifeless member whose strength and adroitness were gone forever.

Sometimes, weary of his seclusion, he longed to go to Paris and his museum; several times he started off by himself and had to be brought back. Thus, it was decided that he should be allowed to go there every other Sunday.

"Why not let him live at the Hôtel Biron during the winter?" I asked the Curator. "He would be much better off there than at Meudon where it is difficult to keep him warm and amused."

"Not possible. Rodin has his own ideas."

"And they have not been proved bad ones."

"He's already been brought there without warning."

"What of it?"

"We must know when he is coming."

My doctor had been urging me to go to the country for a while, but I was reluctant to leave and I asked M. Bénédite to let me do my work on the catalogue in some corner of the Hôtel Biron where I could have the windows opened into the garden.

"No," he said, "you mustn't come to the Hôtel Biron. You know it's one of Rodin's manias. He doesn't want you there; he spoke of it a few days ago. It embarrasses me to have to tell you this [he seemed in no way embarrassed], but it may explain my recent attitude. . . . I suppose you know that Mme Rodin was angry with you on her wedding day."

An angel from heaven would have lost patience with this man.

"What can you mean? Mme Rodin has known me for twenty years. But for me, the wedding you all refused her until she was a dying woman would never have taken place at all. And Rodin has nothing but the friendliest feelings for me."

"Rodin is not very sincere; he will never tell you the truth."

"Rodin is no longer Rodin; the poor man has no will of his own."

"Just try to get him to sign a document in your favour. Then you'll see."

322

"I will certainly do nothing of the sort; he would sign anything I asked him to. That is why you and the others always wanted me to get his signature for any particularly important document or cheque when you suspected that he would refuse anyone else. And now you are trying to make people believe that Rodin is hostile to me."

"You must understand that I am telling you this for the sake of the future and because of my friendship for you," added M. Bénédite, realizing that he had said too much.

Certain things were now clear. Rodin's representative wanted neither the sculptor nor me at the Hôtel Biron. Why? I resolved to bide my time patiently, for I wanted to be near Rodin until he died. If I were not careful he might be forced to sign some sort of paper which would keep me away from Meudon. However, I went again to M. Dalimier and urged him to appoint the museum council. "You are perfectly right," he said. "We'll talk to Cortot about it."

The great musician took down the names suggested by the Minister. He seemed to be listening, not with his ears, but with his big dark eyes, as though he had been given secondary organs for hearing in order to leave the primary ones free to receive musical sounds. But the Painlevé cabinet fell, and M. Dalimier with it; the council of the Rodin Museum was still not appointed.

XV. LAST DAYS

DURING the summer, Rodin had a fainting fit lasting twenty minutes which was very alarming to those who witnessed it. The doctor was present and declared that its origin was digestive and not serious.

Minor intrigues persisted at Meudon and some most peculiar measures were taken. The motor was sold and Rodin's outings were now confined to drives in an uncomfortable carriage from the local livery stable. He saw few of his old friends and far too many new ones. A dentist who dabbled in sculpture was allowed to do his bust, and Choumoff kept on taking photographs, chiefly showing Rodin with M. Bénédite who was anxious to prove publicly his great intimacy with the sculptor. Unfortunately for him, this friendship dated from the time of the latter's mental collapse.

On the 2nd of November, Dr. Chauvet and his wife went with me to Meudon. We found Rodin walking among the chestnut trees; his colour was good, his step less laboured, and his mind less clouded; he complimented Mme Chauvet upon her husband's expert care of him. The new nurse and Mlle Coltat asked whether it would not be advisable, in view of the approaching cold weather, to take Rodin to the south—to Nice or Monte Carlo. "At his age," said Dr. Chauvet, "and considering his failing strength, such a journey would be a serious risk—the trains are few and poorly heated. But, since the heating system here is not in order, he should be moved to a comfortable well-heated apartment in Paris as soon as possible. Otherwise there is the risk of pneumonia."

My repeated appeals to MM. Clémentel and Peytel produced no result, and M. Bénédite was so deeply involved in other schemes of his own that he continually shelved the question of the sculptor's comfort and proper care.

The 12th of November was Rodin's birthday and I went to see him. He was in bed in the little ground-floor room; the nurse told me he had caught cold and had a touch of bronchitis. I talked very little, not wishing to tire him, and he was affectionately appreciative of my visit. Dr. Creton who sometimes replaced Dr. Chauvet came to see him while I was there, but, as he wanted to report to his colleague first, he made no pronouncement.

On returning to Paris I found that an advance copy of my book, published by The Century Company, had arrived from America on the 77th birthday of the man whose life and work it concerned. It had been splendidly produced and I showed it to him the next day. He was still in bed, slightly flushed, and his white hair more striking than ever against the whiteness of the pillows. "Here is something from America for your birthday," I said. He smiled and examined it with childish delight, lifting it from its shiny cardboard box and untieing the wide ribbon bow. "How well they have done it and what a pretty ribbon," he murmured. Then, taking my hand and kissing it, he added: "Thank you, my dear." I showed him some of the illustrations and sat quietly with him for a few moments. His large blue eyes wandered about the room; the wood fire and the partially drawn blinds enhanced the peaceful intimacy of the atmosphere. He was not suffering, and he seemed to be completely absorbed in the enjoyment of the diffused light around him—the sort he had always loved for his work.

At six o'clock, Dr. Chauvet listened to his breathing with his stethoscope. When he had finished he took Mlle Coltat and me aside and said: "The thing I feared has happened. M. Rodin has been allowed to catch cold and his lungs are affected—there are spots already and his condition is very serious."

I was badly frightened and accepted his offer to take me back to Paris so that I could question him further.

"You say his condition is very serious. Does this mean that you will not be able to save him?"

"At his age and in his weakened state it will be almost impossible. If only my repeated orders had been obeyed! I must write to M. Clémentel explaining the situation so that he will not hold me responsible."

Could it be that the great man had come to the end of his life? He did not look very ill. Surely a man of Dr. Chauvet's skill and energy could save him, could at least keep him alive till the opening of his museum!

The next day there was no change, but at noon on the 15th Dr. Chauvet stopped at my apartment on his way back from Meudon. He said that his diagnosis of two days before was, alas, confirmed. Only a miracle could save Rodin. Then he told me of his stupefaction that morning at being asked to wait outside his patient's door until a lawyer with the help of four witnesses had finished getting the sculptor to make his will, when only the previous day he had been in a state of complete mental and physical collapse. Finally the doctor, insisting upon seeing his patient, had found him in a coma. From the bed-room had emerged Maître Ph——, M. Bénédite, and the four witnesses.

During most of the afternoon, Rodin's eyes were closed and he breathed with difficulty. Now and then his eyelids fluttered and he mumbled incoherently. At twilight, a hospital bed arrived from Paris with a mechanical device by which the patient could be gently raised and the bed-clothes changed. The men who had brought it were about to set it up when a fuse blew out and the villa was plunged in darkness. A flickering candle filled the room with leaping shadows and the groaning of tightened iron bolts echoed through the house while the dying man gasped for breath. The scene was fantastic, and painful to us who were straining to catch every sound he made. When the noise had ceased I laid a hand upon Rodin's perspiring forehead—it was comforting to realize that he had heard nothing.

Shortly after six o'clock, M. Bénédite paid a second visit. He was very much startled to find me at Meudon and immediately began to insist, with the corroboration of Mlle Coltat and the nurse, that Rodin had been absolutely lucid all morning. None of them knew that Dr. Chauvet had already reported to me upon his patient's condition.

When the time came to leave, Mme Tirel walked a little way with me. "They're all disgusting," she grumbled. "What hypocrites! That will this morning was a disgraceful business. They got the nurse to give him an injection five minutes before the witnesses arrived. Bénédite is the worst of the lot. Think of the trouble we took to get rid of all those scheming sluts, and now we turn him over to that crafty fox."

The document mentioned by Mme Tirel was not a will, but a codicil to the will made six months before, in which two thirds of his fortune was left to the Coltats, one third to the Cheffers, and a yearly allowance of three thousand francs provided for Auguste Beuret, in addition to what he had inherited from his mother. In the codicil which had now been executed despite the testator's complete insensibility, various household effects and personal belongings were left to Mlle Coltat, his watch to Auguste Beuret, nothing to the Cheffers; and, finally, gratitude for devotion and disinterestedness was offered to his friend Léonce Bénédite whom he now entrusted with the task of selecting and publishing his correspondence and other writings. He then requested that M. Bénédite should succeed him as curator of the Rodin Museum and its annex at Meudon, and appointed him one of the executors of his will, with MM. Clémentel and Peytel.

At eleven o'clock in the morning of the 16th, Rodin's fever was high; his eyes were closed and he was breathing with the greatest difficulty. In spite of the struggle he was making his appearance had changed little. The shadows beneath his eyes had become darker and his mouth was slightly drawn to the right as a result of his last attack. Perspiration soaked his pillow and the nurse lifted his massive head from time to time so that a fresh one could be placed beneath it.

Mlle Coltat was deeply moved as we sat eating our lunch in the dining-room only a few feet away from Rodin's bed. There was no reason to regret his approaching death, for his destiny had been magnificently accomplished; but it was painful to remember the events of the past two years and the insignificant people with whom he had associated in this period of mental collapse.

In the afternoon an injection of serum was given. He moaned a little and tried to push the needle away. Paul Cruet held his hand tenderly and he was soon more comfortable and breathed more easily. But his moist temples pulsated like the flanks of an animal at bay. How grievous a thing is the passing of a soul from its mortal dwelling, and how vain the hope of those who imagine they can alleviate its distress. Theosophists preach resignation and they assure us that our grief merely impedes the flight of the departing soul.

Suddenly—and for me, seated at the bedside, alarmingly— Rodin's voice rose strong and clear, with even a tinge of scoffing forebearance: "And people say that Puvis de Chavannes is not a fine artist!" Even upon the threshold of death his mind was occupied with matters of art. These were his last words.

Mlle Coltat and her sister asked me to tell them, since the end was near, what clothes their illustrious relative should be buried in. I advised against a black suit covered with decorations, which seemed to me both commonplace and macabre, and suggested a long white robe like those he had worn in his studio. They agreed with me, and I went back to Paris immediately to see whether I could find one made of white woollen material. The search was long, but successful at last, and I returned to Meudon after dark with the robe, a batiste pillow, a white silk coverlet, and a little crucifix which the two sisters were anxious to slip into the sculptor's hands. They wanted me to stop for supper, but I could not endure the sight of Bénédite, cold and unconcerned, so close to the dying man's bedside. Everyone except Mlle Coltat was talking excitedly, but soon the room was empty; when I was alone, I leaned over and kissed the burning forehead of the man whose friendship and affection had meant so much to me.

Late that night I heard from a young journalist friend on the staff of *Le Matin* that the famous patient's condition was unchanged; the end came a few hours later. Rodin died on November 17, 1917, at four o'clock in the morning.

The next time I saw him he was lying in the vast drawing-room upon a raised couch. In his ivory-white robe he was like an emperor who, in repentance, had donned a monastic gown: Charles V after his abdication. There was a look of proud serenity upon his pale features, and his hands were like alabaster. I seemed to be gazing upon one of his own works. How far from the wretchedness of this world he now seemed! Eternal silence would be his refuge and his armour henceforth. Nevertheless, almost imperceptibly, at the corner of his mouth, hovered a fleeting and infinitely subtle smile—for Rodin was himself again. His intellect, his shrewd wisdom, his genius—all were there, beneath the massive forehead and behind the closed eyelids and ironical lips.

Visitors thronged the Villa des Brillants and were struck with wonder at the way in which beauty had triumphed over the hand of death. "He is like a thirteenth century effigy," someone whispered. The sculptor Bartholomé was overcome with emotion and had to be led from the room by his young wife. Mme de Ch—— laid a bunch of violets upon the folded hands of the man whose life she had once thrown into such disorder.

When the time came for me to return to Paris, I went to the dining-room to take my leave of the family. Around the table were gathered Mlle Coltat, Mme J——, the nurse, and M. Bénédite. A large sheet of paper lay beside an open leather case. In order to cover the silence caused by my entrance, the nurse said awkwardly: "This is a very good will." Bénédite quickly put the paper back into his case and the two sisters who had just thanked me warmly for my humble efforts now gazed at me with faces like stone. I was weary of all these people. What did they or their ignoble ambitions matter to me, after all?

M. Clémentel had called at Meudon that morning and had promised me an appointment in the evening:

"The scene in that room has been before my eyes ever since this morning," he said when I went to see him. "Sit down. What is it you wanted to see me about?"

"I am so distressed at this tragedy which could have been averted. Rodin's death occurred through negligence—through lack of proper heating at the villa. My poor efforts, alas, were too curtailed. I could accomplish nothing. But we need not try to fix the blame for what is past. The man is dead, but his works survive and they must not suffer. We are all apprehensive about their arrangement at the Hôtel Biron, and the Meudon garden has been ruined."

"Yes," agreed the Minister, "I was greatly disappointed to discover how insignificant *La Porte* and the large figures looked in the chapel. That must be remedied of course—perhaps by means of a false ceiling."

"The chapel will never be a suitable place for them. Rodin would have been in despair. And as for the garden at Meudon . . ."

"Yes, it's frightful," exclaimed M. Clémentel. "I will see to having it put in proper order."

"And I beg you to appoint the administrative council as soon as possible; let it be composed of artists—otherwise M. Bénédite will spoil everything."

"He has had himself appointed curator by will," replied M. Clémentel crossly.

"Which one?"

"The last one—day before yesterday. It all happened without my knowledge." Then he added, amiably: "You must have a job at the museum; your efforts should be repaid both financially and morally."

"Financially, as you see fit; morally—I think I deserve a job." I was well aware that Bénédite would never put up with me at the Hôtel Biron.

"Bénédite tells me he has found ten letters from Rodin proving his enmity towards you," said M. Clémentel with some embarrassment.

"Let him produce them; if they exist at all, they must have been obtained as was the will we have just been discussing and which is just as illegal as the one Mme G—— got from him. M. Bénédite wants me out of the way and he told me that you do too."

"I have no such feeling. I admit that I did not want you to live at the Hôtel Biron. That would have caused too much gossip."

"Why?"

"I have been told that Rodin was your lover."

"By whom?"

"Bénédite."

"And you believed it!" I could not help laughing. "Now I've got a real reason to be angry with you." How could he have been so stupid as to believe kitchen scandal from Meudon?

"Bénédite is full of schemes," he continued. "He's writing a book about Rodin, and he intends to publish his letters."

"Let him do what he likes, just so he doesn't publish anything Rodin did not write. He must be watched and I rely upon you to see that there is no falsifying."

At six o'clock the following afternoon the undertaker's men put the satin-lined coffin beside the bed in the drawing-room. The flowers were removed and for several moments the body lying upon the white sheets looked more sculptural than ever. Then it was placed in the coffin, covered with the white silk coverlet and sprinkled with thyme and lavender. The coffin was then closed and the lid screwed down.

331

The next day the black cloth covering was hidden beneath the folds of a tricoloured drapery and the vermilion and purple silk of his doctor's gown from Oxford University.

The funeral took place on the 24th of November. It was not an official one, the Government having considered such a decree untimely, and it seemed rather surprising that Clemenceau did not realize the symbolic import of such a tribute and its value as a protest against the horrible materialism of the war.

The ceremony was simple, and, except for the stupidity of the official address delivered by the new Minister of Education, M. Lafferre, not without a certain dignity. The low-hanging clouds had a threatening appearance and there was a touch of winter in the air. The façade of the Château d'Issy looked more than ever like a Greek temple. At the top of the steps leading to the grill at the entrance lay the coffin; above it, attached to the grill, was a trophy in the antique manner, and at the two vast window openings had been placed replicas of *La Grande Ombre*. The sky was hung with greyish violet clouds like funeral draperies. No rain fell. The peaceful landscape upon which the sculptor had gazed for twenty years had taken on an austere splendour for his funeral.

The crowd pressed close to the steps of the temple, its sombre colouring heightened here and there by uniforms of horizon blue. The addresses seemed hopelessly inadequate and gusts of wind carried off the superficial phrases as soon as they were uttered. The music of Bach or Beethoven would have been a more fitting tribute to the great man and would have expressed something of the emotion of those gathered round his coffin.

When the addresses were over, Aurel, trembling with rage because M. Bénédite had refused to allow him to speak, urged Séverine, the actress, to say a last farewell to Rodin on behalf of her sex. Bénédite objected, saying that the Minister did not wish any more to be said, whereupon Aurel, with fine courage, called aloud to Séverine who then mounted the steps. The words of this admirable actress were sincerely spoken, with great restraint and simplicity at first—then with increasing warmth and tenderness.

332

Everyone present had longed to hear just such a voice, and, despite the solemnity of the occasion, applause broke out when the last word had been uttered.

The coffin was placed in the tomb; roses were strewn upon it, and I went back to Paris with a heavy heart.

INDEX

339